FISHING BOATS OF BARBADOS

BARBADOS

ROW BOAT

35 c

barbados

Designed and Directed by Hans Hoefer
Edited by Rachel Wilder
Photographed by Tony Arruza

APA PUBLICATIONS

THE INSIGHT GUIDES SERIES RECEIVED SPECIAL AWARDS FOR EXCELLENCE FROM THE PACIFIC AREA TRAVEL ASSOCIATION.

BARBADOS
First Edition (Reprint)

© **1988 APA PUBLICATIONS (HK) LTD**
Printed in Singapore by APA Press Pte. Ltd.
Colour Separation in Singapore by Colourscan Pte Ltd

APA PUBLICATIONS
Publisher : Hans Johannes Hoefer
Editorial Director : Geoffrey Eu
Editorial Consultants : Adam Liptak (North America)
Brian Bell (Europe)
Heinz Vestner (German Editions)

Project Editors
Helen Abbott, Diana Ackland, Mohamed Amin, Ravindralal Anthonis, Roy Bailet, Louisa Cambell, Jon Carroll, Hillary Cunningham, John Eames, Janie Freeburg, Bikram Grewal, Virginia Hopkins, Samuel Israel, Jay Itzkowitz, Phil Jaratt, Tracy Johnson, Ben Kalb, Wilhelm Klein, Saul Lockhart, Sylvia Mayuga, Gordon MaLauchlan. Kal Müller, Eric Oey, Daniel P. Reid, Kim Robinson, Ronn Ronck, Robert Seidenberg, Rolf Steinberg, Sriyani Tidball, Lisa Van Gruisen, Merin Wexler.

Contributing Writers
A.D. Aird, Ruth Armstrong, T. Terence Barrow, F. Lisa Beebe, Bruce Berger, Dor Bahadur Bista, Clinton V. Black, Star Black, Frena Bloomfield, John Borthwick, Roger Boschman, Tom Brosnahan, Jerry Carroll, Tom Chaffin, Nedra Chung, Tom Cole, Orman Day, Kunda Dixit, Richard Erdoes, Guillermo Garcia-Oropeza, Ted Giannoulas, Barbara Gloudon, Harka Gurung, Sharifah Hamzah, Willard A. Hanna, Elizabeth Hawley, Sir Edmund Hillary, Tony Hillerman, Jerry Hopkins, Peter Hutton, Neil Jameson, Michael King, Michele Kort, Thomas Lucey, Leonard Lueras, Michael E. Macmillan, Derek Maitland, Buddy Mays, Craig McGregor, Reinhold Messner, Julie Michaels, M. R. Priya Rangsit, Al Read, Elizabeth V. Reyes, Victor Stafford Reid, Harry Rolnick, E.R. Sarachchandra, Uli Schmetzer, Ilsa Sharp, Norman Sibley, Peter Spiro, Harold Stephens, Keith Stevens, Michael Stone, Desmond Tate, Colin Taylor, Deanna L. Thompson, Randy Udall, James Wade, Mallika Wanigasundara, William Warren, Cynthia Wee, Tony Wheeler, Linda White, H. Taft Wireback, Alfred A. Yuson, Paul Zach.

Contributing Photographers
Carole Allen, Ping Amarand, Tony Arruza, Marcello Bertinetti, Alberto Cassio, Pat Canova, Alain Compost, Ray Cranbourne, Alain Evrard, Ricardo Ferro, Lee Foster, Manfred Gottschalk, Werner Hahn, Dallas and John Heaton, Brent Hesselyn, Hans Hoefer, Luca Invernizzi, Ingo Jezierski, Wilhelm Klein, Dennis Lane, Max Lawrence, Lyle Lawson, Philip Little, Guy Marche, Antonio Martinelli, David Messent, Ben Nakayama, Vautier de Nanxe, Kal Müller, Günter Pfannmuller, Van Philips, Ronni Pinsler, Fitz Prenzel, G.P. Reichelt, Dan Rocovits, David Ryan, Frank Salmoiraghi, Thomas Schollhammer, Blair Seitz, David Stahl, Bill Wassman, Rendo Yap, Hisham Youssef.

While contributions to Insight Guides are very welcome, the publisher cannot assume responsibility for the care and return of unsolicited manuscripts or photographs. Return postage and/or a self-addressed envelope must accompany unsolicited material if it is to be returned. Please address all editorial contributions to Apa Productions, P. O. Box 219, Orchard Point Post Office. Singapore 9123.

Special Sales
Special sales, for promotion purposes within the international travel industry and for educational purposes, are also available. The advertising representatives listed below also handle special sales. Alternatively, interested parties can contact Apa Productions, P.O. Box 219, Orchard Point Post Office, Singapore 9123.

Advertising Representatives
Advertising carried in Insight Guides gives readers direct access to quality merchandise and travel-related services. These advertisments are inserted in the Guide in Brief section of each book. Advertisers are requested to contact their nearest representatives, listed below.

Australia and New Zealand: International Media Representative Pty. Ltd., 3rd Floor, 39 East Esplanade Manly, NSW 2095, Australia. Tel: (02) 9773377; Tlx: IMR AA 74473.
Bali: Mata Graphic Design, Batujimbar, Sanur, Bali, Indonesia. Tel: (0361) 8073. (for Bali only)
Hawaii: HawaiianLMedia Sales; 1750 Kalakaua Ave., Suite 3-243, Honolulu Hawaii 96826, U.S.A. Tel: (808) 9464483.
Hong Kong: C Cheney & Associates, 17th Floor, D'Aguilar Place, 1-30 D' Aguilar Street, Central, Hong Kong. Tel: 5-213671; Tlx: 63079 CCAL HX.
India and Nepal, Pakistan and Bangladesh: Universal Media, CHA 2/718, 719 Kantipath, Lazimpat, Kathmandu-2, Nepal. Tel: 412911/414502; Tlx: 2229 KAJI NP ATTN MEDIA.
Indonesia (excluding Bali): Media Investment Services, Setiabudi Bldg. 2, 4th Floor, Suite 407, JI. Hr. Rasuna Said, Kuningan, Jakarta Selatan 12920, Indonesia. Tel: 5782723/5782752; Tlx: 62418 MEDIANETIA.
Malaysia: MPH Media Services, Lot 2 Jalan 241, Section 51A, Petaling Jaya, Selangor, West Malaysia. Tel: (03) 7746166; Tlx: MA 37402 JCM.
Philippines: Torres Media Sales Inc., 21 Warbler St., Greenmeadows I, Murphy, Quezon City, Metro Manila, Philippines. Tel: 722-02-43; Tlx: 23312 RHP PH.
Thailand: Cheney, Tan & Van Outrive, 17th Floor Rajapark Bldg., 163 Asoke Rd., Bangkok 10110, Thailand. Tel: 2583244/2583259; Tlx: 20666 RAJAPAK TH.
Singapore: MPH Magazines (s) Pte. Ltd., 601 Sims Dr. #03-21, Pan-1 Warehouse & Office Complex, Singapore 1438. Tel: 7471088; Tlx: RS 35853 MPHMAG; Fax: 7440620.
Sri Lanka: Foremost Productions Ltd., Grant House, 101 Galle House, Colombo 4, Sri Lanka. Tel: (1) 584854/580971-3; Tlx: 21545 KENECK CE.

APA PHOTO AGENCY PTE. LTD.
The Apa Photo Agency is S.E. Asia's leading stock photo archive, representing the work of professional photographers from all over the world. More than 150,000 original color transparencies are available for advertising, editorial and educational uses. We are also linked with Tony Stone Worldwide, one of Europe's leading stock agencies, and their associate offices around the world:
Singapore: Apa Photo Agency Pte. Ltd., P.O. Box 219, Orchard Point Post Office, Singapore 9123, Singapore. **London:** Tony Stone Worldwide, 28 Finchley Rd., St. John's Wood, London NW8 6ES, England. **North America & Canada:** Masterfile Inc., 415 Yonge St., Suite 200, Toronto M5B 2E7, Canada. **Paris:** Fotogram-Stone Agence Photographique, 45 rue de Richelieu, 75001 Paris, France. **Barcelona:** Fototec Torre Dels Pardais, 7 Barcelona 08026, Spain. **Johannesburg:** Color Library (Pty.) Ltd., P.O. Box 1659, Johannesburg, South Africa 2000. **Sydney:** The Photographic Library of Australia Pty. Ltd., 7 Ridge Street, North Sydney, New South Wales 2050, Australia. **Tokyo:** Orion Press, 55-1 Kanda Jimbocho, Chiyoda-ku, Tokyo 101, Japan.

Barbados, the 43rd volume in Apa Productions' award-winning *Insight Guides* series, is the result of the hard work and enthusiasm of many talented writers, photographers and editors. Our writers—nearly all Barbadians—have provided an eloquent and in-depth description of their country, culture, traditions and customs.

Hoefer

From the moment founder-publisher-photographer **Hans Hoefer** launched Apa Productions in Singapore in 1970, he wanted to provide travelers with a new

Wilder & Arruza

type of guide—one that would offer a more insightful look at a country than traditional travel books did. He developed the *Insight Guides* series specifically for the "second generation" traveler. A "first-generation" traveler, as Hoefer explains it, is one who requires a book to get him from the airport to hotel to restaurant to tourist attraction and then back home again. And a "second-generation" traveler has transcended those needs, with the assistance of modern travel agencies and personal travel experience. What he needs is a book to explain the *why* of visiting a place instead of the *how* of getting there.

In the case of Barbados, a second-generation traveler probably already knows about the glorious sun, sand and sea he will find there: he wants to learn more about the people, about their lives, their language, their landscape, their art, music, food, history—and their everyday concerns.

New York–based writer/editor **Rachel Wilder** traveled to Barbados—the island she had been visiting annually for nearly 20 years—to seek out the local writers best qualified for the task of explaining the "whys" of Bajan culture to the uninitiated. In Barbados, she found an abundance of talented journalists and authors. She also found, with the help of the Barbados Board of Tourism in New York, one of the world's most talented travel photographers—Cuban–born, Florida–based **Tony Arruza**. The 33-year-old Arruza has traveled exten-

sively throughout the Caribbean, Europe and the Far East. Not only is he an avid surfer and surfing photographer, he also has a natural talent for documenting people in their surroundings. His boundless energy, his curiosity, his excellent rapport with people and his technical expertise make him an ideal *Insight Guide* photographer. During his stint in Barbados, he began work every day before the sun rose and often photographed late into the night. He spent a day at sea with two Bajan fishermen, was "saved" at a Pentacostal church, discovered a remote group of Rastafarians living in cliffside caves that most Bajans don't even know about, "fired" a few with the domino players in a rum shop, joined a candlelight procession of Spiritual Baptists on "Old Year's Night," ate Christmas dinner with a fisherman's family. In addition to providing about 2000 high-quality photographs for this book, he also wrote the feature "A Day in the Life of a Fisherman" on page 90-91.

Included on our expert team of local writers was prominent historian **Trevor G. Marshall**. Marshall is a research officer at the National Cultural Foundation in Barbados and a part-time lecturer on the history of the Caribbean at the University of the West Indies, Cave Hill. He has also taught history at the Barbados Community College. His interests include social history, folklore and music. He writes regularly about history and the arts for *The Bajan* magazine, for the *Advocate-News*, a Barbados newspaper, and for *Contact*, a regional newspaper. He is co-author of the book *Folk Songs of Barbados* and has been the chief judge of the Crop Over Calypso Monarch Competition since 1983.

Marshall was educated at the University of the West Indies, Mona and Cave Hill campuses, and at the University of Waterloo, Ontario, Canada. His piece on the recent history of the island, "Lick an' Lock-Up Done Wid!" begins on page 36. He also wrote "All O' We Is Bajan," a look at the ethnic mix on the island, which begins on page 53, and "A Ship on Land?" on page 65. His "Bajans, Come Back to Calypso!"

on page 235, is about the roots of Bajan music, and "A Very Sweet Thing: The Story of Rum" starts on page 278. In addition to all this, Marshall helped recruit other writers and provided valuable editorial advice throughout the entire project.

Mark DaCosta Alleyne is a 1986 Rhodes Scholar studying International Relations at Oxford University. He holds a B.A. in journalism from Howard University in Washington, D.C. He has worked as a radio broadcaster, newspaper writer and as a reporter and the features editor for *The Bajan* magazine. He wrote two of the "Places" sections: "The South," which begins on page 145, and "The North and East," on page 185.

Annette L. Trotman is the cultural officer responsible for Theatre Arts at the National Cultural Foundation. She has taught English, Foreign Languages and drama at the secondary school level and is a freelance journalist who writes the weekly feature, "Bajan Folkways" for the *Nation* newspaper. She has been the stage manager for countless plays and provides technical production assistance for dance performances, concerts, plays, fashion shows and hotel extravaganzas. She has worked for Stage One Theatre Productions and for "The Guiding Light" on location in Barbados. Her chapter, "Dance and Drama: Street Beats, Stage Treats" begins on page 243.

Addinton Forde, a former English teacher who holds a B.A. from the University of the West Indies, Cave Hill, is also a cultural officer at the National Cultural Foundation. He specializes in Bajan folk traditions. He is a calypso singer and a writer for the *Nation*. His piece "A Religious Mosaic" begins on page 67. He also wrote "The Standpipe," on page 163, as well as providing hundreds of traditional Bajan sayings and their translations from which we culled "40 Bajan Proverbs," on page 256.

Tony Cozier is the island's foremost sportswriter. He is the sports editor of the *Sunday Sun*, the Barbados correspondent for *The London Financial Times* and has been a radio and T.V. cricket commentator since 1963. He has worked for radio stations in England, Australia, New Zealand and India. Cozier was educated at Carleton University in Ottawa, Canada, and is author of the book *The West Indies: 50 Years of Test Cricket* (1978) as well as co-author of a number of other books about cricket. His feature, "Cricket: The National Religion'" starts on page 281.

John Wickham is the editor of the respected literary magazine *Bim*, which has been published in Barbados since 1942. He is on the staff of the *Nation* and is one of the island's most highly acclaimed fiction writers. You'll find his book of short stories—*Casuarina Row*—in most bookstores on the island. His introduction to this guide begins on page 15.

Christine Barrow is a lecturer in sociology at the University of the West Indies, Cave Hill. Born in England, she has traveled extensively in Europe, Africa, the USSR, the USA, Canada, Mexico and the Caribbean, and has lived in Barbados since 1969. She holds a Ph.D. in social anthro-

Marshall Alleyne Forde

Cozier Wickham Barrow

pology from the University of Sussex in England. Her contributions to the book are based on her several periods of anthropological field work in Barbadian villages. Her insightful piece on family life, "Like Family To Me: The Bajan Household" begins on page 77.

She also conceptualized and co-authored with Averille White, her research associate, an unusual feature that provides an intimate look into the everyday life of a rural Barbadian village. It is a letter—in dialect—from a mother to her daughter, entitled "With Love From Maynard's Village: A Letter from 'The Rock'." It starts on page 86.

Averille White is a former secondary school teacher who is now a research assistant at the Institute of Social and Economic Research at the University of the West Indies.

The multifaceted **Timothy Callender** is a talented fiction writer, journalist, painter, sculptor and teacher. His short stories are often broadcast over the radio. He holds a

B.A. in English and an M.A. in painting and sculpture from the University of the West Indies, Mona, Jamaica. His valuable contributions to this book include "A Living Art," on page 227, "From Legends to Literature: A Story-telling Tradition," on page 259, and "The Boyfriends," a delightful short story, on page 264.

Elizabeth Best is a rewrite editor at the *Advocate-News* and a lecturer at the University of the West Indies. She has an M.A. in English Language and Linguistics from the University of York, England. She wrote the chapter on language—"Bajan Dialect: A

White *Best* *Springer*

McGeary *Carter* *Carrington*

Good Cook-Up"—which begins on page 251, and provided much-appreciated editing assistance on a number of other pieces.

Staff of Barbados Museum and Historical Society

Rita Springer is a food writer and author of *Caribbean Cookbook* (1979). Her chapter "Land of Cou-Cou and Flying Fish" is on page 271.

Peggy McGeary has been a secondary school teacher for 15 years. She is especially interested in Bajan folk culture, bush medicine and home cures. She is a co-author of *Folk Songs Barbados*. Her piece "Herbal Cures and 'Itals'" starts on page 276.

Angela Carter is a features writer for the *Nation*, where she specializes in tourism and business. Her articles have been published in *The New York Times* and the *Richmond Times Dispatch* (Richmond,

Virginia). She wrote the travel sections "The West," starting on page 117, and "Central Bridgetown," page 103.

Divya Symmers is a New York-based freelance travel writer with an in-depth knowledge of Barbados. She researched and wrote "the Guide In Brief," beginning on page 290.

Three talented Bajan photographers—**Ronnie Carrington, Stephen Smith** and **Willie Alleyne**—contributed some excellent photographs to the book. .

Special thanks go to Arts Consultant **Robert "Goggie" Ifill**, a dancer, actor, drummer, poet and craftsman who helped shape the book and provided valuable information about all aspects of Bajan culture.

The editor would like to thank the **staff of the Barbados Museum and Historical Society** for their enthusiasm, cooperation and generosity in supplying information and giving permission to photograph items from their fine collection.

We are grateful to Pan American Airlines for their prompt and reliable flights. Thanks also go to BWIA, Bill Hoad of Sunset Crest Rent-a-Car, Richie Alleyne, the Colony Club Hotel, Coconut Creek Hotel, Patrick Porter, the Palm Beach Hotel, the Golden View and Peter Odle. We appreciate the help given to us by the Barbados Board of Tourism, in both New York and Barbados. We also thank Elton Elombe Mottley of the National Cultural Foundation, the Barbados Archives, the Cheapside Post Office, and Price-Waterhouse in Bridgetown.

Other writers, editors, designers and contributors that deserve heartfelt thanks are Kathleen Jonah, Tim Jones, Stephanie Calmenson, Andrea Blaugrund, Jenny Springer, William Bliss Endres, Daniel Smeragliuolo, Kevin McIntyre, Lawrie Kaplan, Dina Ingber, Judy Schwartz, Alison Friesinger, Linden Lewis, Sara Whittier, Rob Seidenberg, Adam Liptak and Vivien Kim.

As Barbados enters its third decade as an independent nation, it has much to celebrate: its unspoiled beauty, its vibrant culture, its long tradition of stable democratic government, its relatively high standard of living, its 95 percent literacy rate, and its proud, hardworking, caring, creative people. This book is a tribute to you, Barbados—happy twentieth birthday!

——Apa Productions

TABLE OF CONTENTS

TABLE OF CONTENTS

OTHER INSIGHT GUIDES TITLES

COUNTRY/REGION

ASIA
Bali
Burma
Hong Kong
India
Indonesia
Korea
Malaysia
Nepal
Philippines
Rajasthan
Singapore
Sri Lanka
Taiwan
Thailand

PACIFIC
Hawaii
New Zealand

NORTH AMERICA
Alaska
American Southwest
Northern California
Southern California
Florida
Mexico
New England
New York State
The Pacific Northwest
The Rockies
Texas

CARIBBEAN
Bahamas
Barbados
Jamaica
Puerto Rico
Trinidad and Tobago

EUROPE
Great Britain
France
Germany
Greece
Ireland
Italy
Spain

MIDDLE EAST
Egypt
Israel

AFRICA
Kenya

GRAND TOURS
Australia
East Asia
California
Canada
Crossing America
Continental Europe

GREAT ADVENTURE
Indian Wildlife

WELCOME TO BARBADOS

"To confess truly, of all the islands that I have seen unto this day, not any pleaseth me so well," said one of the first visitors to Barbados, the Englishman Sir Henry Colt, who arrived in 1631.

For well over three centuries, visitors to its glittering shores have been impressed by this "gem of the Caribbean Sea." Barbados "has an air of neatness, politeness and opulence which one does not find in other islands," wrote a French missionary back in 1700, and it is still true today. Barbados is the only place outside the United States that George Washington ever visited: in 1751, he was "perfectly ravished by the beautiful prospects on every side" of the island.

Barbados is called the "singular island," perhaps because it's a bit off the beaten track, 100 miles to the east of the Caribbean chain, somewhat separated from its neighbors. During the days of sailing conquerers and Caribbean settlement, this isolation provided Barbados with an unwitting defense: it is difficult to sail to Barbados from the other islands because of the prevailing easterly winds.

The island is coral rather than volcanic, and relatively flat, though this doesn't seem so when you're trying to maneuver your car up a steep road in the hilly "Scotland District." The highest point on the island is only 1100 feet above sea level—perhaps that's why Columbus never saw it on any of his trips to the West Indies.

Barbados confirms the theory that the character of a people is molded by the landscape they inhabit. Ever since the English landed on its shores in the 1600s, the entire island has been intensely cultivated, even to the tops of its modest hills. The patchwork of flat, tidy fields which stretches to the sea has produced a hardy, down-to-earth people with a reputation for seriousness, self-assurance and frugality. In the small, crowded space of the Barbadian environment, order and discipline have always been essential. Perhaps that's why Barbados has supplied so many teachers, preachers and policemen to neighboring islands.

Barbadians are not slow to trumpet their own virtues. They firmly believe, as a piece of doggerel from 50 years ago says, that "when the great trump shall blow, all other nations will please stan' back and Buhbadians march up first."

Despite the island's dense population—260,00 people live in a space just 14 miles wide and 21 miles long—Barbadians have one of the highest per capita incomes in the Caribbean and a proud tradition of stable, democratic government. Most houses have running water (pure and drinkable anywhere on the island) and electricity. Inside some of the most modest of the traditional "chattel houses," you're even likely to find modern stereos, TVs or VCRs.

Barbados is a land of contrasts, where the old and the new coexist. International accounting firms sit beside ramshackle "rum shops," a flock of black belly sheep scampers through

Bridgetown traffic, a "tuk band" parades through a village where people are watching "Miami Vice" or "Dallas."

Unlike many of the other islands, Barbados was colonized by just one nation—England. Once called "more English sheself," this singular connection is reflected throughout the island still, in its "very British" traditions, in its nickname "Bimshire," and in many of its place names: Worthing, Hastings, Cheapside and Trafalgar Square, for example.

And little wonder, for when the first English settlers landed in 1627, the only welcome they received was from a multitude of wild hogs; the island was barren of inhabitants and ripe for the imposition of British culture, tropical-style. Quickly, English ways were to coexist with the African heritage of the many slaves brought to work the island's sugar fields. The island remained resolutely British, until 1966, when it became an independent state within the British Commonwealth.

Today's Barbados is a blend of English, African and North American cultures. One local poet has characterized it as "a land of pastel tints and compromise." Over the last ten years, however, Barbadians have gained a new appreciation of their unique cultural heritage. This has encouraged the exploration and celebration of some of the African-inspired aspects of the island's music, dance, art, religion, food, language and family structure.

It is with a new sense of pride that Barbados enters its third decade as an independent nation. It is truly a singular island, as Barbadians know and visitors quickly discover. Barbados may have glorious sunny days, a glistening azure sea and spectacular scenery, but it is a fascinating cultural vantage point as well—an example in miniature of the way history and geography can shape a people and a place.

Preceding pages: Crop Over Festival; St. Lucy coastline; St. Philip coast; Chattel house; At the beach in St. Michael.
Previous page: A welcoming smile from a St. George boy in front of his parent's store; a flying fish emblazons his T-shirt.

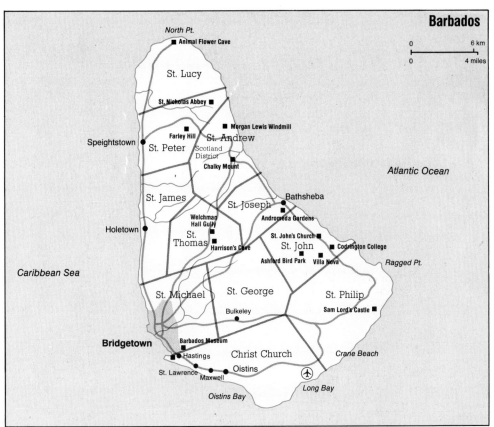

Barbados

North Pt.

■ Animal Flower Cave

St. Lucy

■ St. Nicholas Abbey

■ Morgan Lewis Windmill

Farley Hill ■

St. Andrew

Speightstown ●

St. Peter

Scotland District

■ Chalky Mount

Atlantic Ocean

St. James

Bathsheba ■

St. Joseph

Welchman Hall Gully ■

Andromeda Gardens ■

Holetown ●

St. Thomas

■ St. John's Church

■ Codrington College

■ Harrison's Cave

St. John

Ashford Bird Park ■

Villa Nova ■

Ragged Pt.

Caribbean Sea

St. Michael

St. George

St. Philip

Bulkeley ●

Sam Lord's Castle ■

Bridgetown

Barbados Museum ■

■ Hastings

Christ Church

Crane Beach

St. Lawrence

Maxwell

Oistins

Long Bay

Oistins Bay

0   6 km
0   4 miles

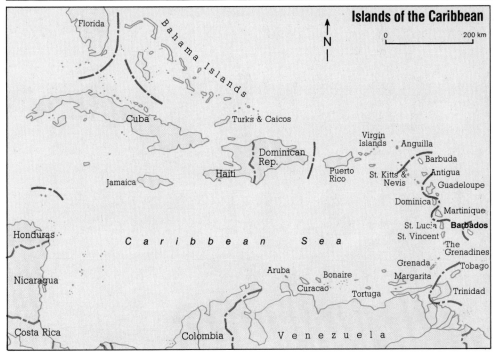

Islands of the Caribbean

N

0   200 km

Florida

Bahama Islands

Cuba

Turks & Caicos

Virgin Islands

Anguilla

Barbuda

Dominican Rep.

Puerto Rico

St. Kitts & Nevis

Antigua

Guadeloupe

Haiti

Jamaica

Dominica

Martinique

St. Lucia

Barbados

Honduras

St. Vincent

The Grenadines

Caribbean Sea

Grenada

Tobago

Nicaragua

Aruba

Bonaire

Margarita

Curacao

Tortuga

Trinidad

Costa Rica

Colombia

Venezuela

A PROSPECT OF BRIDGE TOWN

BARBADOS. 1695 By Samuel Copen.

19

THE FIRST BAJANS

Cannibals and convicts, pirates and planters, slaves and social reformers... A fascinating cast of characters has shaped the destiny of the tiny coral island of Barbados. Though Columbus missed it completely on all four of his trips to the West Indies, Caribbean Indians, Africans and Europeans have all left their mark on this 166-square-mile spot of ground.

The story begins 5,000 years ago, when Amerindians were "island hopping" in the Caribbean, and probably visited Barbados. The Arawaks were the first Indians to establish villages in Barbados, about 400 years before Christ. They came from the area that is now Venezuela, traveling across the sea in canoes up to 90 feet long, which transported women, children, animals, water, plants, idols, navigational devices and weapons. The Arawaks farmed and fished; they also brought with them a calendar system and a unique tradition of pottery-making. Archaeologists have discovered the remains of their villages in what is now Chancery Lane, Silver Sands and Pie Corner.

The Arawak population declined dramatically around 1200 AD, probably because they were wiped out by the aggressive Caribs, a somewhat less sophisticated tribe of hunters and fishermen. The Caribs dominated Barbados for around 300 years.

Many of the Europeans who visited the West Indies in the 16th and 17th Century tell tales of Carib cannibalism. Were they true? Anthropologists now say these Indians probably never depended on human flesh for nutrition, but occasionally did share an enemy's flesh as part of a ritual to promote courage in battle. In fact, the Caribs may have sampled European flesh often enough to have concluded, as one English historian recounts, that "Spanish flesh caused indigestion, the French were delicate in taste, while the English were too tough."

Mysterious Disappearance: Based on claims of "unhumanly" cannibalism, Spanish law justified Indian enslavement until 1542. According to early Spanish documents, many Indians were abducted from

Preceding pages: Samuel Copen print of the Careenage, one of the most accurate views of a 17th-Century port. Left, portrait of a Carib family by Agostino Brunias.

the small Caribbean islands like Barbados and taken to work in the fields and mines on the larger Spanish islands.

Some say it was enslavement by the Spanish; others believe it was famine or disease, but no one knows for sure why all the Indians had disappeared from Barbados by the time the English first arrived in 1627. All the English found was a flourishing population of wild hogs, left behind by Portuguese explorers who had anchored briefly there in 1536.

Soon after the English adventurers landed, however, they persuaded about 40 Arawak Indians from Guyana to move to Barbados and teach them how to grow Caribbean crops.

Traces of both Carib and Arawak culture

"father of the fingers"	thumb
"soul of the hand"	pulse
"my heart"	wife
"he who makes me little children"	son-in-law
"God's plume of feathers"	rainbow
"the pot is boiling"	earthquake
"misshapen enemy" (due to clothing and amour)	European

Near Miss: The sailing voyage from Europe to Barbados is made easier by the currents and trade winds. Even today, it is possible to float on a raft from the Canary Islands to Barbados. Still, the Spanish explorers bypassed Barbados; they settled Cuba, Hispaniola and Puerto Rico instead. It's possible they missed Barbados, being as relatively flat and isolated as it is. But

are still evident in modern Barbados. Whether you are handling a piece of prehistoric pottery, sipping soursop punch or ladling out a pepperpot stew, you'll take a momentary journey back in time. You'll even be uttering the sounds of an ancient Indian language as you use these familiar words:

huracan	hurricane
maiz	maize or corn
canaua	canoe
tobaco	tobacco
hamaca	hammock
sabana	savannah
guayaba	guava

Other Caribbean Indian terms, literally translated, are jewels of creativity:

what's more likely is that the fortune-hunting Spanish were not intrigued by this small island's charms. Its armadas were not interested in settling and cultivating islands, but in snaring precious metals and minerals from existing civilizations, such as the riches of Mexico's court of Montezuma and Peru's silver mines. Benign Barbados, its wealth in fertile soil, was no lure to Spanish fleets.

Barbados' name is Portuguese. At some point during the years of Caribbean exploration, the Portuguese began referring to the island as Los Barbados, meaning "the bearded ones." It's possible the reference is to Barbados' bearded fig trees. Other theories are that Arawaks, bearded men, were then inhabiting the island, or that bearded Africans were among the pre-European "citizens" of the island.

It fell to English explorers in 1625, however, to land near today's Holetown and claim Barbados' 166 square miles in the name of James I, King of England. Captain John Powell led the adventurers.

The first English settlement of the island began in earnest two years later, in 1627. On February 17, eighty English settlers and ten black slaves (captured from trading vessels en route) disembarked on the calm west coast, or Caribbean, side of the island.

Skewed Sex Ratio: The first settlers were an intrepid lot, willing to risk their lives for the promise of colonial wealth and power. Nearly all the initial settlers were men:

growth dramatically. However, if the white settlers did not increase and multiply with gusto, the slave population fared worse still: "Negroes imported to the sugar islands died much faster than they were born," writes historian Richard S. Dunn. "West Indian slave masters soon gave up trying to keep their Negroes alive long enough to breed up a new generation and instead routinely bought replacement slaves year in and year out."

The grim quality of life during the first years of settlement contrasted with the glory of the island itself. Remarked one early observer: "The Land lyeth high much resembling England more healthfull than any of hir Neighbors; and better agreeing with the temper of the English nation."

94 percent of 1,408 migrants from London in 1635 were male, for example. Most were in their teens or twenties: during the 1600s in England, life expectancy was no more than 35. It would prove shorter still on Barbados.

Black slaves—introduced sporadically during Barbados' earliest years by Dutch and Portuguese traders—were predominantly male, too, at first. In fact, during the first 50 or so years of Barbadian English settlement, a severe imbalance of the sexes, black and white, tempered population

Left, carved stone stamp used by Arawak men for body painting. Right, sacred object portraying the deity "Giver of Cassava."

Governor James Kendall, in 1690, declared Barbados "the beautyfulls't spott of ground I ever saw.'

Anything Goes: Beautiful as it was to English eyes, Barbados was miles from home, on the map and in spirit. Life on the island took on an anything-goes quality described as being "beyond the line," that is, outside territorial limits of European treaties. Barbados became a stage for gamblers, fighters and fortune hunters, for political refugees and outcasts, for kidnappers and their bounties.

Many of Barbados' original English settlers were second or younger sons of well-placed Englishmen; these younger siblings would receive none of the inheritance earmarked for first-born sons; they faced financially dubious futures—and Barbados was rumored to be the new frontier. Subsequent migrations were made by political outcasts such as Royalties and Roundheads who had backed losing factions at home. Other newcomers included lower class laborers from England, Ireland, Scotland and Holland without money to buy land. Many agreed to serve as indentured servants on the island for two to ten years, at which time they would be granted a small parcel or a start-up sum by their employers. Unfortunately, few planters kept their promises to indentured servants. Many lower class whites, recognizing their fate, left Barbados for other islands or for North America, especially Virginia and the

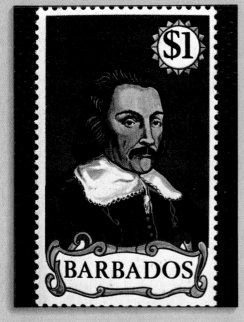

Carolinas.

"The Caribee Islands": From the beginning, the colonizing of Barbados was motivated by economics. The initial settlement was funded, to the tune of £10,000, by a London merchant, Sir William Courteen. Sir William had obtained a deed to Barbados and other "Caribee islands" not already held by any "Christian prince."

The first settlers did not own land or stock, but acted as freeholders or tenants, often keeping a small plot of land and two or three indentured servants or slaves. Profits from tobacco, cotton, ginger and indigo, the original island crops, went to William Courteen and Associates.

During Barbados' first "English" decade,

indentured servants from Europe performed most of the servile and agricultural work. African slaves were a small minority. According to historian Hilary Beckles, the number of blacks on Barbados didn't exceed 800 through the 1630s. Even a decade later, in 1643, the population numbered roughly 37,000 whites to only 6,000 blacks.

If the island were "owned" by one man, at least Courteen proved to be a sympathetic and able administrator. His successor, the Earl of Carlisle (whose name is given to Carlisle Bay) was less of a humanitarian.

The Earl of Carlisle was a Scotsman and a great favorite of the English crown. Recognizing colonization as a profitable business, he convinced King Charles I to grant him rights to the Caribbean islands, including Barbados. Although in direct conflict with Sir William Courteen's deed, this discrepancy didn't prevent Carlisle from sending his own band of settlers to Barbados—to a southwestern bay which eventually became Bridgetown.

Dumbfounded by the turn of events, Courteen enlisted the help of the Earl of Pembroke in restoring his rights to the island. King Charles I granted him his petition for proprietary rights. In a turnabout, however, the monarch then regranted ownership rights to Carlisle, whose will prevailed. The dispute, and especially its outcome, would later be dubbed the "Great Barbados Robbery."

With Carlisle as overlord, Barbados' star temporarily dimmed. Political dueling between Carlisle and Courteen factions on the island sapped the island's economic momentum. Infighting was compounded by drought and a decrease in food production that shook the optimism of the fledgling colony. Carlisle saw to it, too, that his personal profit margin from Barbados exports was substantially increased. The mid-1630s were christened "the starving time" by islanders.

Restless and Scheming: Carlisle appointed as governor a man whose name remains notorious. Henry Hawley, says one account, was "a restless and scheming soul." To appease powerful planter opposition to his appointment, Hawley established, in 1639, a House of Assembly, a "representative" body of citizens added to the island's system of government. Many of the first

Left, the first Englishman to land here. Right, the Portuguese who visited in the 1500s named the island *Los Barbados*, "the bearded ones," after the bearded fig trees.

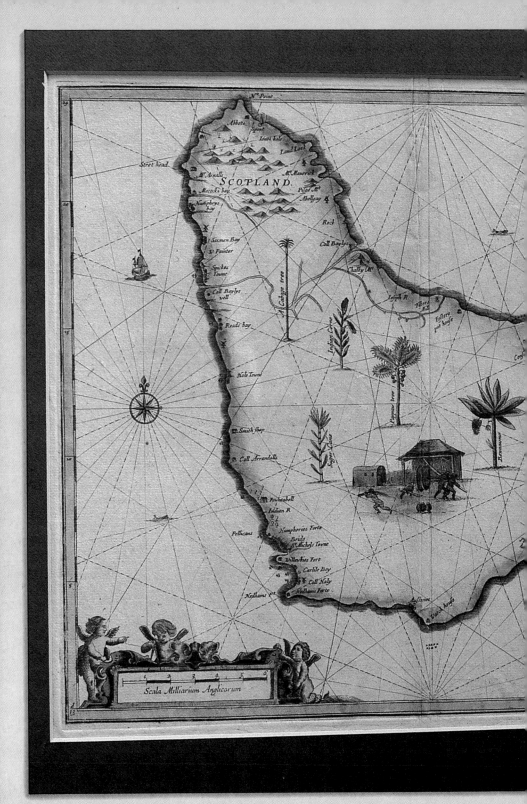

SCOPLAND.

N:. Point

Abbots

Louth hole

Lusd Lord

Stret head

M:. Arnall

M:. Maverick

Becoks bay

Poot M:.

Humphrys bay

Abellsay

Rock

Saxmen Bay

Coll Baylys

S:. Painter

Spickec Toune

Chally M:.

Joseph R.

Coll Baylys well

Indian Corne

Fostere pot house

Readi bay

Nola Toune

Ginginger tree

Sugar Cane

Smith shop

Coll Arrendalls

Fountabell

Indian R.

Pellicans

Humphries Forte

Brids

S:. Michels Toune

Villevhies Fort

Carlile Bay

Nedhams P:.

Coll Haly

Nedhams Forte

Austins

Black hede

Scala Milliarium Anglicorum

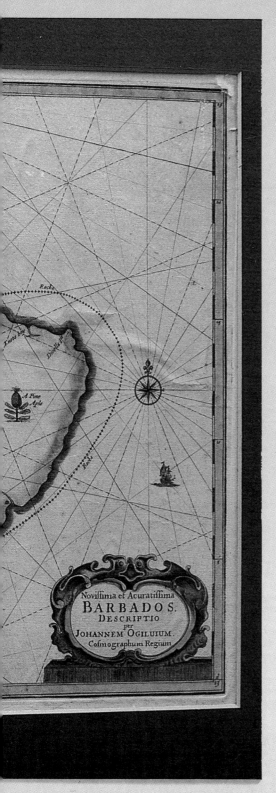

representatives of the Assembly—all white male landowners—were destined to become big planters and heads of influential families.

A Captain Futter, in the 1630s, commented to the island's Judge Read about the character of Barbados' high-appoined officials. "If all whore-masters were taken off the Bench," he inquired, "what would the Governor do for a council?"

Reaping the Sweets: The 1640s were a pivotal decade for Barbados. These were the years in which the colonists "retooled" to manufacture sugar, making Barbados the first British possession to cultivate sugar on a large scale.

The first man to bring sugarcane to the island was Pieter Blower, in 1637; he had learned how to grow and process sugarcane in Brazil. At first, canes were used to produce rum, but by 1642, sugar would be producing sweet profits.

Sugar bred success—immediate success. "There is a greate change on this island of late, from worse to better, praise be God," wrote one Barbadian in 1646. That change was the crystallized and refined juice of the sugarcane.

Everything grew—canes, population and land values. In 1646, one plantation was sold for £16,000—which, according to historian Dunn, was more than the Earl of Carlisle had been offered for the proprietary rights to the whole of the island a few years before.

Barbados's success story was partially underwritten by the Dutch. In the late 1600s, the Dutch dominated European and Caribbean trade. It was the Dutch who brought the planters black slaves from Africa, and offered high prices for Barbados sugar, cash on the barrelhead. Producing sugar was costly, too, and the Dutch came forward with financial backing and sugar-making expertise—a double-barreled enticement.

Of course, the English frowned upon its colony's close ties with Amsterdam. Once Britain's own house was in order, following the civil war which resulted in the formation of the British Commonwealth, Parliament passed several "Navigation Acts" whose purpose was to limit foreign imports to English-owned colonies. In Barbados, for instance, the Dutch had been enjoying brisk business selling foods, provisions and luxury items to profit–rich

Map from a 1671 atlas, *America*, by Englishman John Ogilby, royal cartographer and inventor of the road map.

planters—a seller's market of which the mother country was jealous. In fact, the manufacturing of sugar on Barbados was so profitable that planters were reluctant to "waste' land for the purpose of growing food. As one observor wrote in the 1640s, Barbadians were "so intent upon planting sugar that they had rather buy foods at very dear rates than produce it by labour, so infinite is the profit of sugar workes after once accomplished." In Barbados, the Dutch and English had a captive market with money burning in its pocket.

The Big Get Bigger: Along with sudden wealth, sugar-making dictated two other sweeping social changes on the island. The most far-reaching was the importation of black slaves, in large numbers, to work the hundreds of acres and hundreds of slaves. And the black population of the island increased quickly as slaves were brought in from the west coast of Africa, a practice which would continue for 150 years.

By the 1650s, Barbados' plantation system was intact. The island probably looked then, 300 years ago, much as it does today: heavily cultivated, with very little forest land left standing. A period of unparalleled prosperity was underway—but at a price. When historian Richard Ligon arrived in 1647, an epidemic of yellow fever was sweeping the island. Planters who had begun "sugar workes" were "laid in their dust, and their estates left to strangers."

Price of Prosperity: Sugar meant great wealth on one hand, abject poverty for

labor-intensive sugar fields, mills, boiling houses and distilleries. The new sugar economy also wrought another change: It favored the big planters, or those with investment connections in London, over small planters without access to capital. The reason: Sugar-producing required a sizable initial outlay. And while one acre of land yielded a generous one ton of sugar each year, the cost of initial investments in sugar-making was nearly prohibitive for small planters.

The population shift during Barbados' boom sugar years—roughly 1643 to 1660—was dramatic. The number of whites on the island decreased, as small planters were squeezed out by the giants, who now owned slaves on the other. The notes of Henry Whistler, written during a 1655 visit to Barbados, are even more specific and revealing:

This island is the dunghill whereon England doth cast forth its rubbish. Rogues and whores and such like people are those which are generally brought here.

Without slaves, plantations could not have existed: this was the sad reality of Barbados' economic success.

The slaves brought from West Africa to the West Indies, by the Portuguese and Dutch, were from areas which are now territories of Sierra Leone, Guinea, Ghana, the Ivory Coast, Nigeria and the Cameroons. According to historian F.A. Hoyos, they included such peoples as the Eboes, the Pawpaws and Ashanti, the Whydahs, the Mocoes and Nagoes, the Angolas, the Congoes and the Mandigoes. They came from the Fanti-Ashanti peoples of the Gold Coast, from the Dahomey and the Yoruba and Bini peoples of western Nigeria.

From different tribes and different territories, the blacks who reached Barbados did not share a cohesive culture. Even languages differed. This made communication and continuity of black folk traditions—as well as defiance against white oppressors—difficult. While black traditions are being recalled today with pride and relish, such wasn't always the case; the white planter class discouraged African practices and rituals. Black slaves became,

Police action, sometimes brutal, was a main tactic against uprisings. Slave laws, reports historian Karl Watson, "tried to limit mobility. A pass system was devised to prevent slaves from moving about freely. Rigid laws were enacted for the capture and punishment of runaway slaves ... Efforts also were made to reduce the risk of rebellion by the prohibition of drumming, blowing of horns, ... assemblies."

Barbadian slaves were the property of their owners—a kind of property seen partially as chattel and partially as real estate. Slaves could be sold, or traded against debts.

How Slaves Lived: Living conditions, as might be expected, were abysmal. Slaves were housed in floorless huts, sustained on

psychically and culturally, lost in a white man's world.

During the sugar boom, the slave population grew dramatically—from 5,680 blacks in 1645 to 60,000 in 1684. Slaves outnumbered whites by roughly 3 to 1—a threat to the white overlords which resulted in severe measures of control. Slaves were purposefully kept in awe; they were not discouraged from believing, for instance, that Anglican church services were sessions of evil witchcraft directed against them.

Left, aspects of plantation life: main house, mill, slaves, owner, slave huts. Right, a register listing slaves, with age and race. ("Coloured" means mulatto.)

meager food supplies, and worked six days a week, 12 hours a day.

About three-quarters of Barbados' slaves were plantation field workers. "Their day began at half-past five, when the plantation bell summoned them to assemble in the main estate yard to receive instructions," writes historian Watson. After an issue of hot ginger tea, the field workers divided into three groups. The able men and women were sent out to dig cane holes, to manure, or to cut and crop mature cane. Less able adults, and children and nursing mothers, performed less arduous tasks.

Slaves were usually rationed food weekly. A typical allowance for seven days: 28 lbs. yam or potatoes, 10 pints of corn, 1/2 lb. of

A. Brunias pinx.t et sculp.t

The Barbadoes Mulatto Girl.

fish, 1/4 lb. of salt, 1 1/2 pints of molasses. A yearly ration of men's clothing might be a flannel jacket, a shirt of check, a pair of trousers and a cap. Women might receive a flannel jacket, a gown and petticoat and a cap.

Slaves in skilled positions fared better. With time, Barbadian blacks and the continuing influx of Africa blacks were taught skills mandated by plantation life. Slaves became overseers of other slaves, boilers, distillers, cattle keepers, drivers, grooms, carpenters, blacksmiths, metal workers and tailors. Women worked as stock-tenders and child-minders. Domestic slaves— maids, cooks, butlers—were also generally more trusted, and better treated, than field workers. Wrote a visitor to one raucous household:

> It surprised me on first going to the West Indies to observe the unchecked and even disputatious familiarity of the house Negroes and servants; and at dinners, where much company was present, I have frequently observed them wholly occupied in listening to any good stories and laughing at them much louder than any of the Company.

The rare planter freed his slaves, sometimes upon his own death, according to his will, or as a seeming act of compassion, after the slaves had reached a certain age. Economics as well as compassion were at work—aging slaves were plantation liabilities. Free blacks tended to migrate to the city of Bridgetown, if they did not leave the island.

During Barbados' growing years, interracial marriages were few, according to church records, or perhaps just kept secret. However, interracial liaisons were many, especially between white planters and black slaves and servants. A mulatto population grew up in Barbados, creating a new class of "coloreds" generally treated with more respect and favor, than blacks. It was not uncommon, for instance, for a planter who had fathered a mulatto child to baptize the child into the Church of England and release the child from slavery.

Home Rule: By the 1650s, "the prevailing view in the mother country," writes historian Gary A. Puckrein, "was that England alone should enjoy the market of her colonies."

Accustomed to local rule, the colonists trembled at the notion of home [English]

rule. In 1651, the Barbados General Assembly declared that "being bound to the government and lordship of Parliament in which we have no representatives, or persons chosen by us . . . would be slavery far exceeding all that the English national hath yet suffered."

But home rule was inevitable: Barbados had neither the politican sway, nor sufficient military strength, to declare itself a free state. Barbados was dependent upon its colonial relationship. A blow came in 1663, when the governor Francis Lord Willoughby persuaded the Barbados Assembly to grant England a 4 1/2 percent duty on all exports—a duty that symbolized Britain's ascendancy.

The plantation system received another

shock now, too: A group of white servants was discovered to be plotting an insurrection against the planters. They were no longer able to tolerate dismal living conditions. The conspiracy was found out, and squelched—but not before 18 servants were executed. Open resistance to planters' role was a harbinger of changes to come.

Soon, too, England's Lord Protector Oliver Cromwell would launch his "Western Design," a campaign to seize further Caribbean territories and annex them to the British Empire. Jamaica would come under British rule, for instance, begin to cultivate sugarcane, and force down world market value of Barbados' sugar. It indeed was a new era for Barbados, one

Left, print by Brunias (c. 1790) shows what house slaves wore for special occasions. Right, jewelry found by archaeologists in slave graves.

circumscribed by restrictions.

Volatile Time: The late 1600s proved an especially volatile time for slave relations as well. British Parliament had granted the planters in the West Indies the right to "fight, kill, slay, repress and subdue all such as shall in a hostile or mutinous manner . . . disturb the peace." A trained militia on Barbados became a chief weapon against slave rebellion.

Even so, a 1675 plot by blacks from the Gold Coast of Africa, one that had been painstakingly planned for three years, also escaped notice, and might have succeeded. However, just eight days before the insurrection "cunningly and clandestinely carried and kept secret," a few whispered words were overheard by a house servant, who reported the planned revolt to her white master. The result was 100 arrests and the execution of many of those held.

Scares and plots for rebellion occurred in 1683, 1686, 1692 and 1702. Still, black rebellion was more subdued in Barbados than in Jamaica, for example, where there were more slave and where dense woods provided asylum for hunted blacks. Barbados, so small and highly cultivated, was too wide open for successful hiding. In both Barbados and Jamaica, however, the irony of failed revolt was this: Time and again, carefully constructed plans of rebellion were thwarted when loyal slaves reported the black conspiracies to their masters. Blacks undermined black resolve.

The nature of black protest changed in the 1700s. Certainly, a strong militia—aided by English ships in the West Indies fighting trade wars—helped squelch black uprisings, but black status was changing in some cases, too. Over generations, African blacks became native blacks, or "creolized" blacks. As such, they were favored over slave newcomers from Africa, and considered "capable of instruction." Planters began to grant creolized slaves more liberties. At least in appearance, the slave population generally seemed less aggressive and more loyal than in earlier years. In fact, Barbados gained a reputation for granting more concessions to slaves than any of the other sugar islands.

In 1807, the slave trade was officially abolished by the British Parliament, but humanitarians in England feared it was still going on—though there is little evidence slaves were still being taken from Africa at this time. Nevertheless, in 1815, the British passed a bill which declared that to stop the violations of the new law, all slaves in the West Indian colonies had to be registered.

This caused a furor among Barbadian planters, who saw it as a threat to their right of self-government.

The slaves got wind of the controversy, too, but misunderstood it. They thought that the bill everyone was talking about was not to register them, but to *free* them. Resentment grew as they wondered, "Why Bacchra [white man] no do that the King bid him?"

It is ironic that the ensuing 1816 slave revolt, nicknamed "Bussa's Rebellion," came at a time when food was plentiful and the slaves' working conditions better than they had ever been. But it was the unfulfilled expectation of freedom that caused the insurrection.

Free mulattos and slaves, including one named Bussa, met at weekend dances over a period of months and planned the revolt. Then, on the night of Apr. 14, 1816, cane fields were set on fire on a plantation in St. Philip. The revolt spread, and though it was eventually suppressed by the British militia, it was only after one-fifth of the island's sugar crop was destroyed.

"What I have for some months been dreading has . . . cross to pass," wrote one white planter to a friend. Only one white man was killed, but 176 slaves died in the upheaval and 214 more were executed.

Because of the rebellion, the British government decided to let Barbados pass its own slave registry bill—a triumph for the largely self-governing colony. The 1816 uprising also provided the impetus for further reforms, which satisfied the humanitarians—it was one more step on the road to emancipation.

The humanitarian and abolitionist movements were now irrevocably underway. But it would not be until 1834 that slavery itself was abolished.

In the end, it was a quiet reform. Reported William Hart Coleridge, an influential abolitionist and Anglican Bishop on Barbados:

800,000 human beings lay down last night as slaves, and rose in the morning as free as ourselves . . . It was my peculiar happiness on that ever memorable day to address a congregation of nearly 4,000 people, of whom more than 3,000 were Negroes just emancipated. And such was the order, the deep attention, and perfect silence, that you might have heard a pin drop.

Planters had a busy social life, with much feasting and copious drinking of rum concoctions such as falernum.

LICK AN' LOCK-UP DONE WID!
BARBADOS AFTER EMANCIPATION

Lick an' lock-up done wid,
Hurrah fuh Jin-Jin!
Lick an' lock-up done wid,
Hurrah fuh Jin-Jin!

De Queen come from England
To set we free;
Now lick an' lock-up done wid,
Hurrah fuh Jin-Jin!
    —Barbadian Folk Song, c. 1838

With these joyous lyrics, 70,000 laborers of African descent celebrated their freedom on Aug. 1, 1838. The apprenticeship arm-twisting British abolitionists, a compromise was reached.

On Aug. 1, 1834, the slaves would become "apprentices." For the next four to six years, the ex-slaves were to continue working for their particular plantation in whatever capacity they had previously, while masters would continue to give their laborers food, clothing and shelter. According to the law, masters could expect 45 hours of work each week without pay. In exchange, the apprentices could remain in their meager huts, eating with what utensils

system, which followed the abolition of slavery in 1834, ended on that day. The Barbadian apprentices could now hope that "licks" (whippings) and "lock-up" (jailings) were "done wid" and that "Jin-Jin" (the young Queen Victoria) had come to the rescue. Unfortunately, these former slaves would not see true, harmonious emancipation for more than a century.

It took 40 years of zealous campaigning by British humanitarians to bring about the official abolition of slavery. The white Barbadian planters were, of course, opposed to the plan. They thought of their slaves as objects. Economically, they depended on them. But after years of transatlantic debate between island planters and

they had and sleeping on boards of dried foliage, covering themselves with crocus bag blankets.

Planters were not pleased with the idea of apprenticeship and were severe in their interpretation of this first phase of emancipation. During slavery, for example, children began working at the age of four or five, collecting grass for the plantation livestock. Under the apprenticeship system, however, the 14,000 children under the age of six were no longer required to work. And the planters responded to this by refusing to support young children.

Even the state-supported Anglican Church was sluggish in its efforts to support emancipation. Although William Hart

Coleridge, first Bishop of Barbados, tried to promote peace and reconciliation between master and man and helped keep the transition bloodless, his speech to the slaves on the day they became apprentices offered a mixed message:

Your masters are good men who will continue to look after you when the day of freedom comes. You owe it to them as God's deputies to obey their orders even though you are no longer slaves. Your masters are your fathers on earth even as God is your father in Heaven.

Coleridge was asking his listeners, mostly newly freed slaves, to remain subservient. Essentially, that was the nature of the apprenticeship system—it was a trial period during which planters, laborers and the government could adjust.

Police Protection: The planters were worried that their slaves would emigrate. And if the laborers left the island, the sugar industry would collapse. To guard against this and to keep in check any unruliness resulting from the slaves' first taste of freedom, the Legislature created one of the first police forces in the British West Indies. The transition period was peaceful, however, and emigration was minimal.

For other islands in the British West Indies, this system of apprenticeship may have been necessary, but it was inappropriate on Barbados. The slave population didn't really need a transition period before becoming citizens. Planters didn't have to worry about losing their laborers because they owned almost all of the island's arable land and, at the time, there was no wage competition. Finally, some planters came to believe they could cultivate their land more cheaply with a freed labor force than with apprenticed help for whom they had to provide.

Thus, in early 1838, only four years after the apprenticeship system was installed, members of the Legislative Assembly quickly and with little opposition called for complete emancipation on the first day of August, 1838. The transition itself was simple and gloriously bloodless. The problems of reconciling a large black labor force and a small, wealthy leadership class, however, would take more than a century to solve.

Preceding pages: Detail of 1848 oil, the "Justyne painting," possibly showing planter's daughter returning from European education. Left, "The Freed Slave" by Broodhagen. Right, free and rejoicing.

Legal Shackles: In the first years of emancipation, lawmakers concentrated on making sure that the sugar industry remained active and profitable, keeping the former slaves under control and maintaining the island's reputation for order, good government and loyalty to the British imperial system.

Meanwhile, laborers moved from one plantation to another, looking for the highest possible wages. The planters responded by binding the ex-slaves firmly to the plantations through legal shackles, namely the Masters and Servants Act of Jan. 7, 1840, which established the "Located Labor" system. By this measure, all the freed laborers became tenants on their masters' land. Here, they could live on tiny

"house-spots" at the discretion and whims of the master—and for an additional weekly rent—as long as they provided the kinds of labor they and their ancestors had during the previous 200 years of slavery.

This system was meant to protect the planter class from losing its labor force to neighboring plantations and islands, but in doing so, it stripped workers of most of their rights. The master was legally the sole judge of the rights of his workers when any disputes arose over services required. Any worker who resisted was kicked off his bit of land with four weeks' notice and his crops were taken over and appraised at a value usually below the real value. And if a tenant quit, he lost his house and land and had no claim to the value of his crops.

Because this system was so effective economically, there seemed no pressing reason to change it. Barbados recorded steady economic growth between 1838 and the 1870s. Consequently, there was no "fall of the planter class" as had occurred in Jamaica and other colonies where the laboring classes had more freedom of movement.

The People's Tribune: There was one man who would not allow this virtual return to slavery to destroy the hope of true emancipation. Samuel Jackman Prescod, the son of a slave mother and white father, rose to become a powerful speaker and writer championing the cause of justice, freedom and equality.

redress of their grievances. His retirement from Parliament in 1862 and death in 1871 removed a stalwart "Tribune of the People" from the society at a time when such gifted individuals were sorely needed.

Prescod's demise signaled the end of an era in Barbados, an era in which a man with roots in slavery could provide a strong voice in government. Five years later, the island was in the middle of yet another governmental shake-up, one that pitted whites against blacks, poor against rich. And this time, no strong voice spoke out for the powerless and disinherited.

United Colonies: In 1876, the island was confronted with the "Confederacy Question." The British government proposed linking Barbados with the Windward Is-

---

BARBADOS.

Know all Men by these Presents, That I Elizabeth Holder Inniss of the Parish of Saint Michael in the Island aforesaid, Spinster for divers good Causes and Considerations me hereunto moving have Manumitted, Emancipated, Enfranchised, set Free, and for ever Discharged; and by these Presents do Manumit, Enfranchise, set Free, and for ever Discharge, of and from all manner of Slavery, Servitude, and Bondage whatsoever, to me, or to any Person or Persons whomsoever, the following female Slaves namely, Hannah-Maria, Mary-Hannah, Ruthy and Massey together with their future issue and increase and the said Slaves Hannah-Maria, Mary-Hannah, Ruthy and Massey are respectively hereby declared Free, and entirely Discharged from all manner of Slavery, Servitude, Bondage, Service and Duties to me or to any other Person or Persons whomsoever, so as that the said Slave may henceforth for ever have and enjoy absolute Freedom in Person and Property, as effectually to all intents and purposes, as if they had been born Free, and had never been Slaves.

In Witness whereof, I have hereunto set my Hand and Seal this thirtieth day of January One thousand eight hundred and thirty two.

Signed, Sealed, Delivered, and Acknowledged in the presence of

Eliz. M. Weekes
Jsmes J. Lawson

Elizth. Holder Inniss (S.)

BARBADOS. By the Chief Judge of the Precinct of Saint Michael &c.

PERSONALLY appeared before me, this day, James J. Lawson one of the subscribing Witnesses to the above Deed of Manumission, and made Oath on the Holy Evangelists of ALMIGHTY GOD, that he was present and did see Elizabeth Holder Inniss the Executing Party thereto, Sign, Seal, Acknowledge, and Deliver the same as her free and voluntary Act and Deed.

Given under my Hand this thirtieth day of January One thousand eight hundred and thirty two.

John A. Beckles.

BARBADOS.

In 1843, when the constitution was amended to give Bridgetown, the capital, two seats in the House of Assembly, Prescod won the election for the city, becoming Barbados' first non-white member of Parliament in 204 years!

In the House of Assembly, Prescod fought against open hostility to his ideas and gained some measure of advancement for the new citizens. He helped found the Liberal Party, whose adherents included small landowners, businessmen and mulatto and black clerks, and served as its leader for more than two decades.

Both as a journalist and a parliamentarian, he highlighted the plight of the masses, both white and black, and agitated for

lands in a loose association of British colonies. The current Governor, John Pope Hennessy, tried to persuade the Barbadians of the reasonableness of this scheme, but the island's decision-makers couldn't countenance the idea of becoming a Crown Colony; after all, Barbados had enjoyed self-rule by its own Parliament for more than 230 years. Also, the planters feared they would lose control over cheap labor, and the legislators worried that non-whites would gain more political influence under the new association.

The fear of emigration again swayed public opinion. The whites opposed Confederation because it would provide the masses with a natural outlet for escape to fair wages and gainful employment in other, less densely populated colonies. For the same reason, blacks were in favor of Confederation. This conflict was not to be resolved without bloodshed.

Riots erupted by April 1876 as the black Bajan masses reacted violently to the attempts of the white plantocracy to continue repression through the old system. After three days, eight blacks had been killed, 30 people (mainly blacks) injured and 400 rioters jailed.

In response, the president of the Barbados Legislative Council wrote to the Colonial Office in England to complain that Governor Pope Hennessy had "spread alarm" throughout the island by "exciting that peculiar element in the character of the

The problems spotlighted by the Confederacy Question continued to rage. The non-representational government ignored the needs of the masses, and only 1,300 of the island's 160,000 inhabitants were eligible to vote. In time, however, the oligarchs began to make attempts at improvement.

In 1884, the constitution was amended to include the Franchise Act, making it possible for people with less land to vote. The new act was supposed to remedy the island's gross disenfranchisement of non-whites. But the lower earning and landholding requirements weren't low enough to include the burgeoning, though still very poor, working class.

The Black Knight: Yet these changes were considered epoch-making in Barba-

Negro, which varies according to circumstances from the docility of child to the ferocity of a Savage." And when news of the disturbances reached England, Parliament transferred Pope Hennessy to Hong Kong.

Nonetheless, the people continued to regard Pope Hennessy as a hero; months after his departure, observers reported that many blacks believed Pope Hennessy would someday return in triumph to lift the burden of oppression from their shoulders.

Left, manumission certificate freeing slaves upon a plantation owner's death. Above left, newspaper editor and statesman Samuel Jackman Prescod; and far right, John Pope Hennessy, governor from 1875-1876.

dos, a step towards true democracy. And William Conrad Reeves, a mulatto politician who designed these measures, was praised for having "saved" Barbados from Crown Colony government, on the one hand, and from "mob rule" on the other. He was even knighted—the first black Barbadian to receive such an accolade—and elevated to the position of Chief Justice of Barbados from 1886 to 1902—the first black man in the entire British Empire to hold such a position.

By the end of the century, despite some democratic reform, the white planter class had regained total control of the local Parliament. The Franchise Act of 1884 meant little on an island where whites still owned 90 percent of the land and there were few free villages and no substantial property–holding peasantry, as in other British West Indian colonies. The plantation system with its dependence on cheap labor still dominated the social and economic life of the island.

This time, however, blacks took the course of action so feared by the power-brokers: emigration. Between 1850 and 1914, several thousands of adventurous laborers left for Panama to help build the Canal. Others left for Brazil, British Guiana, Trinidad, Costa Rica and Curacao—anywhere that promised employment and relief from the discrimination that kept Barbadian blacks on the lowest rung of the socio-economic ladder.

talked big and then returned to Barbados with nothing—much to the chagrin of their girlfriends or families. One such case was related in the folk song "Panama Man":

Oh de Panama man 'ent got no money
Still de Panama man want love . . .
But 'e cahn get me wid-out de money
To buy me a taffeta dress!
If de Panama man gwine court wid me,
He gwine treat me like a queen . . .

Nevertheless, many men *did* increase their families' wealth considerably by going to Panama. The Panama money was used to educate their children, raise their standard of living on the island and, above all, to buy land on which they could provide for their own livelihood.

For the first time, laborers were able to

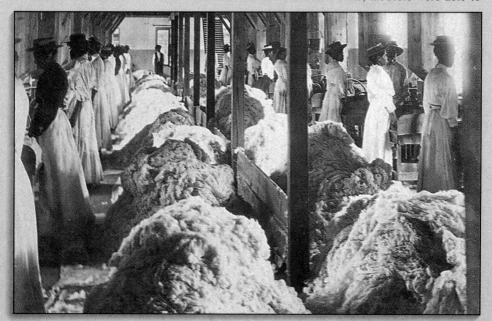

At the time, Barbados' economy was severely depressed. The sugar industry, which had withstood many threats and alarms in the preceding 50 years, was being hurt by stiff competition from Europe and by disease. To cut costs, Barbadian planters were forced to fire laborers. This, in turn, brought greater hardship to the already troubled masses and inspired many more Barbadians to leave the island.

Panama Money: Between 1850 and 1914, 20,000 men emigrated to Panama, where they toiled industriously and sent home money to their families. Most of the men who worked in Panama came back wearing flashy clothes, their pockets stuffed with U.S. currency. But there were a few who

buy arable land from planters, who, with sugar prices down, were sorely in debt. During the gloomy '90s, the price of sugar was far below the cost of production. Between 1900 and 1920, the number of estates fell from 437 to 305, and the major portions of more than 60 estates were actually converted into free villages. While laborers' families battled starvation with remittances from Barbadians in other countries, the planters scrambled to modernize their troubled industry.

The three keys to the salvation of the Barbadian sugar industry—and economy—were the development of fertilizers, the introduction of a new kind of sugarcane and the discovery of new markets.

In 1859, J.R. Bovell, a botanist, and J.B. Harrison, a chemist, experimented with sugarcane germination techniques, dabbled with new cane varieties and studied the incidence of cane diseases in Barbados. Their experiments had profitable results.

Growers began using manures as fertilizer, producing record crops in the 1890s and helping to offset the low price of sugar. By 1900, the old "Bourbon" type cane was successfully replaced by the "white transparent" variety. And the problem of finding a ready market for the product was eased by trade with the United States which began in the 1890s.

Meanwhile, the British government recognized the possibility of an economic collapse in her West Indian islands and, in

Even though the island's economy was in better standing, the Barbadian masses were still in trouble, plagued by the unsympathetic forces of nature. The hurricane of 1898 killed 80 people, blew down 18,000 ramshackle houses and increased the incidence of dysentery and typhoid already common among the poor. Then in 1902, an epidemic of smallpox struck, followed by yellow fever in 1908—all of which greatly increased the death rate.

Yet the government did not improve health or sanitation systems or pay workers enough money so they could improve the quality of their housing and lives. Also, there were not even the meanest social welfare programs for the majority of Barbadians. Children went to "ragged" schools

1897, set up a Royal Commission under Sir Henry Norman to look into the problems of the Caribbean sugar industry. Upon the recommendations of the Commission, the British government invested large sums of money in the West Indian sugar industry. With its £80,000 share, Barbados set up the Sugar Industry Agricultural Bank, a move which made the difference between solvency and bankruptcy for the next 50 years. Bounties on sugar beet were removed, and Barbados again began to benefit from easy access to the British market.

Left, young Bajan women ginning cotton. Right, early photo of members of the House of Assembly.

until they were old enough to work. Meanwhile, higher-class children attended such exclusive secondary schools as Harrison College, Lodge School, Queens College and Codrington High.

Worker's Rights: In 1914, the construction of the Panama Canal was finished, shutting off a dependable outlet for industrious workers. And by the 1930s, workers could only go to Trinidad, British Guiana, Brazil, Cuba or Costa Rica in small numbers.

With few ways to better one's lot, those Barbadian laborers who remained emerged as a peasantry of sorts between 1900 and 1920. The large majority lived in tenantries that were part of the plantations where they worked. And when the depression shook the American, Canadian and British economies in the 1930s, these workers were hit hardest.

New political movements developed in response to these devastating social and economic realities. Dr. Charles Duncan O'Neale for one, a medical practitioner, rose to the cause and devoted his life to fighting for the improvement of the masses in somewhat the same way that Prescod had done 60 years earlier. In 1924, O'Neale founded the Democratic League, the first mass-based, radical political force to be launched on the island in the 20th Century.

The league attracted many non-white, middle-class professionals and sent several candidates to the House of Assembly.

O'Neale won a seat in 1932, and though his health was failing, he left behind the twin legacy of the early "trade union," the Workingmen's Association (founded in 1925), and the League itself. Both of these organizations influenced the formation of the Barbados Labour Party in 1938 and the Barbados Workers' Union in 1941, two particularly powerful groups that fought for worker's rights.

Equally significant to the worker's cause was the emergence of the Garveyite movement in the 1920s and 1930s. Marcus Garvey was a black Jamaican who rallied against oppression of the blacks and wanted to see an exodus from the Americas back to Africa toward the creation of a black nationality.

Garvey spoke to the growing dissatisfaction of the Bajans. Emancipation had occurred 100 years earlier, but equality of the races did not follow. Barbadians took their frustration to the streets in the riots of 1937, inspired by the examples of men like Prescod and O'Neale, who made inroads in government, and Garvey, who offered strong black leadership; in fear of famine and disease, with little hope for education or a parcel of land to cultivate and call home, and with an ever-increasing population threatening to strangle the island with competition for jobs and resources.

Riots in the Streets: Clement Payne was the spark that ignited the social disturbances. Payne was Trinidadian by birth, but both of his parents and his brothers and sisters were born on Barbados. He began advocating the formation of trade unions at public meetings in Bridgetown and incited such a fever among the people that on the night of July 26, 1937, the authorities deported him.

Crowds gathered on town squares to protest his deportation. And as the number of people grew, so did the sense of outrage, which suddenly exploded. The crowds began smashing windowpanes, electric street lamps and anything else that beckoned their stones and their anger.

The rioting lasted three days and spread surprisingly quickly into the more isolated rural areas. Cars were broken into, shops were looted and fields were raided. These responses were prompted less by the deportation of Payne than by hunger and the fear of hunger.

The fervor of these days produced the kind of myths and folksongs that sprang forth out of the excitement of emancipation. One such song is "The Riot Song," a personal and tangible look at the events of this time:

Listen friends to what was composed
De twenty-seventh of July I couldn't show
muh nose.
Civilian wid rocks, policemen wid guns
Doan doubt me friends it wasn't no fun
For everytime dat yuh hear a sound
Somebody dead and somebody wound.

The most colorful account of the riot comes from W.A. Beckles' *The Barbados Disturbances*, a report summarizing the findings of a commission appointed to pinpoint the causes of the 1937 riot. Beckles likens the violent demonstrations to a volcanic eruption:

While the rumblings revealed the presence
of a 'volcano,' it gave no indication what-

ever of the gigantic crash that was to take place shortly after . . . In two days the hot lava that belched forth from the crater had spread its ravages to practically all parishes of the Island . . . Reviewing the situation dispassionately . . . It is manifest that circumstances, and not the qualities of a leader, made Payne, a slim, slight unimpressive stranger, a Moses in our midst.

For the first time, Bajan masses had come to the center of the political stage. Unlike in 1816 and 1876, they consciously challenged the fact 70 percent of the population was still disenfranchised on an island that called itself a democracy and touted its "long and proud tradition of Parliamentary government."

Little England: In 1946, Barbados was in the New World. And because the island's social and economic life was completely bound up with sugar cultivation, the plantation system was more completely preserved than in any other Caribbean colony. And with that system came inequities.

The top of Barbados society, about 2 percent of the population, received approximately 30 percent of the national income. This minority controlled the economic institutions of the island: the great plantations, stores and warehouses. Moreover, the two commercial banks were run by Britain and Canada, further protecting the island's finances from the laboring masses.

Lastly, for almost 300 years this ruling economic group had dominated the government under a franchise system that limited

the most crowded area in the Caribbean, with a population density of more than 1,200 people per square mile. It was the most British colony. in the New World, never having existed under any other flag. Nicknamed "Little England," Barbados sometimes seemed "more English than England sheself," as one Bajan put it. Its church was more distinctly medieval in cultural and religious matters than any other established Anglican church and all other conventional Christian sects derived

Left, Clement Payne, Trinidadian trade unionist whose agitation helped start the labor movement in Barbados. Right, farm workers on strike in the 1940s.

voting rights to less than 4 percent of the population.

But the fervor, anger and sentiment unleashed by the 1937 riots had led to change. The first lasting labor parties were formed. The nature of the constitution, Barbados' relationship to other British Caribbean colonies and the problems of poverty were questioned. And within the next 40 years, the political and social character of the island altered dramatically.

Democratic Vistas: Grantley H. Adams was the primary catalyst for these changes. Between 1938 and 1945, Adams became the acknowledged leader of and spokesman for an emerging mass movement that coalesced around a political party and a labor union.

Adams firmly believed in the British monarchy and the sanctity of the British parliamentary institutions. But he was determined to modernize the Barbadian political system by narrowing the traditional boundaries between the planters and the laboring masses.

In 1938, Adams, along with C.A. Braithwaite and several others, formed the Barbados Progressive League, also known as the Barbados Labour Party. Adams became president of this coalition and vowed to work for greater equality on the island until a time when the island's wealth and resources would be controlled by the government on behalf of the people. Adams' party demanded fair labor laws, including workmen's compensation in case of injury on

the job, and formation of tribunes to monitor wage fairness and factory conditions. It also advocated a slum clearance and housing plan.

The party gained its first political victory in 1940 when it won five seats in the House of Assembly and Adams was able to push through legislation requiring an old age pension and a Minimum Wage Act. But his most pressing task—modernizing the political system—met with strong opposition. A bill to provide for adult franchise was consistently voted down. In 1942, however, the members of the Assembly recognized the mood of the times and agreed to a compromise. The bill passed reduced the income qualification for voters

to £20 and, for the first time, permitted women to vote and to be eligible for membership to the House of Assembly on the same terms as men.

Most important during this time of remarkable change, however, was the realization by Governor Bushe that the constitutionally mandated system of government was, in his own words, "incapable of coping with modern conditions."

The Governor adopted a constitutional change, dubbed the "Bushe Experiment," whereby the Governor transferred the responsibility of choosing an executive committee from himself to a spokesman for the majority in the Assembly. (Adams was the first to serve in this new role of majority leader.) The Executive Committee thereafter was privy to and accountable for decisions made in the House.

Working out the Kinks: These changes—though conceptually sound and well-intentioned—did not make any significant impact because the Legislature was still controlled by white planters. When reforms such as the nationalization of public utilities, paid holidays for workers and adult franchise came up, the two bodies inevitably clashed. By 1949, however, this kink was worked out by limiting the powers of the Legislature to the functions of revision and delay, thereby leaving the ultimate say in the enactment of legislation to the House.

The constitution endured further changes in the next few years, including the formation of ministries for formulating specific governmental policies. In addition, the leader of the Barbados government would become Premier of Barbados, to be supported, after 1958, by a cabinet. With the help of Adams' decisive and influential leadership, Barbados was able to modernize its antiquated system of government in only two decades. The island was clearly heading towards Independence. While Barbados was working towards political modernization domestically, it was also in the process of negotiating for similar changes within the West Indies and in the British Empire. Leaders of the various West Indian islands began discussing—once again—the merits of Federation.

With Adams representing Barbados, a Federation was, in fact, inaugurated in 1958. Unfortunately, it never achieved the kind of momentum needed to grab interna-

Prime Minister Grantley Adams, who effected revolutionary social reforms. Right, Barbadian flag first unfurled on Independence Day, 1966.

The Advocate

BARBADOS, WEST INDIES   WEDNESDAY, NOVEMBER 30, 1966   12 CENTS

Midnight: Darkness encompasses Savannah...then the Barbados flag emerges

BARBADOS IS INDEPENDENT

By Tony Vanterpool

AT one minute after midnight today, Barbados threw off the shackles of colonialism, when during a tense and historic moment at the traditional Garrison Savannah the British Union Flag was lowered and the 166 square mile nation's ultra-marine blue and gold flag with broken trident was hoisted.

A deafening applause came from the thousands and thousands who came from every nook and cranny of the sugar coated territory, braving the threats of inclement weather, to witness the most significant achievement since the freedom of the island's slaves 132 years ago.

And so ended 339 years of association with Britain as a colonial territory and so began the membership of Barbados to the British Commonwealth of Nations as its 26th member.

Barbados' Governor-General-designate, Sir John Stow, raises Prime Minister Errol Barton's right hand as a sign of victory seconds after Barbados became independent today.

Up goes the Barbados flag of ultra-marine blue and gold with broken trident (left), and down comes the British Union Flag. Within seconds of the completion of this operation, Barbados became an independent State within the British Commonwealth of Nations.

Russia recognises Bimshire

THE Soviet Union has declared its recognition of Barbados as an independent and sovereign state.

IMPROMPTU ROAD MARCH

MISS BARBADOS ARRIVES

MISS JUDY ROSITA WALKER, 18, Miss Barbados (United Kingdom), arrived in Barbados last night from London to take part in Barbados' Independence celebration.

Victor's hand is raised

POPE'S CONGRATS

The Queen's thoughts are with us

QUEEN ELIZABETH II has assured Barbadians that her thoughts are with them as they step into independence.

MUD AND WATER ON THE GROUNDS

Traffic jams as thousands flock city

HUNDREDS of Barbadians, young and old, flocked the city last night to window shop and see the buildings and stores which were brilliantly illuminated and gaily bedecked with flags and bunting in Barbados' national colours of ultra-marine and gold.

Vice-president of Lions here

China rejected

748 die in U.S.

NEXT ISSUE

A REMINDER

SPECIAL ISSUE

TODAY'S WEATHER

TV BINGO

Pammastic: proof against any climate in the world

MANUFACTURED LOCALLY
AGENTS:
JAMES A. LYNCH & CO., LTD.
McGregor Street, Bridgetown.

tional attention because each island seemed to have different goals for the union. Also, the Queen maintained legislative authority in matters of defense, external affairs and finance of the Federation, and the Governor had the power to veto any laws passed. These problems led to the dissolution of the Federation on May 31, 1962, only four years after its inception.

When Adams returned from his dealings with the Federation, much had changed in the political and social life of Barbados. And his nemesis, Errol Walton Barrow, had succeeded Adams in his old seat of power. In 1961, Barrow, with his liberal Democratic Labour Party, held the reins of power in the government.

Barrow, the nephew of legendary reform-

Federation from 1962 to 1965, it became clear that Barbados would not receive Dominion status through any union of British West Indian islands. Yet Barbados was ready for a break with her mother country at a time when Britain was clearly liquidating her empire.

Although the decision to proceed to Independence was one of the most significant in Barbados' history, it was accepted with relatively little opposition or fanfare. On Nov. 30, 1966, Barbados peacefully became a sovereign state, a state that had fought many battles for the cause of freedom and equality in the past and could now begin a new life as a free nation.

The actual transition from colony to sovereign state in Barbados involved only a

er Charles Duncan O'Neale, immediately instituted reforms that were severely lacking during the years of constitutional rearrangement. He carried out a program of public works to provide relief for the unemployed, repaired roads, cleared lands and gullies, and sent men to begin work on a canal in the Constitution River.

Finishing Touches: Although he, like all preceding reformers, faced his share of difficulties and opposition, Barrow was able to put the finishing touches on an island prepared for imminent Independence. After Adams' frustrated attempts to consolidate a Federation of the Caribbean from 1958 to 1962 and a subsequent attempt at a smaller Eastern Caribbean

change of titles and functions. Errol Barrow and his Democratic Labour Party were reelected, and four weeks later, amid pomp and solemnity, the new flag was unfurled.

As the fledgling nation's first leader, Barrow served for over 10 years. By 1976, however, Barbadians were ready for a change, and Barrow's DLP was defeated by the BLP. Five years later, the BLP won again, this time headed by the popular Tom Michael Geoffrey Manningham Adams, son of Sir Grantley Adams, who took Barbados confidently into the '80s. He entered 1985 without a political care. But on March 11, he died of a heart attack at the age of 53, leaving his party and the country bereft of his guidance.

Full Circle: Adams' successor, the energetic Bernard St. John, moved swiftly to allay fears of a disintegration of the ruling BLP, continuing the policies of his predecessor with the same dedication.

Errol Barrow, then 65 with 33 years experience in Parliament (a Caribbean record) seized the opportunity. His party hammered away incessantly at the St. John administration as Bardados experienced an economic slowdown.

St. John decided to hold the election constitutionally due by September in May—in order, some say, to avoid the harsh criticism in song that would come from the calypsonians during the summer Crop Over Festival. Despite a massive advertising blitz by the BLP, on May 28 the

forging a new identity. Many of them were also influenced by the Rastafarian movement from Jamaica. But by far the most powerful influence has come from American television programs and music. In 1969, only 6 percent of Bajans owned televisions. By 1980, 69 percent did, and the influence of American tastes and trends became ever more pervasive.

Only in the last five to 10 years have Bajans become interested in trying to preserve aspects of their *own* culture in the face of foreign influences. After its first twenty years as an independent nation, Barbados is finally coming into its own culturally. Now there is an ever-growing appreciation of things Bajan, and a movement to preserve aspects of the traditional

Barbadians went to the polls and voted in the DLP, led by Barrow, by the largest landslide in Barbados history.

Coming into its Own: Although Barbados was politically ready for Independence way back in 1966, it would take years before its unique indigenous culture could flourish. Barbados was well-known for its British-ness and for the conservative, old-fashioned life-style of many of its people.

In early 1970s, inspired by the Black Power movement, Barbadian youths began

Left, burning "Mr. Harding," symbol of hard times, at Crop Over Festival. Right, Kadooment Day Parade at Crop Over, a uniquely Bajan cultural tradition.

culture that are fast disappearing.

The enthusiasm the summertime Crop Over Festival generates is one sign of the new cultural pride. Crop Over originated in the early days of plantation society. Revived in the 1970s and managed by the National Culture Foundation since 1982, it has played a major part in promoting the new cultural awareness, and is largely responsible for reviving the calypso tradition in Barbados. The wildly popular calypsonians are now a major force in Bajan society: they speak for the people, providing social commentary, gentle protest that grows out of concern for their nation, and a constant source of indigenous entertainment that delights Bajans and visitors alike.

ALL O' WE IS BAJAN

All o' we is Bajan!
Bajan to de back-bone . . .
Bajan black, Bajan white,
Bajan hair curly, Bajan hair straight,
Yo' brother red, yo sister brown,
Yo' mother light-skin, yo father cob
skin . . .

This excerpt from local poet Bruce St. John's *Bumbatuk I* reveals something of Barbadians that, given the island's many ethnic groups, may come as a bit of a surprise. That "something" is a sincere and deep-seated national pride, a sense of unity.

There are Afro-Bajans, Anglo-Bajans, Euro-Bajans, Bajan Jews and Bajan Hindus and Muslims. Smaller groups include an American community, a Canadian element, some South American expatriates and an influential group of Arab-Bajans from Syria and Lebanon.

Barbados is one of the most densely populated agricultural countries in the world, and the population is expected to increase from approximately 250,000 now, to 300,000 by the year 2000. Given the propensity of Bajans to "get their quivers full," this substantial population growth is likely to occur, despite the efforts of the local family planning association.

Over 70 percent of today's Barbadians are directly descended from Africans who were part of the greatest involuntary migration in world history—the slave trade. Another 20 percent of Bajans are of mixed black and white blood—described as "brown-skin," "light-skin," "fair-skin," "high brown," "red" and "mulatto." Another 7 percent of the population is white, either "overseas" white (of traditional Caucasian features and skin tone) or "Bajan" white (containing "a tip of the tarbrush," or a small amount of black ancestry). The remaining 3 percent is drawn from the immigrant groups mentioned earlier.

Still, despite this diversity, a national character, or sense of identity, has emerged. Bajans, on the whole, are pragmatic people with a native capacity for wit and irony.

Quick Sense of Fun: Barbadians do not take

Preceding pages: Cocktails at the Colony Club Hotel; Crusaders Fellowship Church, Mt. Hillaby. Left, before class at a private school. All schools—both private and public—require uniforms.

offense easily, a trait which has led some visitors to believe they suffer abuses, particularly bigotry, without protest; actually, this trait has made the social evolution from the modified feudal system prevailing before 1937 smoother.

There is a quick sense of fun among Barbadians, often quite subtle, and capable of being effectively directed, in true British fashion, against any form of pretentiousness. There is a refreshing realism of outlook and a sturdy resistance to change for the sake of change—a characteristic which stands out in sharp relief against the excitability and enthusiasm of other Caribbean peoples. Some have interpreted this Barbadian trait as smart-aleck cynicism, and it is not unusual to hear other West Indians use terms such as "smug," "smart Bajan," and "know-alls" to refer to Barbadians with whom they've had contact.

John Hearne, the Jamaican novelist, offered this analysis of the Barbadian character in the *New World Quarterly* (Barbados Independence issue, 1966):

. . . The Barbadian is a problem. . . . He is English in a way that the rest of us are not. History Englished him by giving him an exclusive association with the former Mother Country. This gave him some values, and a head-start in the development of education; Barbadians have been school teachers to the rest of the (British) Caribbean, at a time when education in Jamaica (a hundred times larger than your island) was at the level of reading, writing and arithmetic . . . In all this Englishness the Barbadian geography has played a significant role. It is the most un-West Indian of the islands in appearance, and in atmosphere . . . It is a sunburnt piece of England, modified by the Tropics, but still and stubbornly a corner of the English countryside, and Barbadians, black and white, have clung to that Englishness. But it has given the Barbadian a wholeness, a selfconfidence and self-discipline that is remarkable and enviable among West Indians . . .

At least in one regard, however, Barbados and Bajans conform to the West Indian norm: there is a slowness of tempo to which the foreigner must adjust if he wants to avoid frustration. This is balanced by a readiness to oblige, exhibited with such unforced courtesy that the recipient of

favors feels no sense of obligation.

Earliest Inhabitants: The story of the people of Barbados begins more than 30,000 years ago, when men of the Far East crossed the Bering Strait, which was then a land bridge, and made their way through the North American continent to the Southern landmass. Others came by way of the Pacific, their skill in navigation bringing them across the vast ocean until they reached present-day Brazil, Venezuela and the Guianas. Thus Barbados' Amerindian ancestors began to migrate from South America to the West Indies. These hunter-gatherers eventually came to Barbados in search of new food sources: they settled in Barbados about 2,000 years ago. These earliest people, the Barrancoid, left relics at

what are now Chancery Lane, Boscobelle and Golden Green. They left Barbados around 600.

Two hundred years later the Arawaks came to the island from South America, traveling to the island in long, narrow, flat-bottomed canoes. They inhabited Barbados for the next 400 years, settling around springs of freshwater in various parts of the island. They grew cassava, corn, peanuts, squash, guavas, pawpaws and pineapples for food; they also grew cotton and tobacco.

The Caribs were the last group of Amerindians to settle in Barbados. This warrior tribe arrived on the island sometime around 1200 AD, and were gone by 1536. They either drove out or exterminated the

Left, dance students take a break from class at a community center in St. James. Right, a woman from the parish of St. George peeks out from the kitchen.

Arawaks and established the island as headquarters for governing the nearby islands of St. Vincent, St. Lucia, Grenada and Tobago. In turn, the Caribs were captured by Spaniards sometime early in the 16th Century and shipped as slaves to Hispaniola. Thus, when the Portuguese, led by Pedro a Campos, first arrived on the island in 1536, the Caribs had vanished.

Off the Beaten Track: Present-day Bajans are slightly miffed that early Iberian explorers by-passed Barbados and did not settle there. Apparently Barbados was off the beaten track—legend has it that Columbus never even saw it because it was so flat. And, after all, the Spaniards had their pick of large Cuba, enticing Hispaniola, mountainous Jamaica, exotic Puerto Rico and

lush Trinidad. So this island was up for grabs until 1625 when some wandering Englishmen "discovered" it, and claimed it as their new colony in the name of King James I. The real settlement began about two years later when a group of 80 Englishmen came across in a ship called the *William and John.* They captured 10 Africans from a Spanish galleon, and the group landed on the west coast of the island on Feb. 17, 1627. Today, this landing is celebrated annually at the Holetown festival.

The English who landed more than 350 years ago were men of substance who came to the West Indies out of a spirit of adventure. The first man to step ashore, William Arnold, was a businessman who

had sold his shop in London to relocate in the sunny Caribbean.

Barbados quickly became the "Brightest Jewel in the English Crowne," despite the fact that St. Kitts was the first Caribbean island settled by the English. To the British, Barbados was reminiscent of the rolling downs of Cornwall and Devon; after they got accustomed to the broiling sun, they soon turned Barbados into a "Little England," tropical style.

Henry Powell, the captain of the first ship of colonists, brought some Arawak Indians from Guiana to teach the new Barbadians how to grow tropical food. This was certainly a key to the successful start of the colony. The settlement thrived, and the English arrived in droves to join the original band of settlers.

Poor Whites: Some of the English who made their way to Barbados were young men of solid families, anxious to make a quick fortune, but others were laborers, indentured to their masters for years.

Gradually, the conditions of work for the poor whites, and the quality of their lives, deteriorated to the level of the African slaves, and these resentful "Christian servants" joined the Africans to plan an uprising against the "higher-ups" and "better-offs," as the planter class was called behind its back. As it happened, the uprising failed and the indentured laborers found themselves worse off for their pains, still treated like slaves and now having to serve even longer terms of indenture. They became a sorry lot, herded into villages on the eastern sea coast and eking out a living by fishing, hunting turtles and land crabs.

The more adventuresome and intelligent of them escaped the island after their indentures were over and went to Jamaica after that island was conquered by England in 1655. A sizable group went on to North America, settling in the Carolinas, speaking their West Country brogue and bestowing a distinctly Barbadian flavor on those colonies. In fact, each year for the past 20 years, Carolinians have made an annual pilgrimage to Barbados, digging into the records of births and baptism lists, searching for evidence that will establish their Barbadian ancestry.

Meanwhile, the original English settlers were joined by some unwilling Scottish, Irish and Welsh men of various classes.

Left, taxi driver Mr. Morris is based in the heart of Bridgetown, city of entrepreneurs. Right, on the job in Speightstown, "metropolis" of the north.

They had been on the losing side in the English Civil War and were exiled, or "Barbadosed." They became bonded servants, and they stayed at the bottom of the social and economic pyramid until the 20th Century. They married their brothers and sisters in defiance of the injunctions of the English *Book of Common Prayer*, thus keeping their bloodlines pure. The fact that they passed on debilitating diseases to their descendants was a price to be paid for their lily-whiteness.

"Red Legs": Over the centuries the Afro-Bajans have ribbed their fellow Bajans about these practices and lampooned them with such nicknames as "Red Shanks," "Red Legs," because the kilts their ancestors wore exposed their legs to the sun, "Ecky-bekky," "white niggas" and "Poor backra-johnnies." "Backra" comes from the West African word *bakara*, which means white man. These white Bajans were also called "Pawgees," a word from a plantation in St. Joseph called the "Spa" or "Spaw," where many poor whites lived.

The sun-intolerance of Celtic skin aside, poor whites did benefit from the generosity of planters who were embarrassed to see their "kith and kin" in such a downtrodden state. Schools, jobs and even clubs were provided for them. The Haynes Memorial School in Bridgetown, Combermere School, the Alleyne School, Harrison's College and Boys' and Girls' Foundation Schools were all founded to help the poor whites pull themselves up by their bootstraps.

Likewise, the Young Men's Progressive Club was established in the 1920s to provide poor whites in the city with an alternative to delinquency. Here they could play cricket, soccer, indoor games and attend lectures, debates and cultural programs. It is interesting to note that the oldest literary magazine in the Caribbean, *Bim*, was started by two early members of the Y.M.P.C., Frank Collymore and Therold Barnes, both descendants of poor whites.

From being scorned and pitied, the Bajan poor whites are now regarded as a remarkable people, "survivors of the crossing," and a group with a romantic heritage. Today they comprise a small minority existing in isolated poverty in the parishes of St. Philip, St. John, St. Joseph and St. Andrew. By the end of this century, these

Miss Gail Prescod, law student and runner-up in the controversial "Miss Barbados" beauty competition.

early settlers will probably not be recognizable as a unique ethnic group. For the most part, they will have assimilated into the middle class, a process which has been underway for the past 50 years.

The Island's Elite: And what became of Barbados' original English settlers? Approximately 20 families dominated the island's history and economic development during the early period of colonization. Even now many of these families still rank among the island's elite, known as "high whites." Sugar exporting was their vehicle to wealth, and many assumed the role of local lords, attempting to recreate patterns of English country life in the islands. An exclusive clique developed: they recommended one another for the Legislature, bestowed knighthoods amongst themselves, sat in the Anglican parish vestry councils and served as Justices of the Peace. These privileges were passed on to succeeding generations.

But first and foremost, the planter class turned its energy to growing sugarcane and producing sugar on the 80,000 acres of land available to them. They developed a deserved reputation as the most outstanding sugar planters in the region, coaxing high yields from the thin soil and driving their African slaves to outstanding effort.

To the planters, "Bimshire," as they fondly called their island, was their only home, and they gratefully spent their adult lives working to show the love they had for the island. Of all the West Indian planter classes, the Bajans were the most devoted to their island, never leaving it to live the life of luxury in England, as the Jamaican plantocracy did.

Today, the great wealth of Barbados' first planter families has been dispersed, but the descendants of these families still remain, along with some of their beautiful and well-preserved plantation houses. But gone is the era of exclusivity which saw the coining of the phrase, "The Sealys talk only to the Piles, and the Piles talk only to God."

The island's "high whites" still speak the purest Bajan dialect, with a rich West Country brogue. You can always tell a Bajan white by his expression "Gaw-blum-muh!" He is a cricket fanatic, a horse-racing addict, and a sturdy believer in the pursuits of polo, tennis, rugby and soccer, a love of which he has passed on to black

Bajans. He named his houses and plantations after the Royal family and British districts and towns, even though he might never have been to England. The white Bajan is a passionate supporter of the British monarchy, of the Anglican Church (termed "the planter class at prayer" by one West Indian cleric and wit) and British institutions. In fact, until Independence in 1966, it was usual for white Bajans to openly support visiting English cricket teams over local host West Indian teams!

"High whites" continue to control much of the commercial and economic life of the island, just as they have since the 17th Century. And many are involved in all things that make Bajans a nation, from cricket to calypso-singing, from cutting

canes to celebrating Crop Over, from eating *cou-cou* to catching flying fish, from loyally drinking Cockspur rum to unswervingly defending Barbados' institutions against reproach or criticism from outsiders.

They heavily influence the island's cultural life as well. It was the privileged class which launched the tourism industry and founded a monthly magazine, *The Bajan*. In the early 1960s, the revival of Bajan folk songs and early calypsoes was spurred by the "Merrymen," a group of four (and sometimes five) Bajan whites still popular today. "Mighty Whitey" became, in 1984, the island's first white calypsonian. Certainly, in the last decades, Bajan cultural life has become a blending of black and white

Left, 77-year-old Mr. King of Martin's Bay has farmed all his life. Right, posing for a shot at Martin's Bay, St. John.

traditions.

Cheek by Jowl: The coming together of blacks and whites in Barbados began during the slave period, when blacks and poor whites lived "cheek by jowl" on the plantation tenantries and in free villages. Afro-Bajan men had children from poor white women, and vice versa. Co-mingling was trickier with the "high whites," however. They didn't mind having a black "outside woman," because, as a rhyme says, " . . . de blacker de woman, de sweeter de tail . . . ", but accepting blacks or mulattos socially was something else altogether. Open race discrimination was practiced in commerce, the civil service and, until the 1930s, within the Anglican Church, where whites sat at the front and blacks were relegated to the

into a white planter-class family in the late 1920s. Sir Grantley was, of course, a "man of the future" at the time: he was a Barbados Scholar, a lawyer, a better-than-average cricketer and a leading agitator for political reform. The marriage caused some raised eyebrows and certainly didn't break down the barriers.

However, Bajans of all groups will tell you that "it doesn't bother anybody." Others will reveal the not-very-secret secret that "black and white Bajans ent gwine marry one anodder, but nuff 'living-wid' does go on dat a lotta people don't know 'bout!" Attitudes are changing, if slowly.

"Bajanized" Blacks: The history of the Bajan black is very different from that of the first white settlers. The Bajan black is a

back. In sports, there were three racially exclusive clubs playing cricket, soccer, tennis and bridge until as late as 1970. Moreover, the last school to desegregate, St. Winifred's, did so in 1970.

While today there is an easy tolerance between the black majority and whites on Barbados, there still remain areas of racial exclusivism and class prejudice. For example, the many interracial couples that are seen on Barbados are almost all foreigners: the number of marriages between black and white Bajans can be counted on the fingers of two hands.

The best-known black politician of this century, the late Sir Grantley Adams, squeezed under the barrier by marrying

descendant of West Africans brought to the island between 1627 and 1807 as slaves. They probably came from the Gold Coast (modern day Ghana) or the area that is now Nigeria.

Unlike Jamaica, Guyana or Trinidad, Barbados was the destination of few African-born slaves after the year 1800. Thus African blacks became "Bajanized" relatively early. This tended to make them less resistant to local culture, with its Anglicized language, religion and customs.

On plantations such as Drax Hall (the largest on the island), Newton, St. Nicholas Abbey, Kendal, Sunbury, Colleton, Bayley's Thicketts and Morgan Lewis, the African natives and their children struggled to create a new way of life. Like those indentured everywhere, they resisted the slave system in whatever way they could. In Barbados, they had no mountains to run to, as in Jamaica or Dominica, St. Vincent or Grenada. There were only two courses open to those who wanted to escape. One was the caves in the middle parishes of St. Thomas and St. George. A second escape was to the island of St. Vincent, 95 miles (153 km) away on the fishing boats of poor whites and free blacks.

The slaves attempted open revolts four times, in 1649, 1675, 1692 and in 1816, but they lost each time, and after each showdown, the whites gained further ascendency. Dreams of freedom thwarted, these oppressed people sometimes resorted to

time there has been a slow yet confident feeling growing among black Bajans that they are as good as the English, Celtics, Jews and Indians who had always been regarded as somehow superior. The agitation of Clement Payne and Marcus Garvey, the performances of Jack Johnson, Joe Lewis and Muhammed Ali in boxing, of Jesse Owens in athletics, Pele in soccer and Gary Sobers, Wes Hall and Charlie Griffith in cricket all prompted new pride.

When black Bajans went overseas, they often became militant and eager to defend the rights of the laboring classes of all races. In Panama, the United States, Canada and Trinidad, Bajan blacks helped organize workers and unions long before such action could be taken on "the Rock" (as Barbados

forms of passive aggression and to indirect trickery, deceit and quiet defiance. Still, the oppressed Barbadians had the reputation of being the most obedient slaves in the region.

A New View: Experience and education eventually proved to be two great levelers, however. Hundreds of black Bajans served in the two World Wars and suddenly saw life in a radically different way. They saw whites doing menial jobs and even being ordered around by non-whites. Since that

Left, execs meet at international accounting firm in downtown Bridgetown. Right, the Forte family on Christmas Day in Queen's Park.

is called by emigrants).

In the 1960s, many of the black politicians who worked towards independence had spent time abroad in their early childhood, and were proud to be black and Bajan. Among these men were Errol Barrow, the Prime Minister, who had been a World War II airman and was trained in London as a lawyer and economist; Sir Grantley Adams, who was trained in London as a lawyer; and Sir Winston Scott, who was to become the first native Governor-General (1967-1976) and had been trained as a medical doctor in the United States. By contrast, the leader of the island's blanket trade union, the Barbados Workers' Union, Frank Wolcott, came by his racial pride the hard way—by remaining on the island and fighting discrimination. These men led Barbados into the 1970s and gave the next generation a new understanding of what it could mean to be a Barbadian.

During this period of ferment, two cultural foundations were formed which heralded the African heritage of black Bajans. Black Night, formed in 1969, and Yoruba Yard, created in 1972, were inspired by the philosophy of Elton "Elombe" Mottley, a confirmed Africanist. Blacks began to challenge the notion that to be a respectable citizen required rejecting African traditions. African folklore and practices were resurrected; school children read the African-inspired poetry of Eddie Braithwaite and the writings of George

vants" to enjoy the "sweets" of Barbados without first becoming part of the culture and supporting the strides she has made in race relations.

To be a Barbadian you have to respect the rights of the people, and this is non-negotiable.

Modern Bajans, in other words, hope that outsiders won't jeopardize a hard-won culture, won't come "mashing our corns." A controversial decision in 1985, to elect a white Canadian as the representative to the International Beauty Queen pageant, inspired this song by Mighty Gabby:

Miss Barbados—never hear 'bout ackee tree
Miss Barbados—never hear 'bout Sir Gary (Sobers) *or even me,*

Lamming, Bruce St. John, Timothy Callender, Austin "Tom" Clarke and Jeanette Layne-Clarke—all literary explorations of what it means to be Bajan.

The "New" Bajans: In the 1980s, a new national consciousness has emerged in Barbados. Ironically, the black Bajan is now more comfortable with whites and the other "original" settlers of the island. However, dealing with the "new" Bajans, recent arrivals of the 20th Century, is a slightly different matter. These groups include Indians and Pakistanis, Lebanese and expatriates of America, Canada, England, Germany, China and the South Americas. According to Eddie Brathwaite's poem "Negus" it is not enough for these "arri-

Miss Barbados—never hear 'bout flying fish
Miss Barbados—never hear 'bout cuckoo dish
Miss Barbados—never hear 'bout nutten so
When she get she Bajan citizenship lemme know!

In the 1980s, Barbadians "ent mekking no sport" about their national pride. After all, it has taken more than 350 years to be able to share in the proud refrain, "All o' we is Bajan."

Above, Mr. Williams of Newcastle, St. John, just awakened from an afternoon snooze, shares tales of life in the old days.

A SHIP ON LAND?

"What a strange idea, but then it is not so strange, considering that we are in Barbados!"
—a visitor's comment

A ship on land indeed. Founded in the 1860s by a retired black seaman, the Barbados "Landship" began as a collaboration of ex-sailors who sought to strengthen the camaraderie which developed among them on the perilous seas, and, at the same time, carry on the sights and sounds of their former vocation. The

founders, seeking to bring discipline and a sense of worth into their "evening years," styled a self-help organization using a naval theme and structure—a land-based "brotherhood of the sea."

Today the Landship has many facets: Not only are they a group of talented performers, they are also a savings and loan society and character-building "club" with many local branches.

Local chapters are "ships," each with a complement of "officers," "mates," "engineers," "doctors" and so on. The "crew" dresses in white bell-bottoms and shirts, British Navy style, complete with epaulettes and ratings. And—call it progressive or just a sailor's answered prayers—women were allowed to come

abroad as "nurses" in the early 1920s.

From the start the most visible aspect of Landship has been its hilarious public performances. With all the starch and shoeshine afforded to a serious review of arms, the sailors, lively and straight-faced, demonstrate their formation marching discipline as only Afro-Barbadians steeped in British pomp and circumstance can. The "wangle-low" is a semi-limbo, the "center-march" is done in time to African rhythm and in a formation that would leave poor Lord Nelson spinning in his briny grave and most civilian onlookers in hysterics. In one dance, the sailors advance with the right hand swinging ahead together with the right foot—shamelessly contrary to tradition!

With titles such as "Rough Seas," "Sinking Ship," "Changing of the Guard," and "Admiral's Inspection," the Landship dances are spoofs of real life situations. They are performed to tuk band music—a sort of fife and drum corps with an African touch, a unique and thoroughly Barbadian accompaniment to the naval masquerade.

The burlesque public appearances of Landship has, over the years, drawn attention away from its more serious purpose: to foster community integrity, self-reliance and leadership. One of its most important features of Landship is the "Meetings Turn," whereby a community pool is funded through regular dues payments by members in order to aid individuals in time of fire, flooding and unemployment. The Landship Movement is truly a credit to the ingenuity and resourcefulness of the Bajan people.

A Religious Mosaic

Religion is not far from hand at any turn in Barbados. From the patchwork of staid Anglican churches (seemingly at least one to every village), to the ebullient "Tie-heads," to Rastafarians hawking coconuts on the street, the Barbadian people are, on the whole, believers and practitioners.

Almost all schools begin the day with prayer, and a substantial amount of radio time is devoted to religious programming.

"Gospel Bag," a weekly newspaper column, informs its readers of upcoming religious activities. It also serves as a local hit parade for new records released by gospel singing groups.

Each Sunday afternoon at three o'clock, CBC T.V. hosts a half-hour of religious choral singing. Island choirs join a year-long waiting list to appear on the popular "Time to Sing."

At last count, there were over 140 *different* religious denominations and sects practicing on the island: among these are Protestants, Catholics, Jews, Mormons, Bahais, Muslims and Hindus.

Religious tolerance is almost as old as Barbados itself. The earliest settlers were British Royalists and Anglicans who, in 1627, claimed Barbados "at one and the same time for the king of England and the King of Kings." Later, at the time of England's Civil War, others fled to Barbados because of their conflict with Oliver Cromwell's Parliament. But when a Cromwellian invasion party gained a footing on the island in 1651, the two opposing factions quickly reached a compromise which proclaimed "liberty of conscience in matters of religion." Ironically, this pact was ratified by the English Parliament in 1652, at a time when religious freedom in England itself was denied.

The colonists' early religious tolerance was admirable, but it also served a practical end: to ensure the stability and profitability of the plantation system. Indeed, the sugar producers were so eager to avoid the disruptive forces of the English conflict that a local custom insisted "whosoever named the word Roundhead or Cavalier, should give to all that heard him a shoat and turkey to be eaten at his house."

An intensely emotional Sunday service at one of the island's many "storefront" revivalist churches.

Yet "liberty of conscience" proved to stretch only so far. Irish Catholics exiled to Barbados as indentured servants were accompanied, at one landing, by 26 teachers and priests. Upon arrival, the teachers and priests were sold into seven years' labor, and many died as a result of the especially harsh treatment ordered for them by local authorities. A trickle of Catholic immigrants followed the first influx, but it was only after a military garrison requested a Catholic chaplain in 1839, and a mission was established, that this faith gained acceptance.

Expedience: By the mid-1600s, sugar was big business in Barbados. Realizing the advantage of a cheap, acclimatized and permanent black labor force over a motley crew of sick, white indentured servants, landowners threw in their lot with the traders and began importing slaves by the thousands.

Unlike the Catholics, who considered it their duty to impart the civilizing force of Christianity to the "heathen" Africans, the British planters refused to let their slaves become Christians, often against the express wishes of the Anglican authorities in Britain. Their rationale, when offered, was primarily one of expedience. It was commonly believed that one Christian could not enslave another. By excluding them from the fold of Christianity, the British insured that the Africans remained fair game.

When the Church of England attacked this excuse in 1691, by declaring that conversion to Christianity did not make slaves free men, the Barbadian planters retorted, "What? Shall they be like us?"

Planters also developed rigid social divisions between Christians and the Africans to maintain order in circumstances in which they were dangerously outnumbered, sometimes by as much as 13 to 1. White indentured servants were given special privileges within the household. Christian ceremonies were always performed in secret in order to play on the African tradition of the secret society, which endows its members with special knowledge and power. This practice, coupled with the staggering control exercised by the planters over the lives of their slaves, created a belief that Europeans were witches and sorcerers, in the classic African sense of one who could cause harm or benefit by harnessing

The organist practices in solitude at St. Patrick's Catholic Church in central Bridgetown.

the powers of nature.

Folk Beliefs: While the massive disruption of enslavement and the intermingling of Africans from very different cultures prevented religious systems from remaining wholly intact, the absence of a Christian missionary effort undoubtedly encouraged the slaves to retain African folk beliefs and superstitions.

Some of these customs persist in diluted form in present-day Barbados. Until recently, the placenta and umbilical cord of newborn babies were buried in the ground near the place of birth in order to link the spirit with its homeland. Long and festive funerals were held to ensure that the deceased's spirit would rest in peace.

Some Bajans still speak of *duppies*, or traveled as a ball of fire in search of blood. If someone found the skin and rubbed it with pepper or salt, the hag could not re-enter, and so died. The last of the hags is supposed to have died in the 1920s.

By far the most notorious of these folk beliefs, however, is the system of *obeah*, a form of witchcraft. The practice is believed to have come from a West African religion called *Obi*. The presence of obeah in Barbados today is a matter of opinion. Many hotly claim that it no longer exists, while most will agree that its power is limited to that segment of the population that believes in it. As one Barbadian author writes, "What you believe in, you die in. If you believe that's a duppy 'pon the roof, then one is there."

spirits of the dead, who roam the earth at night, taking various forms and returning to their favorite "haunts."

Duppies are barred from entering a house by hanging various herbs at the windows and doorways, leaving one's shoes at the door, and scattering sand around the house. (This forces the spirit to stop and count each grain, a task that cannot be completed before daylight.) Gifts of liquor are particularly appreciated, and it's still a Barbadian tradition to sprinkle a few drops from a new rum bottle on the ground "for the spirits."

An especially hideous spirit of the night stalker type was the *hag*—usually a planter's wife—who shed her skin at night and

Obeah "men" can be of either sex, and typically employ a bag of charms which may include rusty nails, feathers, broken glass and pieces of clay to work their magic which can be for good or evil purposes.

"Come-To-Me Sauce": Obeah potions are credited with the ability to make one succeed in one's endeavors and give one control over others. Not a few men are alleged to have been tricked into marriage after unwittingly consuming "come-to-me sauce," which makes its victim irresistibly attracted to the woman who slipped it into his food. Wives are also known to have given their husbands "stay-at-home sauce" to curtail extra-marital philandering.

These potent substances are administered in coco tea or in *cou-cou*, a traditional corn meal dish. Legend has it that one potential victim was saved from a tainted dish of cou-cou and flying fish when the cooked fish began to wink at him.

Control over others can also take more sinister, and even fatal, forms. "Duppy dust"—grave dirt or pulverized human bones—is a particularly dreaded poison, thrown directly on the victim or hidden within his food. Obeah practitioners can "read up the dead" and direct them to wreak the desired vengeance, sometimes by entering the bodies of their poor victims.

As recently as the early 1960s, one such demon reportedly entered the body of an unfortunate woman. Many people claim to have heard the little fellow, called Conrad,

What de hell it could be
Dat every fo-day morning
A man in Della belly.
O Conrad, O Conrad
Conrad come out de woman belly
and he gone to Trinidad
Tra-la-la-la, Tra, la, la, la
Conrad come out de woman belly
and he gone to Trinidad!

Though death is sometimes attributed to the force of obeah, induced insanity is the more oft-mentioned result. Certain bush medicines are believed to act upon the nervous system to produce psychotic states, and just the fear of obeah is said to be enough to drive one mad. In the early 1960s, a young man charged with the murder of his wife's lover had his charge

uttering the foulest curses in a high-pitched voice, and making all kinds of demands on his "hostess."

Nobody knows how or why he tormented this particular woman, but it is known that he defied all efforts of an obeah man to exorcise him. Eventually, the wretched woman was admitted to a psychiatric hospital.

This is no isolated incident, as indicated by a popular folk song:
De mother-in-law said to de son-in-law

Left, Spiritual Baptists, called "Tie-Heads" because of the colorful cloths they wear, in St. Michael. Right, Sunday morning at St. Thomas Church.

reduced to manslaughter on the grounds of temporary insanity due to obeah.

The British did their best to crush obeah from the start, forcing the practice underground. Today, obeah remains on the Statute Books of Barbados as a felony.

Conversion Efforts: Prior to the emancipation of the slaves in 1838, several religious groups antagonized the planting community with their efforts to convert blacks. The Quakers were the earliest and most influential. They ignored a 1676 Act which prevented them from bringing Negroes to their meetings and riled the establishment with their controversial stands on such issues as war and oathtaking in court.

Quaker's Road, in St. Michael is believed to be the former center of the Quaker community. A cemetery west of Government House, and a burial place just north of the St. Philip Parish Church are the only other vestiges of the Quaker religion in Barbados today.

The Moravians, the oldest Protestant Episcopal Church in the world, became known for their support of the slaves under their leader Benjamin Brookshaw. During the slave revolt of 1816, members of this denomination were granted virtual immunity from the surrounding terror. Today, the majority of the 1,200 seats in the Moravian Church on Roebuck Street, once the site of a cockfighting pit, are filled with black Bajans.

The ranks of the Methodist Church were

tional options, majority of ex-slaves joined the Anglican Church following emancipation and the offer of salvation.

To many Barbadians, Anglicanism still represents respectibility and an opportunity for social mobility. Yet, its complete isolation from traditional African belief, and relative lack of "religious zeal," created a sort of spiritual vacuum in the post-emancipation period, soon to be filled by the revivalist sects that were sweeping the American South.

"Store-Front" Churches: Barbados today hosts a staggering number of small sects, often similar in doctrine though different in name. As in some African societies, any man who could be a convincing intermediary between his fellows and his Maker was

also swelled by the newly-freed slaves at whose side it had stood in the darker days before emancipation. Previously, the Methodist minister, William Shrewsbury, had so angered the landed gentry with his "forthright manner" that, in 1823, his church was systematically demolished, its furniture was destroyed, and a proclamation aiming to abolish the faith was posted on the town walls. This challenge to religious freedom was soon answered by Anne Gill, who defied the authorities and rallied her fellow Methodists into a united front. By 1826, the church had been rebuilt on James Street, St. Michael. Over 20 Methodist churches stand on the island today.

Despite the presence of these denomina-

likely to establish a following. Many storefront churches took root in impoverished rural areas. The intensely emotional religious experience they encouraged and their joyous, hand-clapping gospel music was nearer to black African rhythms than the English hymns of the established churches.

Yet, these religions still harked back to a white, Christian God who often did not seem to be listening to His black children. This was true throughout much of the Caribbean, where it seemed that God moved in mysterious, if selective, ways among the white people, but left the blacks to fend for themselves at the backs of the English-built churches or in makeshift churches of their own.

In Jamaica, social inequality and the search for an identity rooted in Africa fostered the Rastafarian movement. It has since had a profound impact throughout the Caribbean.

The movement began, in spirit at least, in the teachings and beliefs of the Jamaican, Marcus Garvey, who founded the Universal Negro Improvement Association. In the 1920s, he called for self-reliance among Africans "at home and abroad." He advocated a "back to Africa" consciousness, and awakened black pride. He denounced the British colonial indoctrination that taught blacks to feel shame and contempt for their African heritage. He urged his followers to "look to Africa, when a black king shall be crowned, for the day of deliverance is at

and the need to regain their heritage that the black race temporarily lost by straying from the holy ways. Thus, the true Rastafarian lives a peaceful and pious life, desiring nothing beyond material essentials, and engaging in contemplation of the scriptures.

A Modern Babylon: At the same time, the Rastafarian rejects the white man's world—the modern "Babylon"—and its greed, dishonesty, lasciviousness, meat-eating habits, "devil soup" (alcohol) and chemical-oriented technology.

The two most obvious external marks of the Rasta—his "dreadlocks" and his proud, strutting walk—are inspired by the image of the lion in Selassie's title, Lion of Judah. Rastas are also known by outsiders for their use of *ganja* (marijuana) as a

hand."

When, in 1930, Ras Tafari was crowned in Ethiopia as Emperor Haile Selassie I, "King of Kings, Lord of Lords, and the Conquering Lion of the Tribe of Judah," many thought the prophecy was fulfilled, and a way of life was born.

Haile Selassie claimed to be a direct descendant of King David, and the 225th in an unbroken line of Ethiopian kings from the time of Solomon and Sheba. His followers stressed pride in their blackness,

Left, members of an Anglican church choir. Right, the ebullient "Tie-Heads" singing at their annual candlelight procession, on "Old Year's Night" (New Year's Eve).

sacrament, a cause of frequent conflict with the police.

Rastafarianism was introduced to Barbados in 1975, and spread quickly. But in addition to faithful adherents, the movement soon began to attract various undesirables, including criminals and the mentally ill. Local youths saw it as an extension of their rebellion against school and home. They welcomed the attention their dreadlocks, cocky strut and colorful garb attracted; Rastafarianism was an excuse, too, to smoke ganja.

Barbadians soon took up arms, sometimes literally, against this wave of "Rascals." Whenever a dreadlocked youth fell foul of the law, there was always a headline to trumpet the fact: "Rasta fined for possession of drugs" ... "Rasta youth charged for larceny" ... "Dreadlocked man arrested" ...

In due course, however, the attention of renegade young people wandered back to the streets—to rollerskating, break-dancing and video games. Criminals, too, realized that dreadlocks no longer afforded them anonymity, and the faddists got bored and cut their hair.

The remaining true brethren more or less accept and are accepted by the larger society. Many have made substantial contributions to the arts and to sports. Some better-known Rastafarians in Barbados are Winstone Farrell, an actor and rhythm poet; Adonijah, a university teacher, jour-

nalist and calypso musician; Ras Iley, another calypsonian; and Ashanti Trotman, a gifted wood craftsman.

Heard God's Voice: The only truly indigenous Barbadian religion is the so-called "Tie-head" movement, founded by Bishop Granville Williams in 1957, after a 16-year self-imposed exile on the neighboring island of Trinidad.

In Trinidad, Williams had been exposed to the Spiritual Baptists, a West Indian revivalist religion with its roots in Africa. Maintaining that he had heard God's voice and seen visions, Williams held his first open-air meeting in the fishing village of Oistins, within days of his return to Barbados. There was a terrific response, and soon after, he established the Jerusalem Apostolic Spiritual Baptist Church at Ealing Grove, followed by its Zion Sister at Richmond Gap.

Members wear colorful gowns, each color symbolic of a particular quality: white stands for purity, cream for spirituality, blue for holiness, gold for royalty, green for strength, brown for happiness, silver-gray for overcoming, and pink for success. Red stands for strength, as well as for the blood of Christ. Both men and women wrap their heads in cloth, hence the name "Tie-heads."

As a native faith of Barbados, the church is closely tied to African religious traditions and rites. Its lively music is often accompanied by much hand-clapping, foot-stomping and dancing. "We can take 'Abide with Me' and make you dance to it," boasts Bishop Williams. This is no mean feat: 'Abide with Me' is an Anglican hymn traditionally sung at funerals and notorious for its dreariness.

The Tie-heads are also known for their mysterious "Mourning Ground" rituals. After accepting the faith, the members are baptized in "living water" and given instruction in the doctrine. The born-again then mourns "a godly sorrow which calls one away from the busy walks of life." The Mourning Ground is a sacred section of the church set aside for this purpose and tended by chosen members. Here, in isolation, the mind is cleansed by prayer and purification for a period of seven to 10 days.

The Spiritual Baptist Church now boasts a following of some 7,000 people, approximately 60 percent female and 40 percent male. This is considered quite an achievement, as the island's seemingly innumerable rum shops tend to deprive the traditional churches of male membership.

Churches and rum shops, in fact, constitute the largest number of non-residential buildings to be found on this island of 166 square miles. And while a Barbadian woman is likely to be found attending services on a Sunday morning, rum shop patronage for men has become a well-entrenched alternative. Indeed, women in Barbados are generally expected to bear the burdens of morality and stability for their families. It is women who are the backbone of the family and the church, and the primary force behind religion's continuing importance on the island.

Left, Anglicans after a Sunday service. Right, the graveyard behind St. John's Church, with sweeping views of the east coast and a tree that loses its leaves.

"LIKE FAMILY TO ME": THE BAJAN HOUSEHOLD

Mrs. Eudora Brathwaite is 55 years old. Last year she married Selwyn, the man she has been living with for the last 26 years and for whom she bore six of her 11 children.

She looks back on her life: "In dem days girls didn't stay on at school like they do now. I left when I was 14 and had to stay home and help my mother do the housework. She work in the (cane) field. When I was making my first child she was so mad. She cuss and carry on and t'row me out de house. But she tek me back when the baby born 'cos she like how it look."

The relationship between Eudora and the father of her first child was short-lived and though he gave her money for the child during its first year, she stayed with her family.

At age 19, she became involved with Deighton. A child was born and she moved in with him. Only two of the four children born to the couple lived. Eudora explains in a matter-of-fact tone: "Women had a lot of children in dem days—some had more than 20. But a lot died."

When Deighton migrated to England to work as a bus conductor, Eudora and her children moved back in with her mother. Deighton at first sent money to them, but later this and all other communication from him ceased, and Eudora was forced to earn money as a domestic servant. Her mother looked after the children. Life was hard, but they managed.

Major Crisis: But then her mother died, and Eudora faced the major crisis of her life—the threat of destitution and the embarrassment of becoming a welfare case. She found a solution: "I had to find somebody to help me with the children. Selwyn was liking me at the time and he had a good job, so I decided to stick wid he."

Before their marriage, Eudora and Selwyn lived together for 26 years and produced six children. In the early years, Eudora continued to earn money to support her children from previous unions. Now these older children contribute financially to her maintenance. But Deighton recently wrote from London to ask that

they join him there. Eudora is reluctant, for she feels she will lose their contributions if they go.

Eudora's changing family pattern is typical of women of her generation and illustrates a number of characteristics of the families of poorer black Barbadians, who form the majority of the population.

A typical pattern for women is that of delaying marriage and entering into a number of different unions, serially and with different men. Often couples start out with a "visiting union," in which the man

visits his girlfriend at her house. Children may be born, and the couple may either move in together and eventually marry, or they may remain casual for a while before ending the relationship. It is not uncommon for a woman to have given birth to children from more than one man. The distinction between legitimate and illegitimate children is of little importance and there is no stigma attached to being an illegitimate child.

While it is accepted that a woman will enter into unions with more than one man during her lifetime, to do so simultaneously and to "have children all about" (from a number of men) is cause for considerable scorn. There is a Bajan proverb that goes

Left, champagne and a kiss for Mrs. Scantelbury from her son Victor; on the table is "peas and rice." Right, "hanging out" in St. Joseph.

"When yuh pick corn 'pon more than one row, yuh don' know where yuh get yuh bag full up." It means that when a woman is involved with too many men, she will not be sure which one has made her pregnant. Most women are careful about this, and they are generally sure about who the fathers of their children are.

Fame and Shame: For a man, however, the situation is different. It is often said in Barbados, "What is fame for the man is shame for the woman." Even when a man is married or involved with one woman, he often continues to maintain a relationship with another woman and produce "outside" children. This is often accepted by wives until money they feel is theirs goes to support the other household.

Even though some women will tell you that "A good live-with better dan a bad marriage," for most, to wear a ring and be addressed as "Mistress" signifies that they have really made it, even though they may have had to wait for years. Weddings are often put off until a couple is well into middle age and childbearing is complete, as in Eudora's case.

This ambiguity towards marriage is the result of expectations about what a husband should be. For a man, marriage means economic responsibilities—not the least of which is the cost of the wedding.

Food for Days: A Bajan wedding is a grand affair! No expense is spared. People nostalgically speak of the country weddings of years ago, especially the elaborate recep-

Though many women work, and have done so since the days of slavery, home and children are their main concerns. Children are so important to womanhood that it is a great insult to be called a "mule," or worse still, a "graveyard" (a term for a woman who has had an abortion). But while one or two children are proof of womanhood, males are esteemed for their success with a number of women and their fathering of many children.

Women are expected to be the carriers of respectability in the community. As one man joked, "Women in de church; men in de rum shop." Respectability for a woman has its roots in the family and the church and is symbolized primarily by marriage.

tions with "food for days." These celebrations were often repeated the weekend after in what was known as a "second day" wedding. As Louis Lynch describes it in *The Barbados Book:*

For days friends had been bringing down trays of ground provisions, dozens of eggs, bananas, water coconuts and live cockerels...masses of corn pone, cassava pone, pudding, sponge, coconut bread, 'black cake', fricasseed chicken, baked ham, boiled salt beef, avocados, lashings of peas and rice and stew, baked pork and fried fish, and to wash it all down, coconut water for the children, cheap red wine or falernum for the ladies, and rum or gin for the lords of creation.

Some of this splendor has died out. Some say it is because people are "too cheap," others that it is difficult to keep up with the rising cost of living. Still, a wedding is an important celebration.

If the opportunity arises, the visitor should stop and take a peek inside the church at the beauty of a bride in white lace, satin or chiffon, the brillance of the bridesmaids, often six or eight in number, the bridegroom and best man in smart dark suits set off with orchid buttonholes. Nothing must be left out of a "proper wedding." Weddings may attract many bystanders to the church, and any perception of skimping, even by the use of a cheaper material for the bride's dress, is cause for "malicious" comment.

a doctor's attempts to obtain information from a male patient:

Doctor: *What is your son's name?*
Father: *John.*
Doctor: *John what?*
Father: *I doan know. You see he can either go in my name or the mother name.*
Doctor: *What is the mother's name?*
Father: *Estelle.*
Doctor: *Her second name.*
Father: *I doan know.*
Doctor: (becoming exasperated) *How many children do you have?*
Father: *Five, but I doan know she last name' cos I doan tek so much notice o'she.*

Paternal Pride: A father often takes pride in his children, especially in their educa-

Something old, something new: marriage, Bajan style, circa 1900 (left) and today (right). Weddings are elaborate affairs where no expense is spared.

Living Separate Lives: "Family is woman's business," and the mother-centered family is another feature of life in Barbados. Ties between the couple are weak and they generally lead fairly separate lives. They usually engage in different leisure activities. Money and property matters are rarely entered into jointly, and as we've seen in Eudora's case, separations are common.

The marginality of the father in family affairs is amusingly recounted by Louis Lynch in *The Barbados Book* as he records

tional progress, but his responsibilities lie mainly with providing financial support. This means he wants to be sure the child is biologically his. Denials of paternity do occur, especially from men in casual, visiting relationships, but then, so do false paternity claims from women.

The financial obligations of fatherhood can be quite onerous for a poor man. A man is reluctant to support children that are not his own even if he is married to their mother and therefore legally bound to do so. Remember how Eudora continued to work to help support her older children from previous unions, even after she and Selwyn were married?

Fathers are expected to support their

children even when he and the mother are not living together or when they are "outside" children, though as we saw in Eudora's case, such support may dwindle with time and then cease altogether.

Men are often accused of being "wut'-less" (worthless) and "vagabonds" in evading their responsibilities to their children. Though these labels may well apply to some, it is not easy for men to keep up with the many claims to their often meager financial resources. As one man put it. "I got a lot of stretching to do with my money. Apart from the woman in the house, I got to give my mother something, plus I got to give some to the ones outside."

Where the father's duty ends the mother's begins, for with the money he provides she performs all the other child-rearing tasks. As Eudora herself put it: "The mother is who raise the child. She does nurse it, feed it, dress it, send it to school and to church—mek sure she raise it the right way, decent-like, with good manners."

The relationship between a mother and her children is close and often lasts to the end of her days. Mothers assume responsibility for their children and take their duties very seriously, always making sure their children are well-groomed and neatly dressed. The sight of scrubbed young girls on their way to Sunday school, all dressed up in pink frills with matching bows in their tightly braided hair, is a delight to visitors and locals alike.

Discipline is strict with "plenty licks and lashes" (slaps)—licks for being late for school and for arriving home late, licks for forgetting to say "good morning" or "good evening" or "yes, please" to your elders. "To spare the rod is to spoil the child," yet as one mother says in George Lamming's classic novel of village life in Barbados, *In the Castle of My Skin*, "When all's said and done they is ours and we love them. Whatever we mothers say or do, nobody love them like we."

Eudora and many other women like her consider themselves mothers first and foremost; they devote nearly all their time and energy to mothering.

Help from Granny: Yet there are times when such duties are by necessity exchanged or passed on to others. It is common for a mother to take a job to earn money and share the raising of her children with someone else.

When Deighton stopped sending money

Homing it up and sporting their finest on a family outing to Queen's Park in Bridgetown.

from England, Eudora took his place as breadwinner and her mother helped take care of the children. "Leaving de child at Granny—dat is my culture," sang the calypsonian Mighty Gabby in "Culture," his 1985 hit about life in Barbados.

The exchanges between female relatives go beyond that of occasional babysitting and borrowing of money, food and other goods. If a woman has a large number of children who prove to be a handful, one or even two may be "adopted" and go to live with an aunt, sister, sister-in-law, or even a neighbor or friend. This is not legal adoption, though the woman assumes full maternal responsibility and may be addressed as "Ma" or "Mum." Children are shared rather than possessed in circumstances like

Eudora's.

Tightly-knit villages and extended families make this kind of cooperation possible. In Barbados, a family can extend beyond the confines of mother, father and children. Supportive networks between female relatives—sisters, mothers and daughters—are especially strong, and sometimes include male relatives as well—uncles, brothers, cousins and grandfathers. These men can serve as father-substitutes when the biological father is not around.

Family relations, then, are flexible and open enough to extend into the wider community. Households may contain a mixture of relatives and friends, often on a permanent basis. Friends may call each other "Sis" or "Brother." A friend is often said to be "like family to me" or sometimes even "better than family to me." Indeed, it is difficult for a stranger to tell who is "family" and who is not.

No Place Like Home: Three generation households are common, particularly those containing grandmother, mother and children. The question of "What to do with mother?" asked by many adults in Europe and America is less of a problem in Barbados, where many grandmothers lead functional lives for much of their old age. The family home continues to play an important part in the lives of many Bajans; it is a haven to which they can return at any stage of life.

Family ties also stretch internationally, and although some links with migrants may weaken, they are likely to be reactivated in later years, as we saw in the case of Eudora and Deighton. Links with migrant family members are maintained by letters, remittances and visits, often for funerals and weddings. Starting in early December planeloads of Bajans laden with gifts arrive "home" for Christmas.

Changing Patterns: But family patterns are changing in Barbados. For example, Eudora's first son Tony married when he was only 24 (14 years before his mother married!). Both he and his wife, Michelle, completed secondary school; he is now a bank clerk and she is a secretary. She has had one child, and continues to work. With the use of contraception, now generally accepted and widely available in Barbados, the couple intend to limit their children to two. Any more would be too expensive and a "keep-back" to their careers. They live in their own house in a new housing development and employ a half-day maid.

Some claim that as Third World countries industrialize and modernize, they will adopt the same cultural patterns as the developed world, with family life becoming centered on a nuclear family household. Maybe so, but tradition dies hard. While Tony and Michelle lead a very different life from Eudora, not everything has changed. Eudora looks after their child while they are at work. Last year Michelle returned to her mother's house after she and Tony quarreled. Michelle suspected he was involved with another woman. True or not, it would be in character for him to have an "out-

side" woman. Though perhaps universal, this behavior is especially common in Barbados. What is changing is that wives are becoming less tolerant of it.

Family Flexibility: Traditional family life in Barbados is often described in derogatory terms as having "promiscuous" and "adulterous" sexual relations, "illegitimate" children, "unmarried" mothers and "absentee" fathers. But there is another side of the picture, one which stresses the flexible and adaptable nature of the family among the poor in Barbados.

Historically, these families have endured the transposition from Africa and the rigors of slavery, and now survive in conditions of unemployment and poverty. Migration also removes adult breadwinners from the family. In many societies, this might cause a crisis in family life. But the Barbadian family adapts relatively painlessly. The weakness of the bonds between couples, at least in the early years of a relationship, and the fact that men and women lead fairly separate lives cushion what seems to be almost inevitable separation.

We must look at these features within the economic and historical context of the society in which they exist. Only then can we come to a full understanding of family life in Barbados, where family duties are constantly being rearranged and reassigned to cope with life's contingencies.

Facts About The Bajan Household

85% of all Barbadians own the houses they live in, but not necessarily the land their houses are built on.

In rural areas, 98% of the houses are occupied by the owners; in urban areas, 75% are.

(In contrast, only 62% of Americans and 47% of Englishmen live in houses they or their families own.)

78% of Bajan children are born out-of-wedlock.

Over 74% of Bajan between the ages of 15 and 44 have never been married, according to the 1970 census.

38% of Bajan households are headed by women.

In the early 1980s, only 20% of Bajan households had clocks in working order.

90% of households have running water.

79% of Bajans have TVs.

24% of the people have cars.

55% of the houses have telephones.

82% have radios.

79% have refrigerators.

The Yearwoods pose outside their chattel house in the parish of St. Lucy. "Chattel" means "movable property."

WITH LOVE FROM MAYNARD'S VILLAGE:
A LETTER FROM "THE ROCK"

Almost every family in Barbados has relatives living abroad. Yet even emigrants think of Barbados, affectionately called "The Rock," as home, and try to keep in touch. The following letter from a mother in Barbados to her daughter in England provides some insight into the everyday life of a Bajan village:

Dear Grace,

I got yuh last letter and I glad to hear yuh keepin' well—yuh old mother here alright too. I hope yuh tekin' care o' yuhself and de cold weather in England 'ent killin' yuh.

white people nose 'cause dey keep slippin' down on my wun. Dese pas' months de pressure 'ent botherin' me so much—de doctor call it hypertension or some such fancy name. I tryin' to keep down de weight like yuh tell muh. I cut down 'pon de starches and tryin' to eat de greens—but dey so expensive doh!

Yuh father still here de same way. Yuh would tink now he gettin' old—he did 65 las' birthday—yuh would tink dat he would change. He still chasin' de women—dey goin' kill he! But I lef' he to de Lord. I know

Yuh mus' remember to use de mixture—dat candle grease and coconut oil and camphor—which I send up for yuh to rub yuh feet 'gainst de cold. Doan' mind de smell—it good.

Yuh ask muh so many questions 'bout so many people here in Maynard's village in yuh las' letter dat it goin' tek a long time fuh muh to write 'bout all o' dem. And muh eyes 'ent so good now. Las' time I went to de doctor he tell muh to wear de glasses all de time but yuh know how it is—Mum 'ent get 'custom to dem yet. Dis old grey head o' mine can't deal with dis new-fangle ting. And besides de glasses mussee mek for

yuh doan like muh to bad talk yuh father and he 'ent all bad—I should know after 50 years!

He still usin' de money dat yuh send good—fixing up de place. We change de winders in de front from de old-time jalousies to glass ones. Dat wasn't so much problem. But dis changin' from de wood to de wall is a real headache. De dust from de cement and de cleanin' up every day after de workmen gone. So far de back part finish—paint up and everyt'ing. It 'ent so much to be done now—Praise de Lord! And I hope he goin' let muh live to see it done.

Yuh know dat yuh sister Shirley daughter staying wid me now. We does call she "Tammy" for short. But she's a sweet girl doh! And helpful too—washin' wares and tidyin' de house and so every mornin'. I gotta admire she 'cause she doan get on like dese young vagabonds o' today. Yuh can't speak to none o' dem 'cause dey 'ent got no respect and no shame neidder. When you did commin' up any big person could correc' yuh and yuh would have to hear. But today dem too hard ears.

But I was tellin' yuh 'bout Tammy. She is church. Well, nobody 'ent see she for a few months very well. And yuh know what—jus' yesterday I did commin' from in town and I butt up 'pon lickmout' Doreen. She tell muh dat Mavis got a baby boy—6 weeks now. And nobody 'ent see it yet. To tink dat Bertha is muh friend and she 'ent tell muh—not a word! But Doreen now—she does know everyt'ing 'bout everybody—she say dat de child ugly, ugly like de Pastor. De Lord does move in mysterious ways!

I going stop writin' for now I goin' to look

bright too yuh know. She jus' pass de exam and she reach near de top. And it does mek muh old heart feel so good to see she steppin' out 'pon a mornin' in she school uniform.

But child I gotta tell yuh dis—yuh remember Bertha daughter dat name Mavis —de foolishy, foolishy one—dat used to play dat she more Christian dan anybody else? And de only place dat she used to go to

Left, outdoor haircuts, such as this one in St. John, are a Bajan tradition. Right, the girls of St. George shake and jam to the beat of calypso and American Top 40.

for someting to put in de pot. I still can't do like de young people and cook Sunday for Monday. I goin' cook some stewfood wid sweet potato, a piece o' pumpkin, some breadfruit and a piece o' pigtail and some light dumplin's—'cause yuh know yuh father like dat. Doan' mind de women—he still doan' eat out. He mussee frighten for what dey might put in the food to mek he bewitch. Doan' mind me—I know he does like muh cookin'.

I doan' know ef I remember to tell yuh but I did get a invitation to Tiny weddin'. At de St. Michael Cathedral—ef yuh please! So yuh know me—I did had to go.

And de talk, girl—everybody wonderin' who de groom is. He name write 'pon de invitation—Sylvester MacDonald Dacosta Broome! Some say dat he livin' in America, some say England. One body say he white, but yuh Aunt Cintie say doan' mind de name—is de skinny little boy dey used to call "Bones"—dat used to run 'bout here barefoot. But she vex 'cause she didn't get no invitation.

For an occasion like dat dis old girl had to look real smart—everyt'ing new from head to toe—hat, dress, shoes, bag and gloves 'cause gloves in fashion now. I didn't bother you 'bout sending de outfit 'cause my meeting turn was commin' up and dat money was sufficient.

De big day come. Riding in de taxi wid yuh father mek muh remember de day we get married. And yuh father lookin' somet'ing like he did den—t'ree piece suit and all. I did feel too sweet.

Tiny did look real good but she mother—I 'ent know what it is dat she had on! De hat did like a upsided-down lampshade. She face didn't make-up bad but de eye shadder did too blue and too tick and when she start to cry all o' it run down she face. Lord what a mess!

De bridegroom look dapper. He is a Bajan—but he been 'way for donkey years. She mussee find he when she went to

England—only 17 days and she come back talking like she swallow a dictionary.

Anyway everybody enjoy duhself. It didn't really nothin' to find fault 'bout—but yuh know de village people. It did a nine-day-talk 'bout here.

But I did tellin' yuh 'bout de changes in de village. Mos' people try to improve de house. Everybody got in electric now. No more oil lamps—doh I still keep mine—one in each room jus' in case—'cause yuh doan' get no warnin' when de light goin' off. Nowadays everybody got dey little fridge and TV—some even got videos.

Mos' people got in runnin' water now but de standpipe still dere. Sometimes we old folk still find weself by de standpipe talkin' like de old days. Look how t'ings change nuh! Yuh remember how you and Shirley get dere 'bout five o'clock 'pon a mornin' to avoid de cussin' and quarrellin' and pushin' in de line?

Mr. Pilgrim rum shop still dere and yuh father still teking one dere in between. But dat is one place I would like to see move from 'bout here. De young boys tek over from where de old men lef' off. Yuh see dem 'pon a Friday or Saturday—as dey get pay. De money dat shoulda gone to feed dem family gone in Pilgrim pocket. Dis is de second house he buildin' now.

Edna doing well too. She 'ent got no more shop—is a Mini Mart now—ef yuh please! And move out to de front road—sellin' all kind o' fancy t'ings. And she doan' trust no more—no credit for we poor people again. One or two girls in de village get work in de Mini Mart doh—so she didn't forget she roots altogether.

But de big news now—Praise de Lord—we get de roads fix. Dat been a eyesore for years 'specially when de rain fall. And if yuh did by a pot-hole when a car passin' yuh would had to gone back home and change yuh clothes 'cause dem did get wet up and dirty. But now de road get pave. No more carryin' de extra pair o' shoes.

Dis mussee de longest letter I ever write in muh life but I goin' stop now. Give muh love to muh grands—How dey doin' nuh? I hope dey behavin' duhself. And muh best to yuh husband.

May de Lord bless yuh, real good.

Your lovin' Mum.

Left, watching the world go by in St. Philip. Right, young "Philipians" never trouble trouble until trouble troubles them, as the Bajan saying goes.

A Day In The Life Of A Fisherman

Above, the clouds whisk by at a steady clip, their shapes altering every minute. The mind's imagination conjures heads of lions, shapely mermaids and gliding flying fish. Below, the white–cap sea pulsates with the forces of wind and gravity. Between these two natural elements is the fisherman.

In Barbados, a fisherman's day begins before dawn. At 4 a.m. Speightstown residents Philip and David are pushing their small rowboat down to the water's edge. Sensing a lull in the sets of rolling breakers, they quickly hop aboard the dinghy and

bucking the swells and current creating a frothy, turbulent sea.

By the time these two brave fishermen reach their destination, shut off the diesel engine and set adrift, light is just beginning to break over the distant silhouette of Barbados' west coast. David begins his chores: inspecting the engines, sharpening hooks, preparing the nets and palm fronds. Philip, turns on the radio to channel 16 and gives fellow fishermen their location and a weather report. He then washes some pots and cups and prepares the day's meal: a

row under the stars to their fishing vessel, some two hundred yards offshore. This pre-dawn ritual is a daily one during the fall and winter months. They start early so they can bring in a big catch of flying fish—one of the island's staple foods and the visitor's favorite treats.

Loading their supplies onto the single engine fishing boat and untying the anchor line, Philip and David get ready to set out on a course twelve miles due west. It's a slow, long journey and a bouncy one too. Near the coast, the island's land mass blocks the strong southeast trade winds, keeping the water smooth as glass. But a mile or so offshore the wind is strong,

stew of macaroni, pork and fish and a batch of hot tea. The two men have some tea, along with cold fried fish and home baked bread, for breakfast.

Now there's light to work by: they carefully dip one net about 60 yards long, with palm fronds attached to each end, in the water. The palm fronds create a shadow: flying fish gather under it to hide from the sun and are trapped in the net. This net will stay out until the end of the day, when Philip, a strong husky man, will haul it in.

The men drop a shorter net about 30 yards long right next to the boat. A chum bucket filled with cut fish and oil dangles

90

from the side of the boat and attracts the fish to the net. David and Philip work this net every hour or so; pulling it in, cleaning it of its catch—usually about 500 fish—and setting it back out again.

In between the hauling and dropping of the net, they spend the time fishing with handlines. One, a thick monofilament with a large hook and live flying fish for bait, is set a fair distance behind the boat in hope of hooking a blue marlin or any of the other large fish that feed on flying fish. They also use smaller handlines, with tiny hooks and

the last crew to be lost at sea.

In the back of each fisherman's mind is the thought that one day his engine may fail to start after a day of drifting. If that happens, he must simply roll with the tides and waves and hope that eventually he will be found by a passing freighter or run aground on the island of St. Vincent or St. Lucia. That's why fishing boats are painted such bright colors: they're easier to spot if lost at sea. This fateful uncertainty has led to the daily sermon and prayer that comes over the boat radio at 9:30 every morning,

cut bait, to catch the fish that are swarming around the chum.

All the while the seas ceaselessly roll and tumble the boat in every possible way. After years of such an environment, though, the two are oblivious to the seven-foot swells. David stares out at the horizon as if in a trance and Philip loudly sings his favorite calypso song. In the background, the non-stop chattering of other fishermen comes over the radio—seamen trading information on their fishing luck and on news of

Flying fish (*Hirundictys affins*) is a delicacy in Barbados. It accounts for 60 percent of the weight of all fish landed on the island.

given at sea by one of the fishermen who is also a minister.

The work is hard, the hours long, the danger imminent and the rewards fair but not great. It is a life that calls to hardy and adventurous souls. Philip and David are two such characters.

At the end of the day they have netted three or four thousand flying fish. On their way back to Speightstown they bag their catch, wash the boat and themselves down, and change into dry, clean clothes. All that is left to do is to hand over the fish to the market vendors. The fishermen then head home for a meal and hot shower, hoping tomorrow will bring the same results.

How To Explore Barbados : "Go An' Come Back"

No matter how addicted you are to sea and sand—and it does have a special allure in Barbados—it's worth tearing yourself away to experience the "other" Barbados, the one many visitors don't see. Though you can learn quite a bit about the island by chatting with the Bajans you'll meet on the beach and in the hotels, it's well worth renting a car or mini-moke to see for yourself.

Of course you will get lost—but that's part of the fun. Road maps are a good guide to the seven main highways on the island, but with 800 miles of paved roads in a country just 14 miles wide and 21 miles long, it's best to just relax and enjoy the adventure of not knowing where you are. You'll never be more than a 20-minute drive from one coast or the other. Just leave plenty of time to reach your destination—and don't hesitate to ask for directions. Bajans speak English and react enthusiastically to any visitor's interest in their country and culture.

For ideas about some offbeat things to do and see, tune into the "Voice of Barbados" radio station (790 on the AM dial). You'll hear ads in Bajan dialect, short stories, the latest calypso hits and announcements of upcoming events—festivals, concerts, picnics, dances—all of which welcome visitors.

To help you find your way around and discover more of its hidden delights, we've grouped the 11 parishes of Barbados into four categories—Bridgetown, The West, The South, The North and East—and mapped out a tour of each section.

So four times you can "go an' come back," as the Bajans would say, taking a separate tour of each section. Or, you can see a fair portion of the island in a single excursion—"one time," as the Bajans would put it.

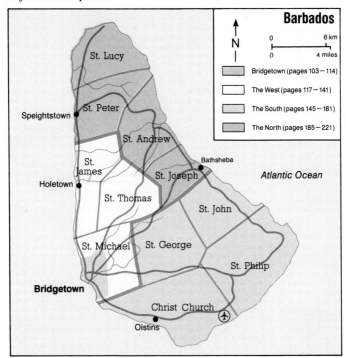

BUSTLING BRIDGETOWN

Though small in size, Bridgetown pulses with all the energy of a major Caribbean capital—and with something that is uniquely Barbadian. In brilliant sunlight, and in the shade of colonial buildings and modern offices, the city hustles and bustles to an ageless quick tempo: women bearing baskets hurry to be first to market; curbside vendors hawk their wares; well-dressed business people hurry towards office doors. A busier, more industrious population—from coconut sellers to international bankers and big-eight accountants—you'll find nowhere else in the Caribbean.

Overseeing it all, at the head of Bridgetown's main thoroughfare, is the **statue of Horatio, Lord Nelson**—probably the city's most popular backdrop for photographs, taking precedence even over the picturesque wharf and the bridges from which the city takes its name.

Yet, the gallant bronze monument, erected in 1813 (preceding the Nelson Column in Trafalgar Square, London, by 17 years), has long been a figure of great controversy. From as early as 1833, people have petitioned for the removal of the statue from its commanding position. It has been an object of ridicule, a dumping ground for garbage and a platform for protesters. But Lord Nelson, sculpted by Sir Richard Westmacott, stands firm, despite the cries of "Take down Nelson and put up a Bajan Man," as sung by the calypsonian, the Mighty Gabby.

As in London, the area around Nelson's statue is called **Trafalgar Square**. Lord Nelson, and the flagship *Victory*, accompanied by other ships of his fleet, arrived at Barbados on June 4, 1805. He was killed in the Battle of Trafalgar later the same year. When the news reached Barbados, patriotic citizens decided to dedicate the square to his memory.

The square is also home to the **Dolphin Fountain**, installed to commemorate the introduction of piped running water to Bridgetown in March 1861. You will also find here the **War Memorial**, unveiled to the city on May 10, 1925. Many Barbadians fought

bravely in World War I, and the decision was made to erect the monument just six months after the Armistice. The names of the dead of that war are listed on three bronze panels. A fourth panel, bearing the names of the dead of World War II, was added in 1953.

Nelson's statue faces west, along **Broad Street**, the main commercial street and thoroughfare through the city. He seems to stand guard over the many transactions that take place on this street from dawn to dusk—the constant wheeling and dealing that give the city so much of its lively, entrepreneurial character.

On Broad Street, the old colonial buildings struggle to retain their old-world charm amidst the steady proliferation of more modern neighbors. Some buildings, like those of Dacosta and Co., C.F. Harrison's and the Barbados Mutual Life Assurance Co., still retain the proud grandeur and architectural flourishes of the turn of the century. All along this street you will find a wide and varied selection of attractive goods, services and banking facilities, rivaling in quantity and style

many of the world's duty-free ports.

Trading on Broad Street goes back to the mid-17th Century. In a statute of 1657, the street was declared reserved "for a market-place and other publique uses of this island." It was then called Cheapside, but today only its western end—where you'll find a modern post office and an old-fashioned farmer's market—still bears that name. During the latter half of the 17th Century, Broad Street was also called The Exchange or Exchange Street because the Merchant's Exchange was situated there.

Settlers and Swamp: Bridgetown was never planned; like many towns, it just grew. It was founded on July 5, 1628, when 64 settlers, headed by Charles Wolverstone, arrived on the spot. The proximity to a swamp, together with the town's haphazard development, provoked criticism from early visitors, including one Richard Ligon who came in 1647. He wrote:

A town ill situate, for if they had considered health, as they did convenience, they would never had set it there; or if they had any intention at first to have built a town there, they could not have been so improvident as not to foresee the inconveniences that must ensue by making choice of so unhealthy a place to live in...

The principal streets of the early town were reputedly laid out by one of Governor Wolverstone's captains, John Swan, who was a surveyor. According to tradition, **Swan Street**, the secondary business street in the city, was named after him.

The city itself derives its name from a primitive bridge built by the Indians to span the waterway. In the early years, such appellations as Indian Bridge, Indian Bridgetown or just simply The Bridge were applied to the town.

Bridgetown now has two bridges, situated to the east of the city. They span the **Constitution River**, which is actually no river at all but an arm of the sea which at one time ran some distance inland. The lower reaches of the river form the **Careenage**, a basin so called because it provided facilities where schooners could be careened and their bottoms cleaned and painted. It was the presence of this arm of the sea which, undoubtedly, influenced the

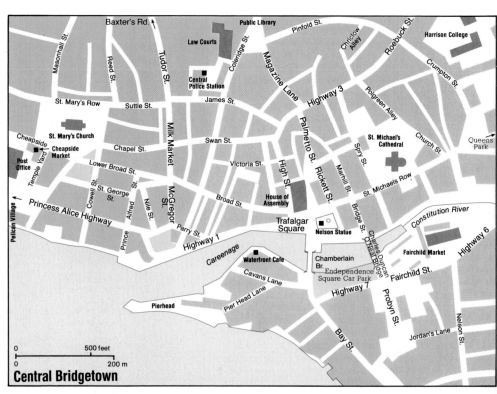

Central Bridgetown

first settlers to choose this site for a town.

For hundreds of years, the Careenage was the berthing place of many small ships from all over the Caribbean. The sea, of course, was the only means of communication between Barbados and the other islands, and the wider world. The busy area around the Careenage was therefore the center of trading and news for the island.

This prominence slowly became a thing of the past as aircraft travel became more popular and facilities for handling cargo at the ports were modernized. Now, instead of seeing bananas, mangoes, plantains and other fruits off-loaded from the old wooden schooners and other vessels, a passerby will admire the sleek, slender–masted yachts berthed in the basin and their affluent passengers sunbathing on the decks.

The bridge which separates the inner basin from the outer is called the **Chamberlain Bridge**, named after Joseph Chamberlain, the great Colonial Secretary who, during the late 1890s, was instrumental in saving the West Indies from European competition in the vital sugar trade. This bridge was once a fascination to visitors, and even the locals, who used to stop to watch it swing back to allow boats to pass into the inner basin where they were careened. But the Chamberlain Bridge swings no more; mechanical problems experienced a few years ago forced the government to make it into a stationary structure.

The eastern bridge is named the **Charles Duncan O'Neal**, after the founding father of the city's Democratic League and the Workingmen's Association, the forerunners of democracy and trade unionism on the island.

On the banks of the Constitution River, next to the Charles Duncan O'Neal Bridge, you will find the city's main bus concourse. This multimillion-dollar terminal on **Fairchild Street** was still under construction in 1986, though the first phase—arrival and departure areas for commuters and an administration block—opened in 1985. It is indeed an improvement over the former terminal, where harried commuters had to fight their way to the buses during rush hours, with very little shelter from the weather.

Shoppers in turn-of-the-century Bridgetown.

On the Waterfront: Across the Careenage at the western end you will find the **Pierhead** and **Willoughby's Fort**. It is not generally known that the fort once occupied a small island. In 1656, Willoughby's Fort was constructed on Little Island by William Withington, who was paid some 80,000 pounds of sugar for the job. Today the Barbados Coast Guard makes the old fort its headquarters.

The Pierhead, once across from the island and now connected to it, originally consisted mainly of pasture, marshland and ponds. Over the years, warehouses were constructed there and on the island, and today these are of enough historic and architectural interest to be preserved by the Barbados National Trust.

One of these former warehouses is the now **Waterfront Cafe**, which as its name suggests, is perched on the waterfront, offering its clients a most spectacular view of Trafalgar Square, the Public Buildings and the upper end of Broad Street. Diners have the option of sitting in the cool indoors or on the sidewalk—European style—to watch the world go by as they savor a flying fish sandwich and a Banks beer.

Leaving the Pierhead and moving east, you will find **Independence Square**, a car park by day and a meeting place by night. Because of its proximity to the main bus terminal next door on Fairchild Street, it is very popular with politicians who stage many of their public rallies there.

Until early in this century, Fairchild Street was a residential area, though today it's the busy provenance of commercial tenants. Colonel John Fairchild, who is remembered in the street's name, was a prominent citizen who lived there in the mid-18th Century. He served as a vestryman of the Parish of St. Michael, a member of the House of Assembly, and was appointed Chief Justice in 1752.

The area between Fairchild Street and Nelson Street was once a disreputable residential neighborhood called **Racoon Quarters**. The origin of the name is unclear, but racoons were once a pest in Barbados, and this neighborhood was probably a haven for these creatures at some time.

In the 19th Century, a devastating cholera epidemic swept this area at

Central Bridgetown, with Careenage. St. Elizabeth's hospital in background, to right.

astonishing speed. On May 14, 1854, a resident of Fairchild Street died under suspicious circumstances. Within three days, similar deaths occurred in Nelson Street and its vicinity. By mid-June the epidemic had spread throughout the island, and by August 6, the known death-toll was 15,243. When the pestilence had completed its course, between 18,000 and 20,000 people had died.

A Moravian minister who lived through the epidemic said the disease *"increased in town steadily . . . until it reached 340 per diem. . . In the most erratic manner it went from street to street, omitting one or two in its course and returning to them when the residents thought they had escaped, and taking off more in such cases than in the street first visited."*

Another bit of history from this area is that in nearby **Bay Street**, the site of the **Harbour Police Station** was once the location of the Hospital for Contagious Diseases, better known as the "Lock" Hospital. This building was constructed after the British government passed an act in 1826 for the better prevention of contagious diseases at certain naval and military stations. The objective was to safeguard members of the armed forces from venereal infection. Constructed in 1869, the hospital was closed in 1887 when the act and its supplements were repealed; the premises were turned over to the Constabulary, the Harbour Police and the Fire Brigade Unit.

Off to Market: Next door to the bus concourse you will find **Fairchild Market**, one of the two big public markets in this city. Though it can sometimes seem that every street-corner in Bridgetown is a mini-marketplace selling everything from baskets and sunglasses to a refreshing drink of coconut water, the public markets are something special. In bygone days, the public markets were a riot of color and full of gaiety, especially on Saturdays when housewives from all over the island came to shop for the week's supply of food. Yams, potatos, breadfruit, lettuce, cucumbers and tomatoes still fill the stalls.

Amidst the development of supermarkets and mini-marts thoughout the island, both of Bridgetown's public markets are slowly losing their appeal

The Barclay's Bank building.

for general shopping. But tradition dies hard in Barbados and every Saturday both Fairchild and Cheapside public markets are lively places—and definitely worth a visit. The calypsonian Mighty Gabby captured the spirit of the market in his song "Bridgetown Early Saturday Morning":

See de women
How dey calling, singing:
'Come for your breadfruit,
Come for your corn,
Come for de apples—
fresh as de morn.
Come for your guava,
Your guava, your guava

Across the street from the public market is **Nelson Street**, the city's red-light district. A residential neighborhood as far back as the 18th Century, it was part of Racoon Quarters. The modern development of the city has passed this area by, but the government has indicated that it will tear down some of these ancient buildings and erect a new housing development along the lines of the others around the island.

It is interesting to note that in the heart of this district is a church, the **St. Ambrose Church**, which was consecrated on Jan. 1, 1858. An extract from the *Barbadian* newspaper of March 14, 1857 stated:

The Rev. Joseph S. Meyers, on his arrival from America, having been placed for a brief period in charge of St. Paul's District, saw at once that there was want of a church—the adjoining Church of St. Paul's accommodating 1,200 in the population of 13,000. The place known as Rebitt's Ground had in it an amount of spiritual destitution startling in the extreme, and was covered with a pall of darkness too deep to be fancied, and only realised by those who have explored the district. The place, once the abode of filth, misery and vice; the scene of cockfights, indignities and other degrading dances; whose very atmosphere was polluted with the dreadful imprecations of the blasphemous, became an object of extreme solicitude to his mind. His appeal was not in vain . . .

Parliamentary Pomp: Back at Nelson's statue, look northward and you will see the neo-Gothic facades of the **Public Buildings**. Erected in the 19th

Shades of city life.

Century, they house many of the island's public records and accommodate the Houses of Parliament.

The earliest parliamentary building, called the State House, was built around 1640, somewhere in the vicinity of Upper Broad Street near High Street. This building was destroyed by the Bridgetown fire of 1668, and for the next 30 years the House of Legislature met in people's homes and public places, often taverns, a situation frowned upon by many. In 1695 Governor Francis Russell proposed allocating funds for a new State House. But it was six years before a building was finally erected in the vicinity of James Fort. Just three years later, this building was assigned for use as the jail, forcing the Council and Assembly back into the taverns and ale-houses. In 1730, when a new jail was completed, the politicians got their building back.

The present Public Buildings became a dream of John Glasgow Grant, a senior member for St. Michael in the House of Assembly, in 1856. A bill was introduced to the Assembly, a committee set up and advertisements published inviting plans and estimates. The west wing of the present building was completed in 1871, and the east wing was ready for occupation by the government in 1874.

It is ironic that it took so long for the physical structure of the **House of Assembly** to be erected when Barbados boasts the third oldest parliamentary body in the Commonwealth, founded in 1639, after Bermuda and Britain.

But the House of Assembly was elaborately done up, with a Speaker's chair and mace, Government and Opposition benches, and a stained-glass window representing the English monarchs from James I to Victoria. Interestingly, the stained-glass window carries the image of Oliver Cromwell, the Great Protector, despite the staunch Royalist sympathies of Barbadians during the English Civil War.

Leaving the Public Buildings and traveling east, you will soon come upon **St. Michael's Cathedral**. This edifice was originally constructed in 1665 to replace the old wooden structure which was located where St. Mary's Church now stands. It was totally destroyed by the hurricane of

Bay Street by day; red–light district by night.

1780, and the present cathedral was built in 1789.

A little northwest of the Cathedral you will find the site of the old Harrison's Free School, founded by Thomas Harrison in 1733. Education was to be free for poor and indigent boys from the parish of St. Michael, but the number of students was not to exceed 25. The school occupied these premises until 1870 when the Freemasons bought the building to use as a lodge.

Towering above the cathedral, the Freemason's Lodge and indeed over all of Bridgetown, is the new **Central Bank** headquarters, rising 11 stories high. It is the tallest building on the island, and its cost—well over $60 million—raised quite a stir among taxpayers.

Along with the new bank headquarters, the government is also constructing a concert hall to seat approximately 500 people. This hall will be well equipped with the most modern features in acoustics and is being welcomed by music lovers as the first of its kind on the island.

Roebuck Hucksters: The Central Bank is bounded on its northern side by **Roebuck Street**, which derives its name from a tavern called the Roebuck, established in the mid-17th Century. The tavern was set up by Thomas Noell, a merchant from London, who sold the establishment in 1659. It continued to flourish for many years, at one time being the favorite meeting place of the Barbados Council and the General Assembly.

It has been claimed that the street was named in honor of the *HMS Roebuck*, a ship of the Royal Navy whose crew allegedly saved the neighborhood from destruction by fire in 1766. But Mayo's plan of Bridgetown, published in 1722, proves these claims to be false, as it definitely identifies the street as "Roe Buck" more than 50 years before the fire.

Roebuck Street today holds a lively concentration of shops, both wholesale and retail. But well before the mid-18th Century, the area was noted for its many "huckster shops"—streetside produce stands. Now selling everything from pineapples to plastics, these stands are a 200-year-old tradition that remains an integral part of Bridgetown life.

Marathon with House of Assembly in background.

110

From the lower end of Roebuck Street to the upper Careenage, including the area around the Charles Duncan O'Neal Bridge, is a district once called Marl Hill or Gravel Hill. It acquired these names because of the nature of the ground. One street in the area retains a part of the name—Marhill Street.

A short walk westward from Roebuck Street will bring you to **James Street** and its environs. James Street, like many others in and around Bridgetown, has important Quaker associations. Early in Bridgetown's history, the Quaker community purchased a plot in this area for use as a burial ground. They lost the property due to the dishonesty of those who held it in trust, and it was sold to the Wesleyans in 1861. It remained in their possession until shortly after World War II, when the Barbados Telephone Company bought it.

Swan Street and the Synagogue: A side street running from James Street to Magazine Lane leads to the site of the old Jewish synagogue. Tradition held that the Dutchmen who introduced sugarcane to the island were Jews, but other researchers say that this race did not settle in Barbados until 1654. In any case, the Jews in Barbados became particularly noted for two things: success in business and the dedicated practice of their faith. They became so entrenched in trade that Swan Street, where most of them had set up business, became known as "Jew Street."

The first synagogue in Barbados, erected before 1664, was seriously damaged by the hurricane of 1831, and a new place of worship was built on the same site in 1833. Regrettably, little remains to remind us of this once elaborate structure. Two of its five surrounding cemeteries have disappeared, and over the years the building was dismantled. Its four great chandeliers went to the private collection of an affluent American; the painting that once decorated the ceiling has disappeared. Its marble fountain, its clock, Chanukkah Lamp and one of its benches, however, rest serenely in the Barbados Museum, saved to show future generations something of this aspect of Barbadian life that has simply faded away.

Another reminder of the Jews is the

"Hucksters" selling vegetables in Cheapside area.

old drinking fountain in the green triangle before the **Public Library**, presented to the city of Bridgetown by John Montefiore in memory of his father. The fountain was set up in Beckwith Place in 1865, but in 1940 it was removed to its present site in Coleridge Street.

On this same street you will find the **High Court**. The site on which it stands is believed to be the first piece of land owned by the Barbadian government. It was purchased on Dec. 5, 1682, by the Governor, Sir Richard Dutton, for the building of a new public warehouse. The warehouse was constructed in 1683 but demolished in 1728 to make room for a single structure to accommodate the Legislature, the Law Courts and the jail. In addition to being a place of confinement for civil and criminal prisoners, the Town Hall Gaol, as it was called, served as a detention center for prisoners of war. An American sea captain named John Manley and his crew were imprisoned there in 1779 and escaped with the aid of a rope ladder.

Placing a Town Hall in the same compound as a jail was an anomaly, and the source of many wry comments from visitors to the island. The prison was finally closed in 1876 by order of the Governor, Sir John Pope Hennessy. Today the buildings house the Law Courts, the Magistrates' Courts, the Public Library and the Police Station.

At the rear of this complex is **Tudor Street**, one of the city's oldest roads. It was on this street that the island's first Quaker meeting house was built in 1670. Because it was illegal for this religious body to meet, their place of worship was closed, the seats torn out, the furniture pulled down and the windows and doors nailed shut no less than four times within the three-year period of 1680 to 1683.

All Night Long: The upper end of Tudor Street leads into Broad Street, but its other end leads into a narrow road known as the "Street That Never Sleeps"—**Baxter's Road**. Every night at dusk, this street becomes an ongoing party, the tiny rum shops and restaurants open their doors, and the air fills with music and an aroma as tempting as anything you have ever imagined. The smell is delicious, but it's nothing

At the Careenage after a day at sea.

compared to the succulent flavor of the spicy Bajan fish or chicken. This is the prime spot for locals and visitors alike to stop at any hour of the night for a drink and delicious snack. In tiny bars the jukeboxes blare and business hops until 4 or 5 a.m. Cooks dish out tasty local food in the one-room, ragged restaurants until the same hour. At one end of the street, local vendors stand over "buck pots," old cast-iron pots, deep-frying fish, chicken and pork—Bajan style—over bright coal fires.

Leading from Tudor Street into the western section of Bridgetown is **Suttle Street** and its extension, **St. Mary's Row**. Until about 1827, these two streets formed what was called Back Church Street, so named because it ran beside **St. Mary's Church**. Suttle Street, until the late 19th Century, was a respectable neighborhood, but now it is nothing more than a back alley devoted mainly to trading in small shops and at doorways. Surrounded by gardens, St. Mary's Church remains the neighborhood's most dignified figure. The church was completed on July 15, 1827, to accommodate the

overflow from St. Michael's Cathedral. Actually, this was the site of the old St. Michael's Church, later abandoned for a more central location in St. Michael's Row.

Continuing from St. Mary's Row you'll find the street and district called **Lake's Folly**, named after an 18th-Century landowner in the area. This area has a violent history: on the night of March 5, 1773, a gang of 12 armed men ventured forth from the neighborhood and went on a rampage through the town, killing two people and seriously wounding another. The night before they set out on the warpath, they formed an "Association," taking an oath to stand by each other until death. To seal this bond, each man punctured his arm with a shoemaker's awl and let three drops of blood into a bowl containing a mixture of rum, gunpowder and brimstone, which they all drank.

Rasta-Mall: Across from St. Mary's Church is another bus terminal, the **Lower Green Station**, which services the northern section of the island. This terminal is supplemented by another public transport system on the Princess

Left, the city of contrasts. Right, St. Michael's Cathedral.

Alice Highway and the privately owned mini-buses which are stationed a few yards west of the Lower Green terminal, at **Temple Yard**.

This area acquired its name from a temple of the Ancient Masons who converted an old naval hospital into a lodge. In this area, behind the mini-bus station, you will see a group of Rastafarians who have set up their own outdoor "shopping mall." Actually, there are only wooden stalls, joined together crudely, from which these artistic and talented young people sell their goods, mainly handcrafted leather products.

The stalls were put there by the government because these vendors, who are easily recognized by their long locks of hair, had taken it upon themselves to erect stalls throughout the city, often on sidewalks where they caused congestion.

West of the mini-bus station you will see the **Cheapside Market**, the second of the city's two public markets. Farther along this street stands the new **General Post Office**. Until recently, the postal services were housed in the Public Buildings, along with the Senate and the House of Assembly. For more than 40 years plans were hatching to construct a separate building, and the task was finally completed in 1984.

At the rear of the Post Office the **Princess Alice Highway** runs parallel to the coast. On the seaward side of this highway, you'll see a small park and then the stunning blue of Carlisle Bay. The Rotary Club of Barbados undertook the project of beautifying this area, right up to the gates of the Deep Water Harbour. The National Conservation Commission took over the upkeep of the park, **Trevor's Way**, named after a young man who was killed in an accident nearby.

Sweet Cargo: Opposite the park is the **Pelican Village**, an amalgam of art galleries, a restaurant and curio shops selling a variety of local handmade items including clothing, pottery, paintings, baskets and straw mats. The land in this area is reclaimed from the sea; indeed, until the 1950s, there was a little island off the shores of Barbados called Pelican Island. The island was joined to the land on the construction of the **Deep Water Harbour**.

After more than 60 years of debate, the new harbor officially opened in 1961. The debate centered on the method of shipping sugar. As competing sugar producing countries began shipping sugar in bulk, Barbados' sugar magnates debated doing away with shipping theirs in bags. Finally, a new bulk sugar store with a capacity to hold 81,280 tons was built on reclaimed land. Sugar arrives at the bulk store from the island's factories and is carried via conveyor belts through underground channels to loading towers. There it is discharged into ships' hatches at the rate of 508 tons per hour.

The harbor provides 1,700 feet (518 meters) of quay space and about 2,700 feet (822 meters) of protective backwater for ships. It offers four groups of berthing areas, can accommodate eight ocean-going ships, and can easily provide simultaneous bunkering for five vessels.

Cruise liners dock here as well, and you can always tell when one is in port. From early in the morning, a stream of taxis stretches from the harbor gates down Princess Alice Highway, ready to carry visitors into the lively hustle and bustle that is Bridgetown.

Left, an entrepreneur on every corner.

114

THE STORY OF RACHEL PRINGLE

Bridgetown's history has its lighter moments. One of them involves a Barbadian hotel owner of the 1700s named Rachel Pringle.

Rachel was the mulatto daughter of a Scottish schoolmaster, William Lauder, and his African slave mistress. According to legend, Rachel became a beautiful young woman who was badly treated by her dissolute father. She was able to escape his cruel hand, however, with the aid of one Captain Thomas Pringle, a British naval officer. Pringle paid an exorbitant price to Lauder for Rachel, and set her up in a house in lower Bridgetown. In gratitude, Rachel adopted Pringle's surname.

Much to Pringle's dismay, his liaison with Rachel was barren. In order to maintain Pringle's affections, Rachel "borrowed" a baby while Pringle was away at sea and presented it to him as their own upon his return. Her ruse was revealed, however, when the rightful mother arrived to claim her baby. Pringle left the scheming Rachel in disgust, but she quickly found herself another wealthy "protector" named Polgreen.

At some time in 1780, Rachel managed to open the island's first modest hotel, starting a Bridgetown tradition of taverns run by black or mulatto women who were favorite paramours of influential men.

Rachel's hotel (on what is now St. George Street) quickly became popular with the British Royal Navy. One night in 1789, a visiting party of Navy officers, led by Prince William Henry (later King William IV), booked in at Rachel's hotel.

The Prince and his companions had their fill of what we might assume was Barbados rum, and in a spree of drunken horseplay, smashed furniture and shattered crockery and glassware. When the Prince topped off his merriment by capsizing Rachel's chair and sending her sprawling onto the ground, she barely uttered a response.

RACHEL PRINGLE of BARBADOES

The next morning, just before the Navy ship sailed, Rachel sent the Prince an itemized bill for 700 British pounds — a princely sum indeed. He paid the bill promptly and Rachel restored her hotel in a more sumptuous style. She renamed it the Royal Naval Hotel.

Rachel Pringle died July 23, 1971. Regrettably, her hotel was destroyed by fire in 1821. But her story lives on, and you can see it reenacted today at the show "Barbados, Barbados," which plays weekly at Balls Plantation.

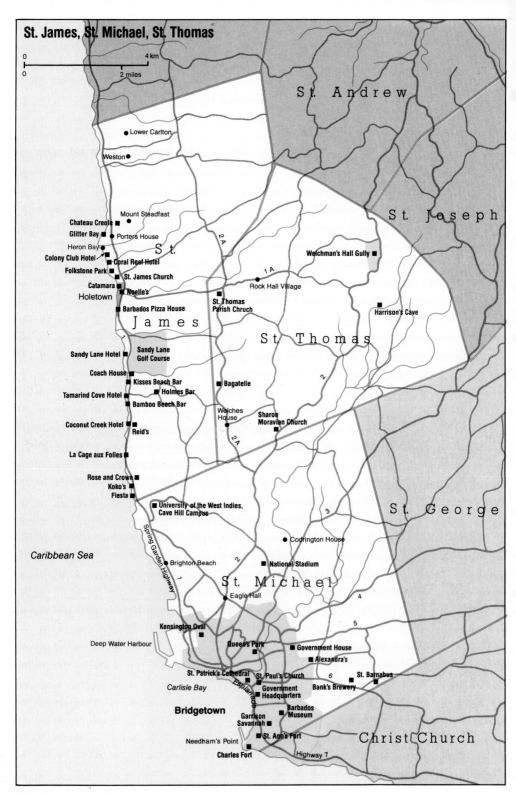

St. James, St. Michael, St. Thomas

ST. MICHAEL: HUB OF COMMERCE

Encompassing the capital city of Bridgetown, the parish of St. Michael is a thriving coastal area, the hub of Barbadian culture and commerce. A traveler, writing about the parish in 1672, said it "hath a commodious road for ships, is a place well frequented and traded unto, and is strongly defended by two powerful Forts."

Steeped in a colorful, tumultuous past—from the bloodthirsty Caribs to the colonial pomp of the British West India Regiment—St. Michael makes a natural location for the **Barbados Museum**, located just south of the capital. There is no better place to begin a tour of this parish than with a trip to the museum, and back in time.

Housed in the old military prisons of the British garrison, the Barbados Museum offers a guided tour of the history of Barbados, from the Amerindians and the Arawaks through the first settlers, the days of slavery, and the development of the island. And the museum's curators have not forgotten the island's natural world; fish of the surrounding seas, and native plants and birds are all represented here.

Most of the galleries are former prison cells, some including their original doors. The two wings at the back of the main building were built between 1817 and 1821, and the main block was completed in 1853.

Here, in the once dim jail cells, are amassed crude artifacts of the native Arawaks, who lived on the island centuries ago; the remains of their warlike conquerors, the Caribs; and relics of the British colonists, including period rooms, a children's gallery filled with historic dioramas, a collection of toys and games from bygone days, and rooms devoted to a fascinating collection of old maps.

The museum's pleasant, open-air courtyard is used for cultural activities including concerts and plays. The popular dinner show, "1627 And All That" is held here every Thursday and Sunday, and a more appropriate stage could not be found for this production, which portrays the history and social rituals of Barbados in song and dance.

The Barbados Museum and Historical Society was established in 1933 by a group of public spirited individuals, led by E.M. Shilstone, who were interested in the history of the island. A few years ago, the government took steps to update the museum in an effort to have it reflect not only the history of the island but also its people's character. The museum is open on weekdays from 10 a.m. to 6 p.m. and on Sundays from 2:30 p.m. to 6 p.m.

Across the street from the museum you will find the **Garrison Savannah**, described in its heyday as one of the finest parade grounds in the West Indies. After seeing the pictures in the museum, you can stand on this green oval and, in your mind's eye, see the brightly colored regiments parade on these grounds.

Carlisle Bay, circa 1750.

A Prospect of Bridge-Town in the Island of Barbadoes.

Today, the Savannah is more often used for horse racing, for which there are two seasons each year, and for soccer and rugby. Early mornings and evenings joggers use the track to keep fit. But if you are lucky, you may be visiting Barbados on one of those few occasions when the armed forces are on parade. On November 30, the island's Day of Independence, the Barbados Defense Force, the Royal Barbados Police Force, the Barbados Coast Guard, along with the Cadets, Girl Guides, Rangers and other groups gather at the parade ground early in the day to march before the Governor General.

Grand Homes and Ramparts: Among the many fine buildings that surround the Savannah, few can challenge the stately beauty of the **Savannah Club** which, with its distinctive cupola tower and clock, has been the subject of many paintings and photographs. It was formerly the guard house of the British Regiment and the venue for the grim business of court–martials and subsequent penalties. The clock tower bears the date 1803 and the building itself was probably completed a few

years later.

South of the Savannah Club stands the **Drill Hall**. It is constructed on the foundation of one of the ramparts of **St. Anne's Fort**, which lies directly behind it.

Construction of St. Anne's Fort began in 1704, but the work was never completed as originally planned. Only the main ramparts survive from that period, indicating the grand design once envisioned for it. The fort today is of a much simpler style. Its walls range from four to 20 feet (one to six meters) thick, and inside are the store rooms, armory and powder magazines as they were at the end of the 18th Century.

Today, the Barbados Defense Force is headquartered at the fort, carrying on some of the same drills and duties that were a familiar sight within these walls over one hundred years ago.

It was the threat of French invasion during the American War of Independence that led to the establishment of the first garrison of British troops on Barbados. As the size of the military establishment increased, Barbados became known as the headquarters of the British forces in the Leeward and Windward islands. But in those early years, it was tropical diseases, not the French, that decimated the British recruits. One report states that of 19,676 soldiers sent to the West Indies from England in 1796, 17,173 died before 1802.

A large number of tombstones and memorials to British soldiers, dated between the years 1800 and 1900, can be found in the St. Michael's Cathedral, and some from a later period can be seen at St. Paul's Church. But most of those who died after 1800 must have been buried in the area behind St. Anne's Fort. The earliest burials seem to have been near the shore, roughly where the Hilton International Barbados now has its tennis courts. Sometime around 1820, the garrison discontinued burials in this area, and began to use a new site, farther west on what is today Highway 7. It is this new burial ground that is today known as the **Military Cemetery**. It is still used for the burial of service personnel, active or retired, and their families.

Next to the cemetery rises the state–owned **Hilton International Barbados** which opened in 1966, the year

Morning trot at the Garrison Savannah racetrack.

the island gained its independence. Located on a street called Aquatic Gap, the hotel shares lovely Needham Point with several other hotels, the Mobil Oil Refinery, one of the island's four lighthouses, and **Charles Fort**, the largest of the defenses built during the prime of the British Regiment.

The beach at **Needham Point** is one of the finest on the island, and a favorite with Barbadians, who flock to the area on weekends and public holidays. One bygone attraction of this beach was a hot water pool, called a "pot" by the locals. Situated a few yards out to the sea, the pot was heated courtesy of the nearby Barbados Light and Power Company. Many people who suffered from arthritis, rheumatism and other ailments used to go for a "bath in the pot." The pot has since been removed, but the beach remains a popular picnic place.

The Light and Power Company itself has an unusual history; it was once a theater where professional actors, engaged by the military, performed for the entertainment of the men of the garrison.

G.W. Slept Here: Continuing along Highway 7 toward the city of Bridgetown is **Crofton House**, at the corner of Bay Street and Chelsea Road. This residence is better known as **George Washington House**, named after the first President of the United States. Legend has it that Washington stayed here while on a visit to Barbados in 1751—reputedly his only voyage to a foreign country. According to the 20-year-old Washington's diary, he and his half-brother Lawrence stayed in a house that belonged to Captain Crofton, who was the Commander of James Fort. Lawrence suffered from tuberculosis, and had come to Barbados hoping to be cured by the invigorating climate. George, who accompanied his cousin, had the misfortune of contracting smallpox on the island, the scars of which he bore for the rest of his life.

Some historians intimate that young Washington's illness was not all bad luck. By surviving the disease in Barbados, he developed an immunity which kept him alive and at the head of the rebel forces throughout the American Revolution, while smallpox all but decimated his troops.

Along the way on Bay Street, you

Heraldry and pomp; clock tower in background.

will see the **Government Headquarters**, which house the offices of the Prime Minister. At the front of the circular driveway, which is bordered on all sides by poinsettias, begonias and hibiscus flowers, stands a bust of the first Premier of Barbados, Sir Grantley Adams.

Across the street, along the seaside, extends the **Esplanade**, with a splendid view of the calm waters of **Carlisle Bay**. This small park, maintained by the National Conservation Commission, is an ideal place to watch the spectacular Barbadian sunsets. What a sight it is to see the yachts riding on their anchors in the bay.

Two Churches and a Baobab: Along this way, two churches soon come into view. The first will be **St. Paul's Church**. Built in 1830, the very next year it was destroyed by a hurricane. Rebuilt in 1832, at one time it was used as a garrison church, and its nave is still decorated with marble tablets bearing the names of many British soldiers formerly stationed on the island.

The other church, at the corner of Jemmotts Lane and Bay Street, is **St. Patrick's Cathedral**. This Roman Catholic church was rebuilt in 1897 in the early Gothic style after the earlier church, on the same site, was completely destroyed by fire. For many years no Catholic priest was allowed to reside on the island, a situation which did not change until 1839 when the Connaught Rangers, one of the British regiments stationed on the island, demanded the services of a chaplain. When St. Patrick's was built, these Irish soldiers attended services there; and to this day their flags and traditional crests adorn the cathedral's walls.

Lower Bay Street leads into Bridgetown, but if you travel along Jemmotts Lane, you will pass the old General Hospital, now the Ministry of Health, and the modern **Queen Elizabeth Hospital**, opened by the Queen in 1964.

At the northern end of the hospital and across Constitution Road is **Queen's Park**, where a giant baobab tree, its girth measuring over 61.5 feet (18.5 meters) has stood for more than 1,000 years. A children's playground has been built beneath the protective branches of this ancient tree.

Left, St. Patrick's Church. Right, street in Eagle Hall area.

Queen's Park is notable for **Queen's House**, which used to be the official residence of the Commanding General of the Imperial Troops. These troops were stationed in Barbados until 1906. The General lived here in stately grandeur, with Nelson Gate pointing in the direction of Nelson's statue in Trafalgar Square, and the Governor's Gate, through which the Governor of the island entered when he came to call. The Park is under the maintenance of the National Conservation Commission, which restored Queen's House and converted it for public use without altering the character of the building. An exhibition hall now occupies the ground floor, and a small theater the floor above. This modern theater presents some excellent productions. The Steel Shed and bandstand, once part of the official residence, have also been renovated.

Opposite Queen's Park stands **Queen's College**, one of the leading secondary schools on the island. The land it occupies was said to have been "a barren common" back in 1818, but the following year the Boys' Central School, later to be known as Comber-

mere School, was founded on the site. A number of other institutions have occupied the spot, but in due course all abandoned the locality with the exception of the Girls' Central School, later to become Queen's College.

Beautiful Belleville: Traveling eastward along Constitution Road and into Belmont, you will come to **Belleville District**. This picturesque suburban area was designed in the 1880s, and the houses retain a delicious 19th-Century grace. Many of the wooden structures have been renovated, maintaining their original architectural lines. The designer of this elegant neighborhood, Sam Manning, owned a residence called **Erdiston**, which is now the home of the Teachers' Training College, and overlooks the 10 avenues that form Belleville.

To the north of Erdiston is **Government House**, official residence of the Governor General of Barbados. Originally called Pilgrim House, it was purchased by the Government in 1736 from John Pilgrim, a Quaker. This sturdily built mansion, survivor of several devastating hurricanes over the centuries, incorporates the typical fea-

All decked out for Christmas Day in Queen's Park.

tures of Barbadian plantation "great houses," with its shady verandahs, arched porticoes, jalousied windows, parapet roof and circular driveway. Its beautiful gardens have been praised by many distinguished visitors.

Bordering the southern side of Government House is Pine Road and the surrounding area of **Pine Garden**, one of the first residential areas in Barbados. In this locality are the houses of various High Commissioners and embassy officials. At the far end of this residential area, on Highway 4, is **Bishop's Court Hill**, named for Bishop's Court, the home of the Anglican Bishop of Barbados.

Also located on Bishop's Court Hill is **Alexandra's**, once considered to be the finest nightclub in Barbados. An impressive building, constructed in the last century, Alexandra's was the spot where the rich and famous flocked to enjoy the nightlife of Barbados during the 1960s and early 1970s. Its reputation has since been tarnished by a more disreputable clientele, and despite several attempts to restore the nightclub to its old, glamorous self, its sordid reputation lives on.

Famous Brew: Moving away from the city, Highway 4 leads along Collymore Rock to a commercial district. The first commercial enterprise you will see is **Bank's Breweries**, where the famous Bank Beer is brewed. Over the years, this beer has won numerous awards and medals for its fine taste and quality of production. With many visitors to the island it soon becomes the hands-down favorite.

Behind Bank's Breweries is the **Wildey Industrial Park**, a new industrial development where a number of factories are located. Further along Highway 4, you will find the **Barbados Institute of Management and Productivity**, where Barbadians take short-term courses in specialized areas such as management and computer technology. You will also notice several commercial banks, car dealers and a shopping center.

The Barbados External Telecommunications, Ltd. (BET) is situated on the **St. Barnabas Highway**, a section of the access highway under construction in 1986 to connect the Grantley Adams International Airport in the south with Speightstown, the island's second lar-

Eagle Hall chattel house.

gest town, in the north.

Along the St. Barnabas Highway modern technological facilities contrast sharply with the quaint, centuries-old villages. Two institutions in this area have encouraged modernization throughout Barbados—the Caribbean Development Bank, and the single television station on the island, the state-owned Caribbean Broadcasting Corporation.

To the west of the highway is **Pinelands**, built in the 1960s, the first housing development developed by the government for low income families. At times subject to heavy criticism, the 1980s have seen it become the object of several beautification projects.

At the northern end of the St. Barnabas Highway, in the center of the traffic circle, stands a statue called **"The Freed Slave,"** which was erected in 1986. Standing defiantly, his head raised slightly towards the heavens, his hands still carrying the broken chains of slavery, he faces the fertile fields of the St. George Valley, as if to say, "It was through toil and sweat in yonder land that I was able to free myself from this bondage." He represents a planta-tion slave named Bussa who purportedly led a slave rebellion in 1816. The statue is the masterpiece of Karl Broodhagen, one of Barbados' best known sculptors.

Coralstone and Columns: A turn west at the roundabout will take you along Two Mile Hill, where you will find the official residence of the Prime Minister of Barbados, **Ilaro Court**. This home was designed in 1919 by Lady Gilbert Carter, the American wife of Sir Gilbert Carter who was the Governor of Barbados from 1904 to 1911. Built of coralstone, the house combines many luxurious and varied architectural features, including Ionic columns and an enclosed swimming pool. It was purchased by the government in 1976.

Two Mile Hill extends to Government Hill, which passes the northern boundary of Government House. A right turn at the junction will take you through Welches to Tudor Bridge and Bank Hall. One more right turn at the Tudor Bridge traffic lights, and you will make your way past **Glendairy Prison**, the only adult correctional facility on the island. It was erected in 1855 and has since been immortalized in a folk song:

Rasta selling coconut water on typical Bajan street.

Send my bail down to Glendairy/. This place is wearisome/Got put in jail/Just for drinking Barbados rum.

This route leads to the **National Stadium**, which was opened in 1970. In addition to track and field events, soccer and cycling, a number of concerts and other cultural events are held here each year. With a seating capacity of 5,000 and standing room for 2,000 more, it is the largest gathering place on the island. Its only drawback is that as an outdoor facility, it is exposed to the vagaries of sunshine and showers; occasionally events must be cancelled due to rain.

Passing the stadium, proceed down Highway 2, away from the outskirts of Bridgetown, and you will be bound for the parish of St. Thomas, traveling into the heart of the island.

The road into Bridgetown will take you past the 300-year-old **Codrington House**, once the residence of Christopher Codrington, an enterprising colonist who arrived in Barbados in 1628 and amassed a large family fortune here. A little further along Spooner's Hill, as this road is called, you will see **Tyrol Cot**, home of the late Sir Grantley Adams, the first Premier of Barbados and the only Premier of the Federation of the West Indies.

When you reach the junction of Eagle Hall, Bank Hall and Black Rock, you will find a densely populated neighborhood, packed with a mixture of small stores offering a wide variety of goods. Rum shops, tiny gardens, chickens, sheep and children compete for space and attention along the crowded streets.

A left turn at this corner will bring you onto the street known as **Black Rock**. On this route, traveling northward, you will see the **Psychiatric Hospital**, reputed to be one of the most up-to-date institutions of its kind in the Caribbean. Black Rock ends at the junction of the new Spring Garden Highway and Cave Hill. A trip up this hill deposits you on the doorstep of the **Cave Hill Campus** of the University of the West Indies, one of three campuses in the Caribbean.

Back on the main road and continuing northward, you will pass the **Lazaretto**, which was once used as a sanitarium for lepers. It now houses the **Barbados National Archives**, including some of the most valuable

documents on the history of the island.

Returning to the junction, and traveling down the **Spring Garden Highway**, which opened in 1984, you will see the first in a string of luxury hotels that bask in the sun along this coastal highway. You will also pass the popular **Brighton Beach**, a great favorite with locals.

Near Brighton Beach, on the inland side, notice the area called **Indian Ground**, where a monument was erected to commemorate the tercentenary of the first landing of the English on Barbados. The monument bears the date 1605, as the year the British first visited the island, though the event really occurred in 1625. In that year, the English landed at Holetown, walked up the beach and erected a sign to mark their presence.

Continuing down the highway, at the junction of Holborn Circle, a left turn takes you to the **Deep Water Harbour** with its large sugar warehouses and molasses terminal. Nearby you will find **Kensington Oval**, which dates from 1882. On the oval, white-clad teams compete in the wildly popular cricket matches.

Below, inside the West Indian Rum Refinery; and right, kids on school vacation at Brighton Beach.

SOPHISTICATED ST. JAMES

Stretching along Highway 1 in St. James is the area known as "the gold coast" or the "platinum coast" of Barbados because of the abundance of wealth along this strip. Almost all the luxury hotels on the island are in St. James—most of them right on the edge of the clear, glittering Caribbean Sea with its white sand beaches.

Here, luxurious homes, many hidden behind long, tree-lined driveways, rival stately plantation great houses and plush hotels. These establishments exist side by side with their more humble neighbors, the gaily-painted Barbadian chattel houses.

Beachcomber's Paradise: For those who like to walk along miles of uninterrupted white sand beach, St. James is the place for it. You can stroll along just to take in the natural beauty of the coastline and gentle azure sea, or check out the other sights of the St. James beach as well: a vacationing movie star, local craftsmen selling their wares, fishermen drying their nets in the sun, a lively game of beach cricket, people roasting breadfruit and flying fish over an open fire, a quiet family picnic on a Sunday.

Luxury hotels abound on this beautiful strip of beach, but there are many reasonably-priced apartment hotels here, too, such as the comfortable **Palm Beach Hotel** in Holetown. The more expensive hotels such as the Colony Club, Coconut Creek, Tamarind Cove, Coral Reef, Sandy Lane, Treasure Beach, Divi St. James, the Sandpiper Inn and Glitter Bay have earned worldwide reputations for excellence. All these hotels are on Highway 1.

The **Colony Club**, for example, has an atmosphere of casual elegance; it has a lovely beach shaded by graceful casuarina trees and a seaside terrace for lunch or a rum punch at sunset. **Coral Reef**, right next door, is delightfully English in its tradition of serving afternoon tea and thoroughly Caribbean with its open-air dining by a moonlit sea. **Coconut Creek**, a little farther south on Highway 1, is a charming hotel perched on top of a coral cliff.

The Rich and Famous: But it is **Sandy Lane** that has welcomed many of the world's rich and famous in the 25 years of its existence. This grand hotel was built by the late Ronald Tree, an Anglo-American who settled in Barbados and wanted a place where his friends could vacation in luxuriant tropical surroundings, while at the same time maintaining the habits and standards of English upper class life.

He spared no expense in the construction of the hotel, traveling far and wide to ensure that only the finest materials and workmanship would go into Sandy Lane. Portuguese masons were brought in to do the bathrooms—and many of the original tiles are still there. Tree designed much of the original furniture himself.

Sandy Lane opened its doors in 1961 to great fanfare and a magnificent first winter. Its fame grew, and people such as Princess Margaret, Claudette Colbert, Jacqueline Kennedy Onassis, David Niven, Tom Jones and Mick Jagger have passed through the porticoes of this grand hotel.

Many of Tree's friends purchased property and built houses around the hotel and its golf club. Now, the exclusive 380-acre Sandy Lane Estates

Preceding pages: Slaloming into the sunset at Discovery Bay. Left, behind the scenes in St. James; and right, a hobie cat ride is easy to find.

has more than 100 luxury homes on its grounds, ranging in value from $350,000 to $3 million each.

Sandy Lane's golf course, nine holes of which were built in 1962 and the other nine added ten years later, is the only 18-hole championship golf course on the island.

Not far away from Sandy Lane, also off Highway 1, is **Sunset Crest**, a sprawling complex of villas, apartment buildings, shopping centers and nightclubs. Designed by a Frenchman in the 1960s, this resort was once a popular haven for visitors from Canada, England and Europe. But during the last five years it has lost many of its clientele because a number of tour operating companies on which the resort depended have gone out of business.

Today, the only vibrant sections of Sunset Crest are the grocery stores and shops—always bustling with both visitors and residents.

First Settlers: Sunset Crest stretches into **Holetown**, the site of the first settlement in Barbados. This was where Captain John Powell and his crew landed in a ship called the *Olive Blossom* on May 14, 1625, and claimed the island in the name of King James of England.

They named the area St. James' Town, but it was later changed to Holetown because the shallow-draft ships could enter the river at this point, reminding the sailors of The Hole on the Thames River.

Two years later, on Feb. 17, 1627, the *William and John* landed with 80 settlers and 10 Negro slaves captured from other ships on the way over from England. A monument in the heart of Holetown commemorates the settlement of the island. Every year in mid-February, the Holetown festival celebrates the discovery of Barbados: streets are filled with stalls selling local food and crafts, music is everywhere, and you can see dance performances and a waterski show.

Behind the Holetown police station is the **James Fort**, which once protected this coastal area. Not much of it is left today, except for part of a wall and one gun. Nearby is **Folkstone House**, also a former fort.

Recently, this area was landscaped by the Rotary Club, which built a

On the beach at the Colony Club Hotel.

playground and tennis courts.

Underwater Park: At Folkstone there is a museum where the marine life that surrounds the island is on display. In the water is a marked "recreational zone" where snorkelers can follow an underwater trail around Dottin's Reef, a seven-mile long reef located about a half mile offshore. Scuba divers can hire boats to take them to the many diving spots on the reef, a habitat for fish, sea anemones, man-sized fans, soft corals and sea lilies. Less adventurous visitors can view the active underwater life from a glass-bottomed boat.

The St. James coast is also a haven for other watersports: water-skiing, parasailing, jet-skiing, windsurfing and hobie cat sailing.

Next to the Folkstone is the **Bellaires Research Institute**, which is dedicated to the study of marine biology with special reference to the island. The institute was set up in 1954 as an affiliate of McGill University, Canada, and its objectives are to improve the agriculture and fisheries of Barbados, as well as to investigate and cultivate new sources of food from the sea.

Also in Holetown is the **St. James Church**, erected on the same site 200 years after the original church was built. The first St. James Church was probably constructed just a few decades after the first settlers arrived, and legend has it that the first 10 to 12 feet from the foundation are part of the original stone church. An old bell, dated 1899, with the inscription "God Bless King William" has survived to this day.

Ronald and Nancy Reagan worshipped at this church on Easter during a 1982 vacation in Barbados.

In the church is a mural of Sir John Gay Alleyne, the Speaker of the House of Assembly in the late 1700s. He was called an aristocrat and a radical, but undeterred by criticism, he succeeded in making the Barbados Parliament a much more effective instrument of government. At the opening of every session, he claimed for society members the privileges claimed by the English Parliament: freedom of speech, freedom from arrest and free access to their representative in government.

Sir John owned one of the plantation

Left, water-ski instructor at Coconut Creek Hotel. Right, Dale Yearwood at Sandy Lane beach.

great houses in St. James—**Porters House**, which is north of Holetown, opposite the Colony Club Hotel. Porters is one of the few remaining plantation houses constructed in the early period of the island's history. The oldest part of the house dates back to the 1700s, but it has not been preserved entirely in its original form. Sections were added in the 1800s as well. The house is furnished with Barbadian antiques, including a big mahogany dining room table and mahogany four poster beds.

Stately Mansion: Nearby is the stately **Heron Bay**, a house designed along the lines of an Italian palazzo. Heron Bay was built in 1947 by Ronald Tree.

Set on 20 acres of parkland, the Palladian mansion includes on its grounds a small lake filled with mullets, a coconut grove and a citrus orchard.

Leaving Holetown and continuing along Highway 1, you'll pass the villages of Mount Steadfast, Weston and Carlton. In St. James, the built-up areas are all along the coast. Traveling inland, you'll see only cane fields interspersed with small villages, mostly situated around plantations such as Orange Hill, Westmoreland and Bakers.

St. James is one of the smallest parishes on the island, but it has a profusion of restaurants. The **Inn on the Beach** is a small hotel that serves flying fish sandwiches right on the beach every day the sun is shining. You can stroll along the shore and munch your sandwiches right by the sea. But watch out for the hot sauce! Its one of the spiciest you'll find anywhere.

Across the street from the Inn is a small **farmer's market** (at Sunset Crest) where Bajan ladies sell locally grown fruits and vegetables—good for seaside snacks. Depending on the season, they sell avocados, which Bajans call "pears," papayas, which they call "paw-paws," mangoes, soursop, passionfruit and a great variety of vegetables good for cooking up a big Bajan stew.

Local Feasts: Most of the restaurants in St. James serve simple, "continental" food adorned with a few local touches. The **Bamboo Beach Bar** offers simple fare accompanied by the sound of waves lapping the shore. A bit more

Sinking the *Stavronikita* to make a new coral reef.

elegant is **Reid's**, where you eat in a tropical garden in the back of the restaurant. And fancier still is **La Cage Aux Folles**, for gourmet French food. If you're in the mood for a burger at an English pub, try the **Coach House**, and stick around to hear a local band play later.

Along Highway 1 there are many restaurants with terraces overlooking the sea, including **Koko's, Fiesta** and further north on the border between St. James and St. Peter, **Giggles**.

Also on the beach is the **Barbados Pizza Hut**, where you can get surprisingly good pizza to take out or eat there.

The **Rose and Crown**, a simple and unadorned restaurant which is also on Highway 1, serves real creole meals. **Noelle's** in Holetown is known for its lobster.

The atmosphere is convivial and the home-cooked Bajan food delicious at the **Catamara**, on a side street in Holetown. There you'll be able to sample the island's superb pumpkin soup, fried flying fish, or stew with "peas and rice." The owner and his wife will join you for a drink, and on some nights there's a guitar player.

Holmes Bar is another rum shop in St. James, and it serves food late into the night. It's at the top of Holder's Hill (off Highway 1 just opposite of Tamarind Cove), and a good place for a nighttime snack of spicy Bajan chicken. This bar, with its blaring jukebox, is a typical rural "hangout."

There's more nightlife in St. James than meets the eye. The popular **Coach House** often has live music—the best bands in Barbados play there—and a big crowd of both locals and visitors.

There's a small but lively disco at **Barbados Beach Village.** And most of the other hotels on the west coast have nightly entertainment, often beginning with a sumptuous buffet. The type of entertainment you'll find at the hotels here ranges from the polished dance performances given by the company "Bim International," to a concert by a children's church choir, to the ubiquitous flaming limbo dancers, to music by a steel band.

Sophisticated St. James is a place to relax and enjoy yourself: bask in the sun and sea, explore the beach, and savor the world's best rum punch.

Heron Bay estate.

ST. THOMAS: LUSH AND EXOTIC

Situated in the heart of the island is the parish of St. Thomas, one of only two parishes not bounded by the sea. Whether you're exploring its limestone caves, walking through a ravine, or traveling over its rich plantation farmland on horseback, you'll find St. Thomas a region of unique beauty.

Three main highways run through this central land; Routes 2 and 2A from St. Michael; and Route 1A from St. James, which meets 2A. Highway 2 begins at the junction near Eagle Hall in St. Michael, and continues past **Warrens,** an old plantation house built in 1686. It is a fine example of what the wealth of sugar harvests could bring planters in the 17th Century.

Just beyond the plantation house stands one of two surviving baobab trees on the island. This massive-trunked tree is about 250 years old. The only other example of this African species remaining on the island is an even larger version, on the grounds of Queen's Park in Bridgetown.

A few miles further along Highway 2 is **Sharon Moravian Church,** built in 1799 by the Moravians, who settled the island in 1765. Arriving from Germany, they were the first group of missionaries whose goal was to bring Christianity and education to the slaves, and the first in Barbados to admit slaves to its congregation.

Sharon Church is one of the few 18th-Century buildings unspoiled by alterations and additions. Its stately tower and handcrafted windows reflect the staunch faith and hard work of the Moravians. Admired by visitors, the church shows a marked architectural influence from the Low Countries of Europe, the birthplace of Moravianism.

Natural Wonder: Next along this route, you will not want to miss the exotic **Welchman Hall Gully,** where tropical plants and trees abound, highlighting the lush natural wonder of this three-quarter-mile (1¼-km) ravine.

The gully is actually a crack in the coral limestone cap which covers most of the island. The area got its name

Preceding pages: cotton field in St. Thomas. Left, Harrison's Cave.

from the Welshman, General Williams, one of the earliest settlers and the original owner of the land.

Sometime around 1860, one of his descendants cleared a portion of the gully and planted fruit and spice-bearing trees, adding to the already plentiful native growth there. For some reason, the gully was allowed to grow wild again soon after, and became a tangled overgrowth of trees, interlaced with a profusion of fruits and flowering plants. For over 50 years this gully remained private property and was visited by only a few curious and adventuresome souls. However, in 1962, the newly-formed Barbados National Trust turned it into a delightful place to stroll through and to enjoy a cool respite from the tropical sun.

The Trust left much of the gully in its natural state, adding only a few flowering plants and visitor facilities. Winding paths lead through the dense green shade of palms and ferns, past brightly colored flowering plants, exotic herbal treasures, such as cinnamon and nutmeg, and breathtaking natural landscape. You may also encounter chattering groups of wild green African monkeys.

In the second section of the gully, pay special attention to one of the many stalactites which forms a massive pillar, and appears to support the rock cliff above. This large pillar—the result of the stalactite and the stalagmite having joined over the centuries—has a diameter of over four feet (more than one meter), making it one of the largest in the world.

And at the northern end of the gully don't miss the gazebo, which looks out to the Atlantic Ocean, and offers a most spectacular view across the hilly section of the island.

In the vicinity of Welchman Hall is a road which bears the name Vault Road, derived from the burial vault of the Williams family, the only remaining building from the original estate. General Williams was a devoted Protestant and, according to legend, when one of his sons married a woman of the Roman Catholic faith, the General was grievously offended. When she died, however, she was buried in the family vault. But the next time the vault was opened, the coffins were found in disarray, and the old General's was

Welchman's Hall Gully.

138

standing upright, as if in indignant protest. The vault was rearranged, with the General returned to his original resting place. But again, the next time the vault was opened, his coffin was found upright. The woman's body was then removed, and the vault has remained in order ever since.

Subterranean Splendor: Just a few yards further along Highway 2 you will reach **Harrison's Cave**, a subsurface phenomenon said to be the only one of its kind in the entire Caribbean. A special tram takes you through the amazing limestone caverns, carved by the slow but steady work of underground streams over the centuries.

This site was known for many years, but it wasn't until 1970 that a Danish speleologist (cave specialist) named Ole Sorenson discovered a new and very interesting section of the caves, the **Crystal Caverns**. Heavy rains that year had caused severe flooding in several areas of the island, and a large quantity of ground water found its way into the underground system where its force eroded a small entrance into this new, unknown and parallel cave. Through this opening, Sorenson dis-

covered several other small passages leading to a large room about 250 feet (75 meters) long by 100 feet (30 meters) wide, and 100 feet high.

The government, encouraged by the National Trust, decided in 1981 to open the caves to the public, and today a tour through the underground system is a breathtaking experience. Indirect lighting enhances the magnificent scene of thousands of gleaming, actively growing stalagmites and stalactites. Near the lowest point of the cave is a 40-foot (12-meter) waterfall which plunges into a large blue-green lake.

In 1985 the caves opened for night tours. This popular night tour is combined with a dinner served on top of the caves, underneath a cliff, where lights that are partially concealed in the branches of the many trees give the effect of actually being inside the caverns.

Best of Barbados: Continuing on Highway 2 from Harrison's Caves will bring you to the east coast parishes of St. Joseph and St. Andrew. Backtrack, however, to Warrens, where Highway 2A branches off from the main highway, and come to **Welches House and**

Plantation, home of the Best of Barbados products.

Owned by Jill Walker, a local artist, the plantation buildings have now been converted into the administrative offices, screen-printing studios and stockroom for the Best of Barbados, a company that produces beautiful crafts and gifts that depict the culture of the island. The plantation started soon after the first settlement in 1627, but the present plantation house dates from sometime around the mid-1800s, probably following the great hurricane of 1831, when most of the buildings on the island were either damaged or totally destroyed.

Leave Welches and continue north along Route 2A and you come upon **Bagatelle Great House**, now a restaurant which has earned a reputation throughout the world for its gourmet dinners. This plantation great house goes as far back in time as St. Nicholas Abbey and Drax Hall, the two oldest houses on the island. The original owner, the first Earl of Carlisle, was once the proprietor of the entire island. In 1651, the property was handed over to Lord Francis Willoughby of Parham and its name was changed to Parham Park House. In 1877, the property left the Willoughby family's hands, lost as part of a gambling debt, and its name was changed to Bagatelle. The great house is now owned by Nicholas Hudson, who displays a picture of Lord Willoughby on the souvenir menus he presents his guests.

Some miles further along the highway stands the indomitable **St. Thomas Parish Church**, which can boast of having suffered more hurricanes than any other institution on the island. Destroyed by the hurricane of 1675, it was rebuilt five years later. Damaged in 1731, it was completely demolished again by the great hurricanes of 1780 and 1831.

First Free Village: Turning off the main highway and traveling inland, you will come to **Rock Hall Village**, an old settlement of great significance to Barbadians. This was the first black freehold village in the country, and possibly the first in the entire West Indies. The Rock Hall story unfolded in the pre-emancipation year of 1820, when the area was part of Mount Wilton Plantation, owned and man-

Roadside poinsettias.

140

aged by Reynold Alleyne Elcock. This young white planter, a man with moral values well ahead of his time, recognized the plight of the slaves and was determined to improve the lot of those who directly depended on him. In a will he made in 1820, he bequeathed £5 sterling per year to each of his 120 adult male slaves, making additional provision for the repairs of their quarters.

Somehow, news of the will and its contents leaked out, with tragic consequences. Unwilling to wait for his master to die a natural death before reaping the rewards, Elcock's valet, Godfrey, decided to take fate into his own hands. It is not clear if he acted alone or as part of a conspiracy, but he slashed the throat of the 32-year-old Elcock one night in 1821 as the master slept.

Godfrey was apprehended at nearby Hangman's Hill and subsequently paid the ultimate penalty for his crime. Because of the murder, the slaves at Mount Wilton had to wait a further 17 years, until the Emancipation Act came about in 1838, to reap the fruits of their generous master's will. They used the money to purchase plots of land at the Mount Wilton Estate and the village so formed became known as Cut-Throat Village. We know it today as Rock Hall.

Other white planters in this parish followed Elcock's example and willed their plantations to their colored (mulatto) children, born to slave mothers. Among these plantation owners were William Ellis, Henry Simmons and George Hewitt. William Ellis' son, Thomas, one of the first colored men to be elected to the House of Assembly, inherited Canefield Plantation; Hewitt left Cane Garden and Bloomsbury to his colored son, who also won a seat in the House; and Simmons' three mixed race descendants inherited Vaucluse Plantation, where Simmons' gravestone can still be seen.

St. Thomas is one of the major agricultural districts in the island and therefore, on your trip through this parish, you will pass fields and fields of sugarcane and other crops. A beautiful way to view this land is on horseback, especially in the early morning, just at sunrise, when the freshness of the earth saturates the air and envelops you.

Fertile fields and plantation house.

THE SOUTHERN PARISHES

They say that the parish of St. George "has no sea," that St. John is "behind God's back," that people in St. Philip are clannish, and that anyone well-educated who lives in Christ Church must be sophisticated and wealthy. Though the four parishes that comprise the southern half of Barbados are more alike than different, some of the startling contrasts between them explain why a small and relatively insular society can be exciting—and full of pleasant surprises.

If you look beyond the familiar attractions in these four parishes, you'll find areas full of unique features that reflect the historical, geographical and social heritage of the island. One of St. George's familiar attractions is the old Gun Hill signal station and the panoramic view of the south that it affords; but don't overlook St. George Church which boasts a hoard of treasures dating back to the 17th Century. And there's Drax Hall plantation, the only estate that has remained in the hands of a single family since the time of the island's settlement. In St. John you'll find treats like Ashford Bird Park, the historic Codrington (Theological) College and the cool eastern retreat of Bath on the coast. But few know about St. John's "Glen Burnie Project," an effort by a group of Bajan naturalists to preserve and promote the island's rustic East. Christ Church features the nightlife in St. Lawrence Gap, the folk heritage of Oistins Town and the popular surf of Rockley Beach. But those who like curious tales will be drawn to the graveyard in Christ Church's Dover Woods, the site of one of the island's greatest mysteries. St. Philip is home to the world-famous luxury resort, Sam Lord's Castle and the "wicked" waves at Crane Beach. But one is less likely to hear about the Woodbourne oil fields of St. Philip, or the changing nature of the land surrounding the Ragged Point Lighthouse—once forgotten and barren. These are but a few of the subtleties of the four parishes. The southern half is a rich area of fertile plantations, resorts and industrial centers, pregnant with contrast, waiting to be explored.

ST. GEORGE'S EARTHLY CHARM

A drive on Highway 3 allows you to explore some hilly areas of St. George, for the most part a flat parish. This road offers one of the best chances of experiencing Barbados' "sugarcane country," which extends for miles through sugarcane estates, and bisects countless tiny villages whose histories are linked to the area's plantation tradition.

Highway 3 starts (as do all the highways of the southern half) in Bridgetown. It is the road that branches off Roebuck Street by the Globe Cinema roundabout and passes through Station Hill, Waterford, cuts through a limestone cliff, and continues on to Hothersal Turning where it swings to the east into St. George.

At Market Hill, the route through St. George splits into three: Highway 3 heads northeast into St. Joseph; a secondary road ahead takes the traveler into the St. George districts of Sweet Vale, Golden Ridge and Redland; and Highway 3B is the third branch, leading east toward St. John.

Highway 4 proper begins at Welches Post Office which is set in a triangle of land bordered by three roads on the outskirts of the city. All the way out of St. Michael, Highway 4 is lined with houses. Some of these form such working-class neighborhoods as My Lord's Hill, the Ivy, Rouen and Salters. The Salters area is actually what Bajans call "but an' boun'," meaning that it straddles two parishes: part of it is in St. Michael and the rest is in St. George.

At Salters, a road which branches

Preceding pages: Windsurfer Trevor Hunte at South Point; Cane fields of St. George.

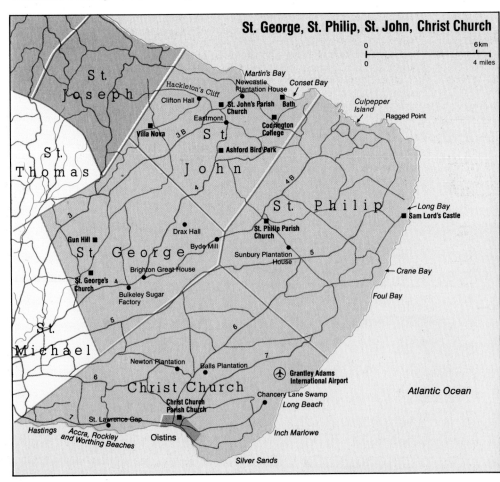

St. George, St. Philip, St. John, Christ Church

St. Joseph

St. Thomas

Hackleton's Cliff

Clifton Hall

Martin's Bay
Newcastle
Plantation House
Conset Bay

St. John's Parish Church
Bath
Eastmont
Codrington College
Villa Nova
3B
St. John
Ashford Bird Park

Culpepper Island
Ragged Point

St. Philip
Long Bay
Sam Lord's Castle

Gun Hill
Drax Hall
St. Philip Parish Church
Byde Mill
Sunbury Plantation House
Crane Bay

St. George
Brighton Great House
St. George's Church
Bulkeley Sugar Factory
Foul Bay

St. Michael
Newton Plantation
Balls Plantation
Grantley Adams International Airport
Chancery Lane Swamp
Long Beach

Christ Church
Christ Church Parish Church
St. Lawrence Gap
Hastings
Accra, Rockley and Worthing Beaches
Oistins
Inch Marlowe

Silver Sands

Atlantic Ocean

0   6 km
0   4 miles

off the highway takes you north, to St. George Church and Gun Hill. If you stay on Highway 4, you'll continue east into the heart of the fertile **St. George Valley**, a region that is steeped in the traditions of the sugar plantation history of the island.

Fertile Valley: Understanding the sugar industry's impact on the character of Barbados is a prerequisite to appreciating the earthly charm of the southern parishes.

Though the days when sugar production rose to over 200,000 tons—1957 and 1967 were the record years—are long gone, thousands of Barbadians still depend on the sugar industry for their livelihood. Across the entire island, cane is grown both by small farmers and on the island's large sugar estates, more than half of which are found in the southern parishes. Together, the small farmers and large plantations produced the cane for the 100,247 tons of sugar that Barbados manufactured in 1985. The island has over 160 sugar estates.

Although Barbados is often described as a flat garden, the mainly limestone island rises in a series of gentle terraces, from west to east, to the 1,100-foot (330-meter) peak of Mount Hillaby, the highest point on the island. In the Scotland district, the chalk and clay have made farming difficult and sometimes impossible. But the fertile St. George Valley is ideal for agriculture.

The Drax Hall estate, set in the Valley on Highway 4, was the first spot on the island where sugarcane was cultivated. The 878-acre estate is the only plantation island to belong to the same family since the 17th Century.

Portable Dwellings: Large estates in the Valley, such as Drax Hall, have been major centers of employment and settlement for as long as sugar has been cultivated in Barbados. Through the tenantry system, peasant families rented the land on which they built their houses, sometimes for generations. Recent legislation, which forces landlords to offer to sell to their tenants, has brought significant improvements to the peasants' quality of life. Now that they have land to call their own, families can build more permanent stone houses to replace the traditional wooden, chattel houses which have

Revelers at "village meet" in Market Hill.

always been built so that they could be dismantled and moved if necessary.

The names of many villages in Barbados are the names of the plantations they were once a part of. For example, in St. George, Boarded Hall is a plantation and a village with its own police station; Drax Hall estate includes the large Drax Hall tenantry where the descendants of the plantation workers now live; Bushy Park, in St. Philip, is better known as a dilapidated car racing arena than as the plantation. It once was Mangrove plantation in St. Philip, now better known as the home of the Barbados Workers' Union Labour College. In Christ Church, Wotton, now a government housing estate, has become synonymous with vivid TV scenes of flooding during the rainy season rather than as a plantation where sugarcane is grown; and Newton plantation now has to take second place in the public eye to Newton Industrial Park, which has supplanted former sugarcane fields.

Valley Plantation is the first large estate on Highway 4 after Salters. Spanning 254 acres, it is now the property of Clarence Shepherd who, for a number of years, managed Drax Hall for the Drax Family, who live in England.

A few miles after Valley Plantation there is the **Bulkeley Sugar Factory,** the only sugar factory in St. George that remains in operation today. Unlike most of the island's six sugar factories, Bulkeley is on a major route and therefore very accessible.

Sweet Nights: It is a great joy for locals and visitors alike to visit a sugar factory at night and watch the sugar and molasses being made. Anyone who wants to visit a sugar factory can arrange a nighttime tour; just call and make arrangements with the supervisor so he can plan to show you the operation and answer your questions. A comprehensive tour of a factory takes at least an hour. Afterwards, your guide is sure to offer you some aromatic "liquor," the brown, hot sugarcane juice that is removed from the mixture just before it crystallizes to sugar. The juice is hot enough to crack a glass container. Bring a plastic bottle with you so that you can take some of the delicious liquid home with you.

Cane fields and sugar mill.

To manufacture sugar efficiently, the island's sugar plantations are grouped into zones, with each plantation sending its cane to the factory in its particular zone to be refined into sugar. Bulkeley produces sugar from cane grown in St. George.

During the grinding season (January to May) Bulkeley and the other five factories collectively can grind over 530 tons of cane per hour. They are capable of grinding an average crop of 1 million tons of cane in 16 weeks.

As recently as 1944, there were over 60 sugar factories in Barbados, but the number gradually declined because of increased production efficiency. Bulkeley is one of the oldest factories still in operation, while the newest (Portvale) was built in 1981 on the St. James–St. Thomas border. Informal tours can be arranged at any time.

Half a mile past Bulkeley, there is a turnpike by a little village where Highway 4 branches into Highway 4B, heading southeast towards St. Philip and Highway 4, which goes northeast, deeper into the parish.

Highway 4B leads from the turnpike to two historic plantation houses.

House with a History: The first, **Brighton Great House,** ranks with St. Nicholas Abbey and Drax Hall as one of the oldest houses on the island. It also has the distinction of remaining in the hands of one family (the Piles) for over 100 years. The first owners were the Wiltshires, who had the property from 1638 to about 1800. Arthur Oughterson bought it in 1802 and sold it to John Gittens Archer two years later. Archer, the first white Bajan to be convicted for the murder of a slave, sold Brighton to Conrad Pile in the first quarter of the 19th Century. Dr. Henry Fraser and historian Ronnie Hughes, in their book *Historic Houses of Barbados,* explain how they used a marble slab in the outer wall of Brighton's south wing to determine the age of the house. On the slab is the name "Wilsheir" and the date 1652. Brightons's roof is supported by mastic columns and 20-foot (six-meter) beams, while its walls are made of a mixture of rubble and corn husks.

Several miles further east on Highway 4B, actually on the eastern tip of the parish where it borders St. John and St. Philip, is the entrance to

"Snow on the mountain" tree in front of chattel house.

HOW SUGAR IS MADE

As you drive up to one of the six sugar factories in Barbados, you'll see tons of freshly cut sugarcane piled up at the front, with a high, overhead crane slowly feeding it into the mill. At the back of the factory are mounds of the golden "bagasses" — what is left of the cane after it has been chopped into pieces and pressed several times by rollers to extract all the juice.

Inside the factory, the cane is chopped and ground mechanically, under a steady flow of water. There, "milk of lime" (calcium hydroxide and water) is added to the diluted juice, and the liquid then passes through a rotating clarifier that removes its impurities.

The milk of lime and the rotation causes the large impurities to settle. The clean juice is then channeled to a series of evaporators, which remove much of the water from the sweet solution and leave a thick, brown

intricate process. He checks the pans often: as the first crystals start to form, he must let in more syrup so that the crystals grow larger and new crystals do not start to form. He also decides when to let the mixture of crystals and molasses (very thick syrup) pass on to the centrifugals.

A centrifugal is a metal basket that spins at very high speeds, throwing the molasses through the holes in its sides while the mixture is sprayed with water to make the crystals as clean as possible. The crystals fall out at the bottom of the basket and are stored in large bins before being taken to warehouses to await export or distribution to shops.

None of the by-products created in the making of sugar go to waste. The bagasses can make chicken feed and hardboard; it is also burnt in the factory as fuel. The mud that is produced when all the impurities are washed away at the chopping and

syrup that is ready to form crystals in the factory's vacuum pan.

The goal at the vacuum pan stage is to produce sugar with crystals as large as possible. One of the most important workers in a sugar factory — the sugar boiler — controls this very

grinding stage is returned to the sugarcane fields as fertilizer because it is rich in phosphate. The molasses is good feed for cattle, horses and other stock. It also makes industrial alcohol and carbon dioxide, not to mention the island's world-famous rum.

another of the island's historic plantation houses, **Byde Mill.**

Although no one seems to know exactly when Byde Mill was built, it is believed that Joshua Steele, who is credited with starting a Barbados Society of Arts and Crafts, initiated construction on the site. Steele, a fellow of the Royal Society, London, leased the Byde Mill estate in 1777. He also owned the adjoining Kendal plantation in St. John where Richard Ligon—one of the most quoted historians of the island—spent his three years in exile in Barbados (1647 to 1650). Ligon's book, *A True And Exact History of Barbados,* was the earliest recorded history of the island.

If you turn onto Highway 4 instead of 4B at the turnpike, the road will take you to what is perhaps the most revered and renowned great house in St. George, **Drax Hall.** From the turnpike, the road gently climbs, passing through the large village of Ellerton and alongside the new housing development of The Mount. The houses on The Mount are perched on a pleasant, breezy ridge that commands one of the most spectacular views of the St. George Valley.

Jacobean Gem: A long, narrow driveway goes from the road to the Drax Hall great house which is completely hidden by trees. James Drax, who, with his brother William built the Drax estate in the mid-1600s, told historian Richard Ligon in 1650 that he intended to return to England, but it is questionable that he would have bothered to build the large Jacobean mansion if he did not intend to live on the island. No one knows the exact age of Drax Hall—but it was probably built sometime in the 1650s. In *Historic Houses of Barbados,* Fraser and Hughes write:

There is a length of copper guttering at Drax Hall that bears the date 1653, but this does not prove the date of the present house. The copper drain pipe may have been used originally on an older house and reused on a later house if rebuilding occurred. Architecturally, however, Drax Hall is typically Jacobean, a stately English manor house in a tropical setting. It has steep gables, corner finials, casement gable windows, and an exceptionally fine Jacobean staircase and ornately carved

hall archway of mastic wood. These all firmly suggest a pre-1700 date. Although a much plainer house than St. Nicholas, it is equally dramatic.

The massive Drax Hall estate dominates a great deal of the eastern section of St. George, and its influence is reflected in the names of some of the settlements and areas nearby. Within a four-mile (6½-km) radius, you'll find Drax Hall Jump, Drax Hall Woods, and Drax Hall Green.

Middle Class on the Move: The influence of the plantations is somewhat less evident in the parish's western section which is reached by the secondary road that branches off Highway 4 at Salters. Like its neighboring parishes—St. Philip and Christ Church—St. George is rapidly becoming a desirable area for residential development in Barbados, and hence a home for the island's middle class.

Some areas of recent middle-class residential development in St. George are Rowans, Fairview and Walker's Terrace. Interestingly, all these areas are on elevated parts of the parish, and some house owners are lucky enough to enjoy magnificent views of the St.

Right, amber waves of cane.

George Valley.

The western parts of the parish have been tagged in the island's physical development plan as one of the areas of "significant population increase" during the decade between 1970 and 1980. St. George's population grew an average of 23 percent every year for those 10 years. In comparison, St. Michael's population grew only 0.06 percent, and St. John's grew by 0.4 percent.

However, in certain areas of the parish the population declined. This was mostly in the sugar belt above the second cliff in the St. George Valley. The Barbados government has attributed this to the increased mechanization of agriculture—the number of jobs on the sugar estates fell from 8,000 to 4,000 in that same 10-year period.

The secondary road that branches off Highway 4 at Salters leads to **Charles Rowe Bridge,** a heavily populated section of the parish where there is a petrol station. Charles Rowe Bridge leads up a gentle incline to two major attractions in St. George, the parish church and Gun Hill.

Hurricane Survivor: The **St. George Church** is about half a mile up the road

from Charles Rowe Bridge. Built in 1784 for a mere £600, the church is the oldest ecclesiastical building in Barbados. It survived the 1831 hurricane; the chancel and the tower have been added in 1923 and 1953 respectively.

St. George Church is the site of "The Resurrection," the altar painting by Benjamin West, the first American President of the Royal Academy. There is also a sculpture by Richard Westmacott, who also sculpted the statue of Lord Nelson in Bridgetown's Trafalgar Square.

After passing the parish church, the road becomes steeper, rising up from the valley toward **Gun Hill.** The milk-white limestone lion on a cliff on the left side of the road is the first part of Gun Hill you'll see. From the lion, you can look up and see the old Gun Hill military signal station above. The Barbados National Trust has preserved it as a historic site. The limestone lion was sculpted in 1868 by Henry Wilkinson, the Adjutant-General of the Imperial Forces stationed in Barbados. Two inscriptions are carved in the rock of the lion's base. The first includes the name of the sculptor, his rank and the date he completed the project. Then there is the affirmation: "It (the British Lion) shall rule from the rivers to the sea, and from the sea to the ends of the earth." An inscription to the right of the sculpture lists the four military workers who helped Wilkinson.

Scenic Signal Station: The signal station itself, which can be reached by car through an entrance further up the road on the left, has been praised by many writers because of the incredible view it offers and the healthful quality of the surrounding air. Historian Robert Schomburgk's description of the view from Gun Hill in 1848 holds true today:

The ridge of cliffs, a continuation of those in St. John, traverse St. George and reach their greatest height near Gun Hill, where there is a signal-post and a convalescent station for the soldiers of the garrison. The air here is considered very salubrious, and the view from the station, over the rich and fertile valley to Bridgetown and Carlyle Bay, is extensive ... no stranger who visits Barbados should omit seeing this spot ...

Left, old-time donkey cart. Right, Gun Hill Signal Station.

152

The inscription on the stone reads:

✚ DOMINABITVR·A·MARI·VS·A
HEN·IOA·WILKINSON·
CEN·COHPED·IX·BRITAN·
TRIB·CASTR·SCVLPS·
A·D·MDCCCLXVII
AD·TERMINOS·ORB

ST. JOHN: SOMETHING FOR EVERYONE

The sight of expansive sugar plantations, dotted by tiny villages, continues in St. John, but the parish has more hills than St. George, and its entire northeastern section is dominated by Hackleton's Cliff, which runs north into St. Joseph. History buffs, nature buffs and those who like to chat with residents of a small fishing village will find St. John a delightful parish.

Hackleton's Cliff is 1,000 feet (305 meters) above the sea and offers one of the most panoramic views of Barbados' east coast, capturing the scenery from Pico Teneriffe in the north to Ragged Point in the south. It is said that the cliff was formed several million years ago when waves on the island's east coast eroded the limestone cap, leaving the area that is now known as the Scotland District. Hackleton's Cliff, a limestone ridge jutting out above the Scotland District, is said to be the point at which the erosion stopped.

Heading into St. John are two main arteries: Highway 4 and Highway 3B. Highway 4 enters St. John at Woodland Plantation and it leads, via a side road, to one of St. John's newest attractions—**Ashford Bird Park**.

The bird and animal sanctuary is part of the **Ashford Plantation**, which is still a working estate of 197 acres. The present owner, Mrs. Rosie Allan, is but the most recent of a long list of people who have owned the estate over the years. The most famous owner of Ashford was Ferdinando Paleologus, a descendant of the imperial line of the last Christian Emperors of Greece, who held the plantation from 1649 to 1670. Paleologus' tomb is in the graveyard of St. John's Church, not far away.

The bird and animal cages are arranged along a paved track that goes around the great house. Visitors thus walk though the yard of the plantation house. A small admission fee is charged. Among the birds are an African Grey Parrot, a parrot found on the nearby island of St. Vincent called Vin, the Plumheaded Parakeet, White Doves, a Cockatiel and a flock of pigeons that fly freely about the yard.

Ashford also offers a rare opportunity to see much of the island's plant life in one place. The extensive list includes grapefruit, orange, shaddock, mandarin, passion fruit, mango, pawpaw, golden apple, banana, sugar-apple, soursop, breadfruit, mahogany, royal palms and bay-leaf. You'll find many flowering plants as well, such as hibiscus, orchids, ixora, stephanotis and the Honolulu Wood Rose.

Ashford, near the center of the parish, is a good point from which to survey the surrounding scenery. The road that leads off Highway 4 to Ashford Bird Park meets a junction at the northern end of the plantation yard. One road leads east through miles of plantation land to eastern St. John, the other is a northerly route to Highway 3B.

Magnificent View: Highway 3B takes you towards the historic **St. John's Parish Church** which is nestled by a little road that leads off the highway. The church is set upon a cliff that overlooks coastal St. John and the Atlantic Ocean.

Although a stone version of St. John's Church was built as early as

1660, the present building was built in 1836 after the church was totally destroyed by the hurricane of 1831.

St. John's pulpit is constructed from six different kinds of wood: ebony, locust, Barbados mahogany, manchineel, oak and pine. The church also contains an interesting sculpture depicting the Madonna and Child with the infant St. John.

Ferdinando Paleologus' tomb in the graveyard at the back of the church has an intriguing history. Ferdinando was a descendant of the Byzantine Imperial family and thus was buried according to Greek custom. His coffin was therefore placed in a different position from the others in the vault with his head pointing to the west and his feet to the east. In 1844, nearly 200 years after Paleologus died, the rector of the parish (apparently curious to find out whether the story about the coffin's arrangement was true) ordered the lead coffin opened. All skepticism about the nature of Paleologus' burial was put to rest when his skeleton was found inside imbedded in quicklime according to the Greek custom.

The view of the rugged St. John coast from behind the parish church is guaranteed to instill in anyone the urge to explore this beautiful area. The road from the church goes north, and at the T-junction, you swing left onto a road that leads directly into the fishing village of **Martin's Bay**. Before that, you'll pass **Newcastle Plantation House**, one of the many historic great houses that dot the landscape of St. John.

Norma Nicholls, who once lived at Newcastle in the days when it was a private home, paid stirring tribute to her former residence in an article that appeared in the August 1977, edition of *The Bajan*, Barbados' sole monthly magazine:

Memories of Newcastle where I spent most of my holidays as a child, come flooding back. Newcastle in the morning, the smell of almonds—West Indian almonds—of roses and the sea. Blowing up from Martin's Bay, the sea breeze brought with it the aroma of burst almonds in the driveway and my aunt's roses which grew in a small bed just below the drawing-room window. Pungent, refreshing, exhilarating, I would take

Unusual Anglican church.

deep breaths and drink it all in, as I sat on the window-sill of the front bedroom, looking down at the horses as they muzzled away at their oats and corn in the long concrete trough which stood nearby, the sunshine rippling on their flanks, their tails swishing in contentment.

In the same article Ms. Nicholls referred to a gardener at Newcastle named Thomas, who was "*a descendant of the Scottish political prisoners who had been banished to the West Indies in the 17th Century: his eyes were as blue as the seas and he always had a tale to tell.*"

"Red-legs": There is no doubt that Thomas was a "red-leg," a group of people who today are concentrated more in St. John than in any other parish of the island. Legend has it that the term "red-leg" was used by the English to describe the Scotsmen because the kilts they wore exposed their legs to the sun. But for generations in Barbados it has been a term for the poor whites who settled "below the cliff." The "red-legs" have lived mainly in the area below the cliff northward into St. Andrew. Their presence is linked to the many caves below the cliff where white indentured servants and escaped prisoners hid successfully from the advancing authorities in the early days of the island's settlement.

Toward the end of the 1800s and until it ceased operation in 1930, the old Barbados railway passed through Martin's Bay. The road at Martin's Bay, which runs along the coast, today basically follows the train's path. A hiker can follow the path from the Bay along the coast and into the parish of St. Joseph. Aside from the abandoned train tracks, this region, known as **Glen Burnie**, remains a wild and rugged place, unspoiled by civilization.

Just like Home: A group called the Barbados Outdoor Club has banded together to ensure that Glen Burnie's natural beauty is preserved. The Club lore has it that an early settler—probably an ancestor of one of the "red-legs"—must have named it after Glenburnie in his native Scotland because the landscape reminded him of home.

The Glen Burnie Project is working to establish a Tom Adams Memorial Park in memory of the late Prime Minister of Barbados who died sud-

Villa Nova.

denly on March 11, 1985. (Prime Minister Adams was responsible for zoning the entire coastal area—which includes Glen Burnie—from Ragged Point, St. Philip, to North Point in St. Lucy, as natural parkland.)

The group is also planning to construct an "historical village" at Glen Burnie. Their proposal states that:

Through this village, locals and visitors would be able to really experience and understand the true way of life of our people—both past and present—and many local people would also be able to find employment by operating their own stalls or houses within the village. In addition, and flowing out of the village, would be other recreational and educational activities, such as sporting events, nature walks and hikes through the surrounding area and camping facilities for visitors and Barbadians alike, so that the breathtaking beauty of our country may be enjoyed to the fullest.

The plan also entails rebuilding a section of the old railway which ran along the coastline in the Glen Burnie area. The group intends to clean up the

coastline which, they lament, has become a "virtual dumping grounds for garbage and unwanted household items."

The rich plant life that flourishes below Hackleton's Cliff has also captured the Outdoor Club's watchful eye. Dubbing it the "Forgotten Forest," they sing its praise:

It is the last surviving piece of tropical jungle to be found in Barbados, and is a natural habitat for all the Robin Hoods, Huckleberry Finns, Tom Sawyers and Robinson Crusoes of today—regardless of their age or occupation. The size and shapes of the trees, the profusion of tropical fruits, the beautiful butterflies, the birds, bees, pawn flies, lizards, and the now deserted homes of the early settlers, the deep caves of the ancient Caribs, the upside-down bats which now live in these caves, the winding foot paths, cut out of the rock so many years ago by some hardened hands, all serve to remind us of the people who lived amongst these trees for so many years—black and white, in perfect harmony, and so healthy and strong.

The idea of the Glen Burnie Project has been less than popular with the public, despite a very impressive public relations campaign complete with a slide show, a video and hikes of the area. Government leaders once ridiculed the project (especially the proposed rebuilding of the railway) at a sitting of the House of Assembly. Thankfully, however, because the area is officially a national park, Glen Burnie is guaranteed to remain a hiker's paradise, "historical village" or not.

Picnic Spot and Satellite Dish: The road into Martin's Bay also takes you out. There is a four-cross road at the top of a hill by the exit and a southward turn leads towards the local picnic spot of **Bath** as well as the historic **Codrington Theological College.**

Two miles past the junction, a road branches off at the left and meanders down a hill to Bath. Although Bath was a thriving plantation in the days when "sugar was king," it is now better known as the site of the massive satellite dish which links the island to the outside world, and as a park where Bajans come to picnic on public holidays. At the junction on the

Cutting up the catch at Martin's Bay.

hilltop, the road which continues from Martin's Bay, goes south, up a steep hill, and on to Codrington College, two miles away.

Christopher Codrington III, whose estate led ultimately to the establishment of St. John's Lodge School and Codrington College, came from a long line of Codringtons who owned land in St. John. The first Christopher Codrington came to St. John from England and bought land there in 1642. Codrington's son, Christopher, went on to become Deputy Governor of Barbados in 1668. The Codrington of Codrington College fame was *his* son, who served a stint as Governor of the Leeward Islands.

Born in 1668, the third Christopher Codrington died a bachelor in 1710. He attended All Souls College, Oxford, and later studied law at the Middle Temple. He was made a fellow of All Souls College because of his outstanding intellect.

Poverty and Chastity: In his will Codrington left 10,000 pounds for the "Society for the Propagation of the Gospel in Foreign Parts" to establish an educational institution on the island.

He wanted:

. . . a convenient number of Professors and scholars maintained there, all of them to be under vows of poverty and chastity and obedience, who shall be obliged to study and practice Physic and Chirurgery as well as Divinity, that by the apparent usefulness offered to all mankind they may both endear themselves to the people and have the better opportunities of doing good to men's souls, whilst they are taking care of their bodies.

Despite Codrington's best intentions, his will was contested by his family in England. The court case dragged on for several years until the Society eventually won. The College did not start until 1748, nearly 40 years after his death. Then there was the problem of finding men willing to live under monastic vows. However, by 1760 the first deacon of Codrington College, Philip Harris, was ordained.

The College has a beautiful campus with lush and peaceful grounds. The complex of coralstone buildings stands on a cliff 360 feet (110 meters) above the sea, looking out over a magnificent

Abandoned sugar factory and working satellite dish at Bath.

view of **Consett Bay.**

Bajan Safari: If you take the road that passes by the front of Codrington College and follow it south, you'll go down a steep hill. At the bottom of the hill you'll find the entrance to Consett Bay on the left. The road which winds down to the Bay is notoriously uneven and poorly maintained. Prepare yourself for an adventure, something like that of a safari. The thick bush and trees that crowd the road are home to a number of wild green monkeys, one or two of which are likely to bound across the road in front of any automobile that drives through their territory.

Apart from Codrington College, most of St. John's historical buildings are plantation houses, the most well-known of which is **Villa Nova.**

Villa Nova is open to visitors five days a week for a small admission price. You can get there by swinging north off Highway 3B at Four Cross Roads, and making a left turn at the first junction, about a mile away. The house is nestled beneath a cool canopy of trees on a hill overlooking the Wakefield vegetable estate, the source of much of the packaged carrots, beans and other vegetables that the island consumes.

Built in 1834, Villa Nova is furnished with antiques of Barbados mahogany from the period. It was once a great house for the plantation now known as Wakefield and is considered to be the island's best example of a 19th–Century plantation house.

In 1966 Her Majesty Queen Elizabeth II and Prince Philip were luncheon guests of the Earl and Countess of Avon at Villa Nova. They planted two portlandias in the garden which have grown well over the years. When the Earl's health deteriorated, his doctors advised him not to travel far from Great Britain. In 1971 he sold the property to Mr. and Mrs. Ernest Hunte, who still live here.

Tip-Top Shape: The Huntes and their staff keep the property in top shape. The collection of antiques in the house was added to by Mrs. Hunte who did regular rounds at local auctions. The tour of the house isn't complete without a tour of the garden.

Two other interesting great houses lie east of Villa Nova: Clifton Hall and Eastmont.

To get to **Clifton Hall**, take a right out of Villa Nova's gate, go to the bottom of the hill and then swing left, heading east. Clifton Hall is just off this rambling road, two miles (three km) away. With an arcaded verandah on three sides and a double staircase that leads to a central porch, Clifton Hall is a prime example of Georgian architecture. Unlike Villa Nova, Clifton Hall is not open to the public and any tour of the inside of the house would have to be arranged privately with the owners.

Eastmont, another private house, can be reached by following the road from Clifton Hall as it heads south into St. John. This great house is not only significant architecturally as the prototypical 19th-Century great house, but it has symbolic importance as well. Miller Austin, a mulatto blacksmith, broke the monopoly of the white plantocracy in St. John when he bought Eastmont in 1895. The property has remained in his family since then. His daughter, Mrs. Lucy Deane, was to eventually inherit the estate. Her son, the Hon. H. Bernard St. John, Q.C., M.P., became the third Prime Minister of Barbados on March 11, 1985.

Road from St. John's Church to Martin's Bay.

THE STANDPIPE

Today, almost all island homes have running water. But modern plumbing is a relative Johnny-come-lately: a generation ago most Bajans trekked to the village standpipe to fill their buckets with water.

Because daily trips to the standpipe were part of every villager's daily routine, it became a community center of sorts—the place where people gathered to gossip and exchange news, where young men and women flirted, and where children played marbles and pat-a-cake.

Almost everyone had to use the standpipe; friends and foes alike would meet there. It was practically impossible for people "who didn't nuse to 'gree" to avoid one another at the standpipe. It was probably the venue for more fights than any other place in the village, as rivals exchange insults and sometimes even blows. Tempers shortened, too, as the queue for water grew longer. Trying to jump the line would be met with the indignant question, "You in know that you come and find me?"

If those who went to fetch water at the "pipe" did not want an unscheduled bath, they had little choice but to assume a finely poised carriage, for water buckets were carried on the head. Some women can still transport them long distances without spilling a

drop. Men often brought water home in washpans, which meant walking with 70 or 80 pounds on their heads. Some held a bucket filled with water in one hand while riding a bicycle down rough cart roads.

A standpipe tradition, too, was the pipe cleaner, who would arrive on occasion with official–looking brooms and scrapers. He would often demonstrate his authority by taking his cool time at his job.

Today, the standpipes are still there, and sometimes you'll see a passer-by stop for a drink of the pure, fresh water that flows from any of them. But gone are the days when they were the center of the vibrant social life of a Barbadian village.

ST. PHILIP'S RUGGED BEAUTY

Although St. Philip is the largest parish on the island, it is one of the least celebrated. This has stemmed partly from its distance from Bridgetown, and from the fact that in the past it was not productive agriculturally.

"Philipians," who are distinctive even in their manner of speech, have developed an unusual homogeniety because of their parish's isolation. This feeling of community among the people of St. Philip is especially strong during the Crop Over calypso competition, when they support their homegrown calypsonians, particularly the champion, "Red Plastic Bag."

Now that St. Philip has emerged as one of the most productive and fastest growing parishes, it has become less isolated. It has some of the finest hotels on the island. The Government, in its Physical Development Plan for the '80s, has identified St. Philip as an area of "significant population increase." The increase, according to the Government, has been because of the availability of low-cost lands not required for intensive agricultural production. St. Philip's population of 18,500 now logs in at third behind Christ Church (40,300) and the most crowded parish, St. Michael (99,000).

Highways 4B and 5 are two of the main roads into St. Philip. Highway 6 also leads to the parish, entering it from Christ Church and running through St. Philip's oil fields.

Tales of Treachery: St. Philip is perhaps best known as the home of **Sam Lord's Castle**, one of the island's major attractions. The castle, which is located on a cliff above **Long Bay**, can be conveniently reached by Highway 5. For the traveler driving through the parish, Sam Lord's Castle is always easy to find since signs pointing the way pop up at almost every turn.

Sam Lord's is now a Marriott luxury resort, but it is steeped in history and folklore, and the "castle" is the main part of the hotel. One of the most well-known characters of Bajan folklore, Sam Lord, has been the sub-

Preceding pages: near Ragged Point. Left, a "Philipian" checks out what's happening.

166

ject of at least one book (*The Regency Rascal* by Lt. Col. Drury) and a record produced by Barbados' world-famous calypso group, the Merrymen. He imported craftsmen from Europe to build his regency mansion around 1820. The construction took three full years.

As the "castle" shows, Sam was a man of lavish tastes who apparently felt no qualms about spending money he did not often have. He died with a debt of £18,000. But what Sam Lord is best remembered for is his treachery. He apparently put lanterns in the trees at Long Bay to trick ship's captains into thinking that the harbor was safe. When the ships were unwittingly wrecked on the rocks, he would plunder them. Legend has it that Sam Lord's treasure is buried somewhere on the grounds of his castle, but whether this is actually the case is anybody's guess.

James H. Stark, in a guide to Barbados published in 1903, described the mansion before it was changed into a hotel and commercialized. Stark wrote:

> Within a hundred yards from the sea, stands a large house known as 'Long Bay Castle', or as 'Lord's Castle'. The building is of a pretentious style, the rooms are large and lofty, and the tall mahogany pillars of the dining room have a fine effect. The house is too large, and its situations too remote for the wants of most Barbadian families, therefore, it has been unoccupied for years and is slowly going to decay.

Some time after Stark's visit, the property was bought by the Cooke family. And, in 1942, a consortium of Bajan businessmen bought the castle from Mrs. George Cooke and turned it into a hotel. They converted the north and south open porches into castellated wings and terraced the gardens to the east. Since then the castle has changed hands twice and now, as a Marriott resort, offers lodgings that are among the most expensive in Barbados, second only to the plush Sandy Lane on the western "gold coast" of the island.

Two of Sam Lord's Castle's outstanding architectural features are the classical mahogany columns and the beautiful plaster ceilings, equal to any in Europe. Inside the old building you **Ragged Point.**

get a chance to see some of the furniture Lord had originally imported for the mansion, as well as his own four-poster bed, mahogany wardrobe and mahogany sofa. The castle is said to be haunted, of course.

Pink Sand: Another elegant and picturesque hotel, **The Crane**, is about two and half miles (four km) to the southwest of Sam Lord's Castle. It is perched above St. Philip's rugged coastline. Stairs built into the bluff lead to a beach of very fine, pinkish sand and a surf that provides excellent waves for riding.

Rusticity and Ruins: Today, luxuriant trade winds still caress the Crane Hotel. For generations, **Crane Beach**, to the north of the bluff, has been a popular location for picnics and swimming. In recent years, erosion has come to the Crane, but on holidays one can still find many swimmers riding the waves, enjoying the rustic nature of the place and exploring the old ruins on the northern end of the beach.

There was once a wharf at what is now called **Crane Bay:** boats traveled daily between Bridgetown and the bay to deliver goods. The area got its name from the massive crane used to unload the boats.

A mile to the south of Crane Bay is **Foul Bay**. The bay earned its not very enticing name because it was a "foul" or bad anchorage for sailboats from Bristol and London. It has traditionally been a popular picnic-spot for Bajans. You'll find a species of plant called sea grape (*Cocoloba uvifera*) in abundance there.

A number of other bays line the St. Philip coast from Ragged Point in the east to Salt Cave Point in the south, including **Palmetto Bay**, **Bottom Bay** and **Cave Bay**.

The coastline north of Ragged Point is an area of cliffs and battering surf that does not have such friendly bays.

Ragged Beauty: Just off the coast about a mile and a half to the north of the lighthouse at Ragged Point is Barbados' only colony—**Culpepper Island**.

Culpepper Island is no more than 25 by 35 yards in size, and it's about 20 feet above sea level. A channel about 35 yards wide separates the island from the coast. But the channel's depth makes it impossible to wade to the

Crane Beach Hotel.

island; one has to swim. In *Exploring Historic Barbados*, Maurice Hutt wrote:

> On the island one has that sensation of being in a small world of one's own, reached by one's own physical efforts, not by some mechanical contrivance, which is always rewarding. And as in all intimate contact with wild nature, one feels a close kinship with the natural forces of the earth which is beyond the price of rubies.

The most easterly part of Barbados, the spectacular **Ragged Point**, is known for its high limestone cliffs and pounding surf. A lighthouse there was once open to visitors but is now closed. However, the cliff on which the lighthouse stands is a popular spot for those in search of solitude and a pretty view.

Following the road from Ragged Point north, taking all left turns and therefore keeping to the west, brings you to the more fertile and agricultural regions of the parish. After passing through the tiny villages of Marley Vale and Bayfield, the road leads back to Highway 4B at Thicket. The highway runs through plantation land below a steep ridge to its north for about four miles (six km) until it reaches **St. Philip Parish Church**.

Plantation Relics: A road at the western end of the church's graveyard leads to another place worth visiting in St. Philip, **Sunbury Plantation House and Museum**, which is about a mile-and-a-half down the road.

Sunbury House was opened as a museum in 1948 by the present owners, Mr. and Mrs. Keith Melville. They bought the great house separately from the plantation, along with six acres of land.

The two-and-a-half-foot thick walls of the house date back to the 1660s. Flint and other hard stone not indigenous to Barbados was used on the walls, brought over from England as ballast for schooners.

Some of Sunbury's other architectural features include old fashioned jalousies, frame sash windows with storm shutters and a turned mahogany staircase.

At Sunbury, you'll see tools, kitchen equipment, and other relics from the plantation era, such as restored old buggies and ox carts. Housed in what

Left, hoops on a hot day. Right, beach near Sam Lord's Castle.

used to be the yam cellar, the well-displayed exhibition is open to visitors during the day, five days a week, for a small admission fee.

Sunbury has its own rocky driveway that runs into Highway 5. A drive across the highway leads directly to a secondary road that is a straight route to Highway 6, one mile away. If you turn right at the junction with Highway 6, you will be heading toward the Woodbourne oil fields in the western corner of the parish, where it borders Christ Church. Highway 6 pierces through Woodbourne, and the small blue and yellow pumps are on what once used to be agricultural land.

Black Gold: Production of petroleum started at Woodbourne in 1972 when the General Crude Company struck oil. The discovery marked a new phase in the search for petroleum in Barbados which dates from the 1970s. Before the success in St. Philip, some other parishes had been explored with few or no rewards.

The oil fields at Woodbourne were nationalized by the Barbados government in 1982, and a National Petroleum Corporation (NPC) was set up to implement public policy on crude oil and natural gas production.

The Barbados National Oil Company, a subsidiary of the NPC, was also started to manage production at the Woodbourne oil fields, whose 76 wells are now the sole source of flowing crude oil on the island.

Nationalization of the oil field was important to Barbados' economy. It came amidst severe world recession and was among the measures taken by successive Barbados governments to reduce the island's oil import bill. It also confirmed the public sector's confidence in the island's fledgling petroleum industry. Already the oil from Woodbourne supplies 50 percent of Barbados' petroleum needs. There is optimism that Barbados can become self-sufficient in all products that can be made from Barbados crude, such as gasoline and kerosene.

Are such hopes grounded? Perhaps. In 1982, the year of the nationalization, the island witnessed a reduction in its oil import bill for the first time in its history. It stood at BDS $76 million, down $16.5 million from 1981's figure of $92.5 million.

Playing dominoes.

SURFING AND SWINGING IN CHRIST CHURCH

By the year 1652, Barbados was neatly divided into 11 parishes. But since that year the country has seen two attempts to further subdivide the island. The first effort was to create a new parish named All Saints. The second was to split Christ Church in two. Neither plan met with success, but those who wanted to divide Christ Church must now be turning in their graves, proclaiming "I told you so!"

Because of its beautiful southern coastline, with its string of sandy beaches and wonderful surf, Christ Church was the first parish to develop in the early days of Barbados' tourist industry. Its population grew at such a steady pace that the Christ Church coast is now the most built-up on the island—with enough people, money and action for any parish.

In the 1970s, real estate developers inevitably discovered Christ Church too, as they rushed to meet the demands of people eager to escape the urbanization of Bridgetown and the congestion of St. Michael. It rapidly became dotted with a number of middle– and upper class housing areas, particularly along the coast. Because of the sudden boost in population, a number of businesses found it profitable to set up shop, making the parish a center of commercial activity.

The entire Christ Church tourist belt is serviced by the well-trodden Highway 7, which runs almost parallel to the sea from Hastings to Oistins, at which point it swerves up Thornbury Hill and heads northeast toward the Grantley Adams International Airport. The other artery through Christ Church is Highway 6, which passes through the middle of the parish and across the farmlands that dominate the parish's northern half. Because the Christ Church coast has gained a reputation as the island's premier tourist playground, many forget that, like most other parishes, it also boasts thriving sugar plantations. These estates, with names like Bentleys, Staple, Grove and Newton, dominate the north of the parish as much as hotels, apartments and guesthouses do the south.

Chic Battle for Hastings: On the journey from Bridgetown via Highway 7, the first part of Christ Church you will reach is **Hastings**, an area that, as its name suggests, is steeped in military history. A number of old red buildings line the left side of the road as you enter Hastings. These were once barracks for St. Anne's Fort, just off Highway 7 to the north. (Read about the fort in the chapter on St. Michael parish.) Once humble soldier's quarters, they are now the chic residences of private tenants—and apparently the envy of many, since the waiting list for these apartments is very long. A military hospital and surgeons' quarters also graced Hastings in the fort's glory days; and the residential areas Marine Gardens and Navy Gardens, off Highway 7 to the south of Hastings, were the sites of a naval hospital and quarters for the Admiral and his staff.

The coastal stretch from Hastings to Oistins at one time featured some of the island's finest beaches. Regrettably, the pollution of the seas that has accompanied the development of Christ Church's coast has all but killed the reefs of the south coast, thus

leaving the beaches exposed to the ravages of erosion. With the loss of tons of sand, beaches like **Accra**, **Worthing** and **Dover** are now but a shadow of what they used to be.

Yet, here in the Eastern Caribbean, where few islands are blessed with many white sand beaches, vacationers still find the Christ Church beaches a delight. The Government is also making efforts to preserve the beaches and protect the marine habitat through a program of laying artificial reefs.

To top off a day of surf and sand, many people enjoy the south coast's lively and varied nightlife. The action heats up at the major night spots clustered along **St. Lawrence Gap**, which branches off Highway 7 by the Worthing Police Station. Each club is unique, with its own ambience and following. Some of the names to know are the **Ship's Inn**, **After Dark**, **Unicorn One** and **The Planetarium**.

Unicorn One (at the Southern Palms Hotel) and the Planetarium (at Dover Beach Hotel) are known as the rage of the younger set. The music is mainly American disco and some Caribbean calypso, and you can be certain that it is loud. After Dark, on the other hand, is Barbados' answer to a North American club for young urban professionals. On weekends it's jammed with men and women in their late twenties and early thirties.

If you work up a big appetite with all that swimming and dancing, you're in luck. St. Lawrence Gap is also where you'll find many of the island's better restaurants—from the American cuisine of **Boomers** to the Chinese treats of **Suzie Yong** to the Caribbean variety of **Witch Doctor**. **Pisces**, located at the water's edge in the St. Lawrence Gap, features seafood and drinks in a romantic setting.

Another venue off Highway 7 that offers some nightlife and good dining is **Maxwell Coast Road**. A residential area with a more restrained character, the restaurants here include **Tourist Trap** and **Flanagan's**. Many of the hotels, such as the **Welcome Inn**, **Sand Acres** and **Shangri La**, also serve meals.

Austin's Oistins: Half a mile east of Maxwell Coast Road on Highway 7, you will come upon the fishing town of **Oistins**. It got its name from an early

South Coast.

settler, Austin (which people pronounced 'Oistin') and is of importance not only for its large fishing fleet but for its historic past.

It was at Oistins in 1652 that the so-called "charter" of Barbados, or Articles between the Royalist supporters in Barbados and the Commonwealth naval forces anchored in the bay, were signed in the Mermaid Tavern. Onerous to the Royalists, these articles pledged the islanders to loyal obedience to Cromwell and his Commonwealth Parliament. Unfortunately, the historic tavern no longer exists.

In daily life, Oistins is better known as a fishing capital beyond compare. For generations, Bajans have traveled to Oistins Bay, on foot or by bus, to buy all types of fish caught offshore. The town was also the focus of social activity for the south coast. But the face of Oistins has undergone quite a sea change in the past 20 years.

The transformation began in the early 1970s when the cinema at Oistins was torn down to make way for a shopping plaza built at the eastern end of the town, on the corner where Highway 7 swings northeast up Thorn-

bury Hill. Over the years, the modern **Oistins Shopping Plaza** has housed a launderette, a Barclays Bank, a supermarket, disco, boutique, video tape club and electronics shop. Then competition, in the form of **Southern Plaza**, sprang up at the west end of town. Its lure for one-stop shoppers has always been a branch of **Super Centre**, one of Barbados' largest supermarket chains.

The government got in on the act by building a $10 million fisheries terminal to facilitate Oistin's traditional industry—the capture and sale of fish. The new terminal occupies 4.2 acres of land, most of which was reclaimed from the sea. By providing modern, comfortable facilities for fishermen and vendors, the Government has encouraged the modernization of the industry. For example, ice machines have now been installed at Oistins, vital to the growing number of long-distance fishing boats that have replaced the smaller launches.

But the sea somehow remains the center of life in Oistins, and the catches the same: dolphin, shark, barracuda, snapper and, of course, the ubiquitous flying fish. At times, shoppers can find

Fishing boats at Oistins Bay.

Old Wives, a succulent fish that is not as large as a shark or barracuda but can be prepared the same way. In the old days, before the fish terminal, women selling fish stood at the roadsides calling out "Fish! Fish!" and the day's prices. Today, going to Oistins for fish is not too unlike a trip to the supermarket, except that the vendors may well approach you in the parking lot, even before you leave your car, to entice you to their stalls. In times of plenty, flying fish can run as cheap as eight for a dollar. Out of season (during the months that don't end in 'r'), you might be asked to pay as much as two dollars for four fish.

The Great Coffin Mystery: On the ridge overlooking Oistins is the **Christ Church Parish Church**. At its present location, Christ Church Parish Church has gained international notoriety as the site of the "great coffin mystery." This event, which occurred in the Chase Vault in the church's graveyard, is regarded by some as one of the wonders of the world.

George Hunte, in his book on Barbados, described the strange happenings. He wrote:

The trouble at the Chase Vault began on 9 August 1812. When it was opened for the interment of Colonel Thomas Chase, two leaden coffins inside were discovered by workmen to be in an unusual position, while the coffin of an infant, Mary Ann Chase, had been moved from one corner of the vault to another. Twice in 1816 and again in 1817 a state of confusion was found when the vault was opened for burial of other members of the family. The Governor of Barbados, Viscount Combermere, was present on 7 July 1819 when the coffins had been restored to order after the interment of Thomasin Clarke. He made impressions with his seal on the cement which masons had put on the outside of the entrance to the vault. On 20 April, 1820, Viscount Combermere visited the vault. The cement was unbroken, the seal intact. The Governor then commanded the entrance to the vault to be broken and sent a man inside. The man discovered one huge leaden coffin standing up and resting against the middle of the stone door. He also noticed the infant's coffin lying at the far end of

South coast sport.

the vault where it had been thrown with so much force that it had damaged the wall of the vault. The publicity associated with this official discovery caused the family to remove the coffins and to bury their dead elsewhere. The vault remains unused to this day.

Clues to Slave Life: To the northeast of Oistins, farther inland, you will find another of the treasures of Christ Church—**Newton Plantation**. You can reach it by following Lodge Road east for a mile and a half (2½–km) until you reach a four-way crossing. A left turn onto the road heading north, and then a right turn into a white marl gap a few yards away leads directly into Newton Plantation yard.

In the 1970s, the excavation of a large slave burial ground at Newton revealed valuable information on slave life in early Barbados. Professor Jerome Handler, the American who supervised the expedition, and Dr. Fred Lange reported their findings in the book *Plantation Slavery and Slave Life in Barbados: An Archaeological and Historical Investigation.* They wrote:

Newton and its slave population typified medium to large-size Barbadian sugar plantations. Because Newton, as a plantation, so well reflected island-wide characteristics, and because its slave community also seems to have typified the Barbadian pattern, we assume that in their mortuary beliefs and practices Newton's slaves also displayed characteristics that were found elsewhere. In general, we believe that the findings of the archaeological investigations at Newton's slave cemetery can be extended to indicate patterns that also existed in other Barbadian communities.

In 1985 the National Cultural Foundation recognized Newton's historic value by making it the venue of the ceremonial delivery of the last canes, so launching the Crop Over Festival. During the program, Barbadians were taken on a guided tour of the plantation yard, which still maintains a pattern similar to what it had in the days of slavery, with the manager's house on an incline overlooking the rest of the yard.

Inch Marlowe Swamp: If you ignore Highway 7 at the junction at the east-

South coast sports fans.

ern end of Oistins (where the highway goes up a hill to the northeast) and take the road going straight ahead, you will be heading towards the southernmost tip of the island. This area of land which bulges out on the bottom of the island, contains a number of large middle– and upper class housing developments beginning on the coast and spreading inland.

After leaving Oistins, the first right off the road leads to Enterprise Coast Road, which runs parallel to the shoreline for a while before shifting inland, to become enveloped by houses on both sides. The road extends southeast through a number of residential districts—**Atlantic Shores**, **Silver Sands**, **Ealing Park** and **Inch Marlowe** among them—that have sprung up within the last 20 years. The area's only hotel, the **Silver Sands**, nestles on the coast below a cliff.

By taking all right turns after passing the road that leads down the cliff to the hotel, you will soon come to Inch Marlowe.

Many years ago Inch Marlowe was swampland, connected to the **Chancery Lane Swamp** beside it. The Inch Marlowe Swamp was drained to make way for tourist development, which many felt was ideal for the area because of sandy **Long Beach** that runs along the edge of the swamps.

Long Beach stretches for a mile and a half (2½–km) from the cliffs below Paragon (an area to the south of Grantley Adams International Airport) to Inch Marlowe Point. A desolate spot, often forgotten by the populace at large, the entire beach and swamp once belonged to the Chancery Lane Plantation.

In the early 1970s, big plans brewed for Long Beach. Commonwealth Holiday Inns of Canada drew up blueprints for a four–story hotel on 10 acres of beachfront property. The **Long Beach Club** opened on a scenic bluff overlooking the beach. A few years later, the Penthouse Apartments and the now abandoned Arawak Inn rose from the sands. A journalist, writing in Barbados' monthly *Bajan* magazine, expressed the prevailing optimism when he wrote:

Here is an entire area, literally bursting at its seams, on the threshold of what could be, provided our tourist

Left, local talent. Right, enjoying a cold Banks at the Ship's Inn, St. Lawrence Gap.

climate remains healthy, another boom area—a virtual second gold coast.

But over a decade later, Inch Marlowe and Long Beach remain more wasteland than hot spot. The Holiday Inn plan has become a faded dream, and the only tourist-oriented activities here are the Surf View Condominiums, owned by expatriates who use them as winter homes, and the Long Beach Club, which has managed to survive.

Long Beach and Inch Marlowe are generally perceived as out of the way, the "outback" of Barbados. Until recently, it was used as a shooting range by hunters. (The only other spot for this sport in Barbados is Graeme Hall Swamp, along the Christ Church coast, between Worthing and Lawrence.)

In 1966 a group of archaeologists unearthed the remnants of Arawak and Carib settlements near Chancery Lane Swamp. It was an exciting discovery, for the pottery they found was very different from any seen before on the island. It indicated that the first inhabitants of Barbados were agricultural and that they settled on the island about 600 AD.

Wandering Cricketers: No description of Christ Church would be complete without a word about Barbados' national sport, cricket. It so happens that Christ Church is home to the island's oldest cricket team, the Wanderers. The club's field is at **Dayrell's Road**, to the north of Hastings, east of the Garrison Savannah. Any weekend during the latter half of the year, a visitor can stop by and savor the sound of ball against willow and participate in a very unique Bajan experience.

The Wanderers started in June 1877, at a time when only the soldiers at the Garrison, and the Lodge School, St. John, had proper pitches. In the beginning, the club was elitist, but it had to adapt and admit blacks as the society changed.

Bruce Hamilton wrote in *Cricket in Barbados*:

If the soldiers may be called the missionaries of modern cricket in Barbados and Lodge the pioneers among the local people, to Wanderers must certainly be given the credit of setting the game on a permanent footing and keeping it there."

Twilight stroll.

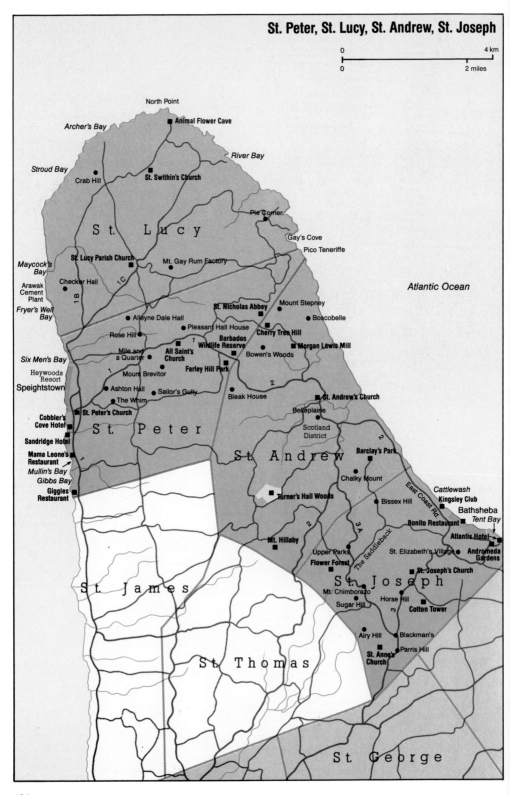

St. Peter, St. Lucy, St. Andrew, St. Joseph

0   4 km
0   2 miles

North Point

Archer's Bay

Animal Flower Cave

River Bay

Stroud Bay

Crab Hill

St. Swithin's Church

Pie Corner

St.   L u c y

Gay's Cove

Pico Teneriffe

Maycock's Bay

St. Lucy Parish Church

Mt. Gay Rum Factory

Atlantic Ocean

Checker Hall

Arawak Cement Plant

Fryer's Well Bay

1 B

1 C

St. Nicholas Abbey

Mount Stepney

Alleyne Dale Hall

Boscobelle

Rose Hill

Pleasant Hall House

Cherry Tree Hill

Six Men's Bay

Mile and a Quarter

Barbados Wildlife Reserve

Morgan Lewis Mill

Heywoods Resort

Mount Brevitor

All Saint's Church

Bowen's Woods

Speightstown

Ashton Hall

Farley Hill Park

1

Sailor's Gully

2

The Whim

Bleak House

St. Peter's Church

St. Andrew's Church

Cobbler's Cove Hotel

Belleplaine

S t.   P e t e r

Scotland District

Sandridge Hotel

S t.   A n d r e w

2

Mama Leone's Restaurant

Barclay's Park

Mullin's Bay

Gibbs Bay

Chalky Mount

Cattlewash

Kingsley Club

Giggles Restaurant

Turner's Hall Woods

Bissex Hill

Bathsheba Tent Bay

Bonito Restaurant

2

3 A

Atlantis Hotel

Mt. Hillaby

2

Upper Parks

St. Elizabeth's Village

Andromeda Gardens

East Coast Rd.

The Saddleback

Flower Forest

St. Joseph's Church

S t.   J o s e p h

S t.   J a m e s

Mt. Chimborazo

Horse Hill

Sugar Hill

3

Cotton Tower

Airy Hill

Blackman's

Parris Hill

St. Anne's Church

S t.   T h o m a s

S t.   G e o r g e

THE NORTH AND EAST:
WILD PLACES, OPEN SPACES

It is to the north and east coasts that both Bajans and visitors go for escape. Here, the scenery is stunning and the people are among the friendliest on the island. Rugged hills and gentle slopes are bordered by a stretch of narrow coastline with sweeping bays and some postcard-spectacular views. The Atlantic crests over treacherous reefs and pounds over the shore, mangling the huge rock formations on the beaches—in dramatic contrast to the turquoise calm of the island's western side.

The countryside lies like a patchwork quilt, decorated at intervals with tenantries, small clusters of houses on the peripheries of plantations. The occasional great house, flanked by graceful cabbage palm avenues, stands like a sentinel.

Relics of the past spring like surprises from all corners of the landscape: the ruined walls of mills that once ground sugarcane, overgrown gullies once the beds of flowing rivers, picturesque bridges that crossed those rivers.

In this beckoning region, you'll see the colorful chattel houses of St. Lucy, the green rolling hills of the Scotland District in St. Andrew and St. Joseph, the fishing villages of St. Peter, and along the coasts of all these parishes, some of the world's prettiest picnic spots.

Hotels, fast-food restaurants and other markers of modern living are few and far between in the north, but an intricate network of good roads make exploring easy. The rural northern parishes are for those in search of wild places and open spaces.

RUSTIC ST. JOSEPH

The smallest parish in Barbados, St. Joseph is bedecked with old plantation houses and cabbage palm avenues. Along its meandering coastline, sculptured rocks jut from the foaming Atlantic and wind-eroded sea grape vines hug the deserted sandy beaches.

Highway 3 leads into the isolated parish from St. George. On its way to Joe's River Plantation, Highway 3 descends down **Horse Hill**, one of the steepest roads in Barbados. Here the traveler will find banana, mango and soursop trees in abundance: the overhanging greenery creates a welcome coolness on hot days.

From Horse Hill and Joe's River, there is a magnificent view of the **Scotland District**, a rustic roll of hills and valleys, rural villages and grazing sheep. The district reminded early British settlers so much of Scottish scenery that they named it after Scotland. The area is completely different from the mainly flat limestone cap that occupies the rest of Barbados. This rugged region, where the roads are uneven and steep, consists of folded and faulted sedimentary rocks—sands, clay, shale and conglomerates. These rocks were probably formed 60 to 70 million years ago when the area that is now Barbados was just a muddy sea. Earth movements then caused the rocks that were to become the bottom layer of Barbados to sink deep beneath this sea. A second layer of white, clay-like rock built up over the original rock. A final layer, this of coral, then grew on top of the second layer. The earth moved again and the entire island emerged from the sea. Over the years, tidal waves which beat upon the eastern side of the island gradually removed the coral cap there, exposing the sands, clays and shale of the Scotland District.

At **Joe's River Plantation**, a Bajan legend finds its home. According to local historian Edward Stoute:

The legend is that at some period during the eighteenth century, the owner of the property died leaving an infant son as heir. He left the child's uncle to see after the estate and to take care of the child. The uncle was a schemer and desired to possess the estate for himself... One fine day the child and his nurse disappeared and could not be traced.

In due course the wicked uncle died, and it is claimed that two pairs of horses which were put in succession to the hearse refused to draw it, and that he was eventually buried on the estate... After the death of the uncle, this mansion became known as a 'haunted house,' for it was claimed that the ghost of the nurse and child were frequently seen walking around. It is also claimed that during alterations to the house a very thick wall was removed, and to the surprise of everyone, two skeletons, one of a child and the other of an adult were discovered. These were given a decent burial and the ghosts were never seen again... this old mansion was demolished around the turn of this century.

Panoramic Views: Horse Hill is on the northwestern tip of **Hackleton's Cliff**. This is the point where the tidal waves of thousands of years stopped their erosion: it is a ridge of limestone jutting above the sedimentary rocks of

the Scotland District. From **Malvern Plantation**, which is on the edge of the cliff, there is a panoramic view of hills and dales.

After Highway 3 descends down Horse Hill it meanders to **Bathsheba**, the fishing village on the east coast where many families have lived for generations, and a number of wealthy folk from other parts of the island own beach houses. Bathsheba's "**Soup Bowl**"—named so because the surf there is very foamy—is a good place to surf. Soup Bowl's surfing competitions, generally held in September, always draw large crowds.

Before Highway 3 reaches Horse Hill, it branches into Highway 3A which goes west into a little-traveled rural area of St. Joseph that is almost virgin in character. The adventurous traveler who is willing to seek out the scenery and talk to the villagers will not be disappointed. Highway 3A leads to such rural villages as **Sugar Hill**, **Chimborazo**, **Spa Hill**, **Fruitful Hill** and **Cane Garden**, on St. Joseph's northern border.

Highway 3A also takes you to the **Flower Forest**, a beautifully landscaped area of exquisite flowering plants and tropical trees, with winding paths and spectacular views. Early in the morning or within an hour of dusk, you may spot a monkey. The Flower Forest is open seven days a week; there is a small admission fee, and a snack bar, gift shop and rest rooms.

A road that branches off Highway 3 to the right at Horse Hill leads to **Cotton Tower**, another site that offers a panoramic view of the Scotland District. The Tower, at the end of Hackleton's Cliff, was one of a string of old military signal stations used by the British during the years of colonialism when communication was difficult. A few years ago it was restored by the Barbados National Trust and is now open to visitors.

Cotton Tower is set among rolling cane fields and from its balcony there is a clear view of the Parks Road Saddle Back to the north and Buckden Gully to the south. To the east, a matter of yards away from the Tower, are the abandoned ruins of Buckden Plantation House. The Tower's caretaker is Mr. Cespert Mayers, the man responsible for the beautiful gardens at

Sugar is the main crop of Barbados and the number two foreign exchange earner.

188

the base. A tailor by profession, he has a wide knowledge of the area.

Above Horse Hill is the **St. Joseph Anglican Church**, rebuilt in 1839 after the original one was destroyed in the 1831 hurricane.

Fraser and Hughes in their book *Historic Churches of Barbados*, relate an amusing tidbit about the church's history:

> *The story goes that the Vaughn family and the Blackman family were competing to donate land for the new church. The Vaughn family won because they demanded only a single family pew, rent free, in perpetuity, while the Blackman family had demanded two pews!*

Mythological Treasures: After the road winds down Horse Hill, the signboards name almost every nook and cranny of this rugged region. To the south of Bathsheba are two of Barbados' most alluring treasures, and both have taken their names from mythology.

Andromeda Gardens is named after the maiden in Greek mythology who was chained to a rock. The gardens are owned by the island's foremost horticulturalist, Mrs. Iris Bannochie. They are named after Andromeda because they are set on a cliff.

Mrs. Bannochie started the gardens in 1954. A stream bisects the six-acre profusion of exotic flowers and plants, which includes many varieties of orchids, bougainvilleas, hibiscus, heliconias, palms, cacti, succulents, ferns and shade-loving ornamentals. Mrs. Bannochie has acquired plants for the beautiful and exotic Andromeda Gardens from horticulturalists all over the world. The Gardens are open daily.

Below Andromeda is **Tent Bay**—the only place along the rugged St. Joseph–St. Andrew Coast where fish is landed. Barbados has 25 landing areas in all—so it's unusual to see such a long stretch of coastline with only one.

Overlooking Tent Bay, down what must be the world's steepest driveway, is the world-famous **Atlantis Hotel**. This simple but very pleasant place, with a reputation for the best local food on the island, took its name from the legendary continent of Atlantis, reputed to have occupied what is now the entire North Atlantic.

Atlantis is the oldest hotel on Barbados, where balconies and sunlit rooms

Black belly sheep.

look onto the dazzling blue ocean. The island's best known novelist, George Lamming, lives here for part of the year. Lunch on the terrace is a memorable experience: cooling trade winds caress you as you savor delicious seasoned Bajan fish or chicken and gaze out at the colorful fishing boats and the vast Atlantic. Be sure to try the coconut pie, too—a real island delight. Every morning at dawn, guests can watch one of the oldest rituals of Barbados: the communal launching of the fishing boats, which have to maneuver through a dangerous S-shaped channel before heading out to sea.

Breathtaking Beauty: The road north from Andromeda Gardens and Atlantis Hotel is a winding, hilly one that leads to the **East Coast Road**.

The East Coast Road goes from St. Joseph into St. Andrew and follows exactly the path of the old railroad to Belleplaine. At the St. Joseph end of the road there is a conglomeration of quaint, breezy beach cottages on both sides, rented by both local and foreign vacationers. At the small **Bonito Restaurant** you can get fresh local seafood and crab.

The road goes through an area called **Cattlewash**, where you'll see sea grape vines and windblown coconut groves. **Kingsley Club** is a delightful old world hotel in Cattlewash, known for its great fish and chicken "cutters" (local sandwiches on buns).

The vigorous trade winds make the surf beating against the East Coast beach particularly violent and hazardous to swimmers. However, at low tide, the beach and coral reefs along the East Coast Road are just the ideal places for exploration.

Coral reefs are native to warm, tropical seas such as the Caribbean. Though they are fragile ecosystems, they grow rather quickly—brain coral, for example, increases its diameter by one or two inches each year. Over long periods, corals can build up large expanses of rock.

The scenic East Coast is full of unexplored places and popular picnic spots. Thousands of Barbadians gather here on holidays, but it is enticingly deserted on regular workdays.

The fishing village of Bathsheba, with Atlantis Hotel in center.

ALL ABOARD FOR BATHSHEBA

Barbados once had a train that operated from 1881 up to 1938 and was a wonderful means of transport linking many beautiful scenic places such as Bath, Martins Bay, Atlantis Hotel, Bathsheba, Kingsley, Dan and Belleplaine. In those days the roads left much to be desired, and most of the motor cars in Barbados were incapable of ascending the terrific hills such as Cleavers Hill above Powell Spring Hotel or Round House Hill or even Horse Hill. If one took a chance and drove down to Bathsheba it was essential to leave well before sunset to get over the hills.

Bathsheba and Bath were not then served by buses and when one went on holiday, which many families did, it meant going for a month or two. This necessitated packing up and bringing down by train suitcases with clothes, bed linen and pillows, large quantities of canned goods such as salmon and condensed milk, PY canned salt butter and hundreds of pounds of Wallaba wood in bags to be fed into the old wood and coal cookers. Ice was always brought down two hundred pounds at a time and this had to be got up to the house and into the ice box.

Yes, it was quite an undertaking to pack

up and go to Bathsheba by train in those days. The train used to leave Bridgetown on afternoons around 4 p.m. and frequently there were heavy landslides in the Consetts cutting or Bath section which meant that a crew had to be summoned to work shoveling the earth from off the train lines. This sometimes took two or three hours and, of course, mothers always had to have emergency rations easily available for the children so that if a serious delay was encountered there would be a picnic meal to keep everyone happy until the line could be cleared. The train station in Bridgetown was located in what is now the Fairchild Street Market and the journey from there through all of the intervening stations to Bathsheba usually took around three to four hours. When the train, after many adventures, managed to come puffing around the Beachmount Hill corner it always gave three loud hoots of triumph and all of the people at Bathsheba would flock to the station to welcome it.

My favorite was No. 3, which was a very powerful engine, and we knew all of the guards by name. Sometimes letters or messages or packages used to be sent down

by these guards and they knew who was in every house. Very few people ever shut doors or windows in the houses occupied and stealing was non-existent.

Yes, there was a train in Barbados and it was loved and looked forward to all day. During August Bank Holidays special excursions used to leave Bridgetown about 6 or 7 a.m. and fifteen or sixteen carriages would be filled with holiday excursionists with their picnic baskets visiting Bathsheba for the day, and, of course, there were always a few people who got rather tipsy, as it was then called, and did most amusing things. These excursions were known as "outings" and were very popular with Sunday School excursionists and other groups. Around 4 p.m. the train began to hoot and they would all flock back into the carriages and the train then pulled out puffing loudly for Bridgetown.

— excerpt from *The Bridge: Barbados* by Patrick Roach

ST. ANDREW: HILLS AND DALES

St. Andrew is not the smallest parish, but its population is small—just over 6,500—and so it has managed to keep much of its virgin character. Some of the hills and dales of the Scotland District in this parish are relatively unexplored, despite their unmatched beauty. The villagers of St. Andrew know one another well, and, because the parish has been isolated for generations, have perfected the art of interdependence and neighborly courtesy.

The East Coast Road enters the parish of St. Andrew at **Barclay's Park**. This popular picnic area has shade, tables and benches, a snack bar and rest rooms. Barclay's Bank International created the 50-acre park in 1966 as a gift to Barbados, to commemorate its Independence.

From Barclay's Park the road runs along the coast for about a mile before veering west into **Belleplaine**, the quaint community that is one of St. Andrew's largest settlements. The village of Belleplaine has a long-standing place in Barbadian history and folklore because it was at the end of the old railway route. In bygone days, Bajans who were uninitiated in the wonders of the Scotland District delighted in going on the lively train excursions from Bridgetown to Belleplaine. One modern researcher relates that:

A string band consisting of guitar, violin, mandolin and saxophone accompanied the revellers. The excursionists danced to the lively tempo of the band at various sites en route. Two wooden horses (crudely built merry-go-rounds) were operated at Belleplaine and provided a singular attraction at the end of the train journey.

Though the train no longer exists, these rides to Belleplaine have been preserved forever in a popular Bajan folk song about the ever-resourceful Bromley, a government sanitary inspector of the day, who also owned a horse-and-buggy taxi service and operated a brass band. He occasionally sponsored free train rides from Bridgetown to Belleplaine—gala occasions for the laboring class. In the song, Bromley denies a young lady's request for more than one kind of free ride:

Yuh hear what Bromley tell de gal,
Yuh never go down Belleplaine outa me . . .
Yuh never wear dat gol' ring outa me . . .

The road from the East Coast meets Highway 2, the major artery through St. Andrew, at a T-junction in front of the Alleyne School, one of the oldest and most outstanding high schools in Barbados.

History and Adventure: A turn to the right on Highway 2 is the route to the historic St. Andrew's Church, Morgan Lewis Mill, Cherry Tree Hill and the rugged, little explored Morgan Lewis Beach. If the visitor heads north by turning left on Highway 2, the road leads to the pottery works at Chalky Mount, Turner's Hall Woods and Mount Hillaby, the island's highest point.

St. Andrew's Anglican Church is a mile away from the Alleyne School on Highway 2. It bears a proud place in Barbadian history since it was one of the few churches to survive the terrible 1831 hurricane. The church was in disrepair by 1842 and the present

building was built in 1846.

The road north from St. Andrew's Church winds through **Walker's**—the district that is the source of all the sand used for construction in Barbados.

The Scotland District has a reserve of over 132 million tons of sandstone. The main deposits are in St. Andrew and St. Joseph. Top quality glass cannot be produced from Barbados sands, but green and amber glass can be made.

The Walker's sand dune, which towers over the roadway, has been extensively mined for several years. It alone has a reserve of 16 million cubic meters of sand which would last, at current rate of usage, for another 100 years. Conservationists have recommended that only 10 million cubic meters of sand from the dune should be removed to prevent serious ecological damage to the area.

A turn right by a bridge after passing Walker's leads to **Shorey Village**. It is a quaint little community that is closely knit. Shorey villagers are proud of the fact that their community produced one of the greatest cricketers in the history of the West Indies, Conrad Hunte.

The story of truckloads of supporters from St. Andrew going down to Kensington Oval to cheer on Conrad Hunte when he appeared for the West Indies is now a part of Bajan cricket folklore. Today he is still so much revered by the people of Shorey Village that their cricket team in the Barbados Cricket Association's annual competition is named after him. The team is particularly good, too, and it can be seen in action on the village green on any weekend drive through Shorey Village.

500 Windmills: On leaving Shorey Village, the road ascends a steep hill to **Morgan Lewis Mill**, open daily to visitors. It is the only intact Barbadian windmill left on the island, and its wheel house and sails are in perfect working order. It is a good example of the Dutch windmills that were introduced to the island by Dutch Jews who came to Barbados from Brazil and pioneered the cultivation and the manufacture of sugarcane.

The working parts of the mill, you'll soon learn from a tour inside, were manufactured by the George Fletcher firm of Derby, England, in 1908. The Fletcher firm has a worldwide repu- **Morgan Lewis Windmill.**

tation for machinery used in sugar manufacture.

The slaves who worked on the sugar mills generations ago were specially trained and did not have to work as hard as the field slaves. The mill gang of about eight men had as one of its chores the task of moving the mill sails into or out of the wind by pulling and pushing the long tail tree. Heavy wind was just as bad for the grinding of sugar as was a light breeze. Squally wind would rotate the mill out of control and the vibrations could make the entire mill collapse.

At one time there were over 500 windmills on Barbados, all grinding sugarcane. Indeed, grinding sugarcane by windmill was practiced well into the 20th Century in Barbados.

The view becomes truly spectacular when one goes up the hill further to **Cherry Tree Hill**, a steep mile away from Morgan Lewis Mill. Visible from here is most of the Scotland District, including Belleplaine, Chalky Mount and Hackleton's Cliff in the far south.

At Cherry Tree Hill the road levels out and leads into the parish of St. Peter. The title Cherry Tree Hill is a misnomer for the long avenue that is lined by mahogany (not cherry) trees. The avenue is about 600 yards (550 meters) long, and the mahogany trees are so old and established that they form a cool canopy over the road, the trees from both sides of the road coming together about 20 feet (six meters) into the air.

The type of mahogany tree found at Cherry Tree Hill was introduced in Barbados sometime in the late 18th and early 19th centuries, according to some sources. The trees grow slowly, but can now be found in all parishes of Barbados, even though Cherry Tree Hill offers their most picturesque arrangement.

Isolated Beach: Before you leave St. Andrew for St. Peter via Cherry Tree Hill you should take the time to explore the little-known, isolated beach that is below the cliff from Morgan Lewis Mill. You'll get there by swinging right onto a narrow road after leaving Morgan Lewis Mill and before getting to Cherry Tree Hill. This road leads directly to the large village of Boscobelle, which straddles the parishes of St. Andrew and St. Peter. However, before you reach Boscobelle, turn onto the overgrown road that branches off the route. This leads down a cliff covered by thick foliage to one of the most isolated spots in Barbados—**Morgan Lewis Beach**. The road leading to the beach is not indicated on even the most detailed maps of the island. It is a pleasant white sand beach about two and a half miles (four km) long.

Morgan Lewis Beach is the best position from which to view the desolate coastline that runs for miles, past Green Pond, Long Pond and Lakes Beach to the East Coast Road. There are no houses or structures of any kind in this untamed region. It is not difficult to imagine it as the location for a film about an abandoned island.

Another point in the parish which affords an unusual view of the area's scenery is **Bleak House** which is on a limestone ridge at the western edge of St. Andrew, close to the St. Peter border. It is reached by following Highway 2 after it passes St. Andrew's Church, up Farley Hill in St. Peter, and making the first left turn after passing Farley Hill Park.

The view from Bleak House is of the

Green monkey.

entire Scotland District amphitheater in all its glory, complete with white waves lashing against the east coast beaches.

The house itself was built in 1886 as a kind of "bachelor great house" by an eccentric, Charles Peddar. Richard Goddard, a Barbadian businessman and head of the local Duke of Edinburgh (Exploration) Awards Scheme, now owns the property. The house has 166 acres of land with it, and Mr. Goddard is trying to make it as productive as possible by raising pigs, black belly sheep, chickens and cows, and growing plants such as pawpaw.

Highway 2 south from the Alleyne School leads directly to the interesting **Government Agricultural Station** on the old Haggatts estate. The station is the headquarters of the Soil Conservation and Rural Development Scheme in the Scotland District, which was started in 1957.

The Haggatts station is well-known for its research into fruit tree production, the development of forestry for the area and fish farming. It also plays a key role in the prevention of soil slippage and erosion in the Scotland District.

Nutritious Cherries: Haggatts is actually in a valley, bordered by the hills of St. Simons and Mount All on the west and Chalky Mount on the east. The valley is dominated by Haggatts' extensive orchards that produce such fruits as mango, citrus and the world-famous Barbados cherry (*Malpighia glabra*).

The cherry is famous because of its extremely high Vitamin C content. Just one Barbados cherry supplies a day's requirement for the human body. The cherry also contains riboflavin, niacin and thiamin. Under good conditions, the plant can fruit up to 10 times a year.

At the Haggatts station the road branches into a "Y," the right arm of which leads to the tiny village of **St. Simons** and Turner's Hall Woods at the end of the cul-de-sac.

The Caribbean's foremost gospel singer, Joseph Niles, spent his formative years in St. Simons. Niles has distinguished himself as a prolific producer of albums (he cut 15 in 14 years, beginning in 1970) and as a gifted interpreter of songs from the Negro spiritual tradition.

Outside the Chalky Mount rum shop.

Primeval Forest: Turner's Hall Woods on the slopes above St. Simons is the last remnant of the dense forest that carpeted Barbados before it was settled in the 1600s. Here you can see what those early adventurers must have seen when they first set foot on the island. This area of thick tropical foliage, including cabbage palm up to 130 feet (40 meters) tall, covers 46 acres and runs in a northeasterly direction from Mount Hillaby, at heights ranging from between 600 to 800 feet (180 to 240 meters) above sea level. Thankfully, the Woods have not been developed and remain relatively unspoiled complete with an overhead orchestra of birds and monkeys.

Cutting down trees such as those found today at Turner's Hall Woods (including Spanish oak, beef wood, fustic, candle wood and silk cotton) was the task of the early colonists of Barbados. In those early days any clearing was solely for agricultural purposes. In 1631, Barbados was still "so full of woods and trees" that one Sir Henry Colt was unable to train 40 of his musketeers. Historian Richard Ligon reported in 1657 that the first English settlers found a landscape which was "so grown with wood as there could be found no champions [open spaces] or savannahs for men to dwell in."

A hole in the ground inside the Woods which leaks out natural gas and can be lit with a match is an indication that the land at Turner's Hall is also rich in minerals. Back in the valley by the Haggatts orchards, a road leads off Highway 2 on the left up Coggins Hill towards **Chalky Mount Village**. The residents of Chalky Mount live mostly in wooden houses, many of which are built on the sides of hills. A narrow road that should be negotiated carefully meanders along ridges through the village.

Chalky Mount proper is not accessible by road. The traveler must park where the road ends and hike to it. It is 550 feet (170 meters) above sea level and looms over the East Coast.

Chalky Mount Village is home to the island's celebrated potters. And not surprisingly, it has one of the largest reserves of clay in the island. This scenic area is dominated by a brownish-red soil, evidence of its clay consis-

View of Atlantic Coast from central St. Andrew.

tency. The main clay deposit of 77.8 million tons is at Morgan Lewis. However, clay is now mined only at Chalky Mount and Greenland. The clay taken from Greenland is used to manufacture bricks.

The Chalky Mount potters can make almost anything out of their clay and they delight in having spectators watch them shape the rough brown or white blobs into handsome objects. Local creations include "connerees," special pots to preserve meats and to make "pepperpot," and "monkeys," which are water jugs that keep water cool and reportedly make it taste better. Much of the local pottery is glazed to a shining red ochre finish.

The craft of the Chalky Mount potter, using his machine or kick-wheel, has been handed down through families of the village for generations. Surnames such as Devonish, Harding, Springer and Cummins are likely to be found on clay pieces.

Soon after passing the Coggins Hill exit, Highway 2 branches in two at Bruce Vale. The left branch leads into the St. Joseph village of St. Sylvan's, or Dark Hole, as it is more popularly

known to Bajans. The right branch is the route through Baxter's towards Mount All, White Hill and Mount Hillaby.

Road on a Ridge: The road through **Mount All** and up **White Hill** is the first exit on the right. Like most of the roads in the Scotland District, this is perched on the back of a ridge. It offers some spectacular views as it climbs up.

The road leads into the village of **Hillaby** after it reaches the top of White Hill. Hillaby is a larger settlement than Belleplaine but it has not yet been blessed with a police station or post office like the village in the valley below. If you're in this area on a Saturday, you'll find a truly local treat for sale at the rum shop in the nearby village of **Gregg Farm**—homemade "pudding and souse," a traditional Bajan dish.

To get to the summit of Mount Hillaby, go left at the T–juction at the top of White Hill. A swing to the right leads down to **Mose Bottom**, a point which offers a splendid view of the deep ravine on the northern side of Mount All, Haggatts in the valley, and the eastern reaches of St. Andrew and St. Joseph.

Highest Point: After you swing left and take the second left off the road, you will soon find yourself on the summit of **Mount Hillaby**, 1160 feet (350 meters) above sea level. There is no fanfare here, at the highest point on the island—no park benches, no stalls vending souvenirs to visitors, no snack bar; in fact "The Mount," as the people of Hillaby call it, is deserted most of the time.

The summit itself is actually a chalk hill with a dirt cap. On top of it the only indication that it is Mount Hillaby is a stump of cement with a metal cap with the simple inscription "Inter-American Geodetic Survey/Do Not Disturb/-Hillaby/1953."

Here on the summit it is breezy, cool and quiet. The view to the south includes rolling fields of agricultural land with the telecommunications antennae at Sturges and Mount Misery furthest away. To the north, there are the settlements of White Hill and Gregg Farm, and the land slopes up on the west to St. Peter's eastern ridge. The view to the east from Mount Hillaby is the most spectacular. It is of stunning ravines, gullies and hills.

Left, Kemeta Belgrave in Shorey Village. Right, The Potteries at Chalky Mount; the potter is John Springer.

SCENIC ST. LUCY

In St. Lucy, the parish that caps the northern end of Barbados, you'll find the island's most dramatic scenery. Adventurous travelers will delight in exploring its untamed terrain. Along its rugged coastline, the powerful, relentless surf of the Atlantic beats against steep, jagged cliffs. Bajans call St. Lucy's foaming breakers "white horses."

St. Lucy also offers the best opportunity to see the Barbadian chattel house in all its glory. These little cottages are arranged in small villages that dot the vast plain of sugarcane fields that make up most of the parish. The number of households here is hardly vast: today it stands at just over 9,000.

As the population of the parish and its wealth grow, the small wooden chattel houses so characteristic of Barbados are being replaced by generally less interesting stone bungalows. The best examples today of chattel houses are in the villages of Greenidge and Connell Town near Archer's Bay.

In the villages of St. Lucy several stone ruins of old peasant dwellings are still standing today. Presumably these were the homes of folk fortunate enough to own the land on which their dwellings were sited. In the 1970s it became popular to describe these old houses as slave huts from the 19th Century that needed to be preserved. But writer Norah Francis, writing in the May 1974 issue of *The Bajan* Magazine made a valuable contribution to the debate:

> *In fact, the houses that slaves lived in are not in existence today. They were small and made of organic materials called wattle and daub. Their roofs as well as those of the stone huts of later date were thatched with materials such as trash or plantain leaves. These houses were usually square or rectangular and consisted of only two rooms, occasionally three.*

Touring St. Lucy: Traveling north from St. Peter along Highway 1, you'll pass Heywoods on the newly-built Speightstown by-pass, then reconnect with the old Highway 1 on the edge of coast at Six Men's Bay. The fishing communities of Six Men's, Half Moon Fort, Fustic and Checker Hall line the coastal road as it enters St. Lucy.

The route goes up a steep incline at the village of **Checker Hall**. Here you'll see a typical Bajan "rum shop," where the men of the village gather to drink and socialize. They are likely to be engaged in either a heated discussion of politics or cricket, or playing a serious game of dominoes.

At the top of the hill a road on the left leads to the **Arawak Cement Plant**. The factory has its own jetty that extends out into the Caribbean, to the south of the secluded Maycock's Bay. The plant was built on the northwest coast of the island to take advantage of the calm water–loading facilities as well as the close proximity to the raw materials used in the manufacture of Arawak's Portland cement.

From the cement plant the road meets Highway 1B at a four-cross road. A swing to the left is the route to the northernmost tip of Barbados. A drive straight through the four-cross roads junction leads to St. Lucy's Church and the Mount Gay Factory.

Turn left, and you'll see beautiful

Maycock's Bay stretching for about a mile along the shore. Two steep paths lead down to the beach; one of them takes you to the ruins of the old **Maycock's Fort.** Treasure is said to be buried under the fort.

An overgrown track on the eastern limits of the Barbados Defense Force base leads to the **Harrison Point Lighthouse.** A path down a thickly forested cliff at the base of the lighthouse accesses the secluded coastline. Here loom large rocks that have been so eroded by the sea that they assume eerie characteristics. Some of St. Lucy's sea cliffs are thought to be more than 500,000 years old.

Boots, Boots and More Boots: The Barbados Defense Force base is out-of-bounds to strangers. Armed soldiers patrol its limits. It used to belong to the U.S. military before it was handed back to the Barbados government in the late 1970s.

On the coast, east of Harrison Point, is **Archer's Bay**, a very popular picnic spot with Bajans. The road into Archer's Bay is at the Crab Hill police station, here the visitor won't find tables, benches and rest rooms, but will

encounter a rocky track that leads to a grassy expanse shaded by a grove of casuarina trees, just a short walk from a cliff with a magnificent view of the sea. A path winds through the wooded limestone ledge and down to a sandy cove.

Surf and Spirits: Near the village of Crab Hill, over one of the many narrow dirt roads that go through fields of sugarcane, is the place the island's serious surfers call **Duppies.** In Barbados, "duppies" are ghosts, and this area is well-named: tales of huge sharks and mysterious happenings abound here.

When the wind is blowing from the north, surfers flock to this little known, isolated area to ride the 15-foot swells. If the surf's up at Duppies, there will be local teenagers sitting on a bench under the almond tree at the edge of cliff, munching on sugarcane and watching the surfers.

From Crab Hill, another road leads eastward towards the **Animal Flower Cave**, a wave-eroded cavern which derived its name from the tiny sea anemones (seaworms) growing in its rock pools. Here stalactites and stalagmites grow towards each other from

Fishing through a hole in overhanging rock.

ceilings and floors, and the seaworms indeed look like flowers as they open and close their tentacles.

The cave, which is run by the brothers, Pancho and Manuel Ward, is open to visitors for a very small fee. The land around the entrance to the cave consists of barren rock, much like a moonscape; it's difficult to imagine that this region produced sugarcane in bygone days as the Animal Flower Plantation.

The Wards have the island's largest collection of business cards stuck on the walls and roof of the refreshment stands near the cave's entrance. They hope to make it the biggest collection in the world and gain mention in the *Guinness Book of World Records*.

Pancho and Manuel serve delicious homemade lemonade at their refreshment stand, and more potent drinks as well. Don't be surprised if Pepita,their pet black belly sheep, comes over to your table to greet you. You'll see herds of black belly sheep all over the island (even in Bridgetown!), but Pepita is probably the only one who likes to drink 7-Up straight from the bottle, and she's always willing to demon-

The Animal Flower Cave.

strate this feat to visitors.

The road south from the Animal Flower Cave goes by the abandoned **North Point Resort** at Middle Bay, and to River Bay.

Constructed in the early 1960s, North Point was once a popular Barbadian hotel. Management problems forced it to close in 1977, and it has since fallen into disrepair. The hotel has the island's only Olympic-size swimming pool (now empty), a facility missed by competitive swimmers.

Adjacent to North Point are the interesting remains of what used to be artificial salt lakes. Water was pumped from the sea into the ponds and left to settle and dry out, leaving the salt. The salt lakes were closed in the 1940s.

Breathtaking Bay: South and North Point is the well-known area of **River Bay**. It has been the destination of Bajan bus excursions for generations. The Bay gets its name from a stream that meets the sea at the inlet. From the hills above, it is a breathtaking sight. Visitors enjoy exploring the wind-eroded landscape and dry riverbed or just relaxing under casuarina trees. The bay is chiseled into the chalk and

limestone rock. Close to land, shallow water hugs moss-covered boulders, while further into the ocean turquoise waves break in laundry-white surf.

Now and then a fountain of spray appears from below, and a salty breeze caresses the face of anyone lucky enough to inhale the pure air transported over 2,000 miles of ocean.

River Bay is full of picnicking families on weekends and holidays; but during the week chances are you'll have this scenic spot all to yourself.

From River Bay a road leads west back into the center of St. Lucy and towards the parish church. **St. Lucy's Parish Church** is one of the first six parish churches on the island. The original structure was already in existence by 1629, and was reconstructed after damage from the 1831 hurricane.

A road meanders up a cliff, from the parish church to **Mount Gay Distillery** in the east, about a mile away.

Mount Gay is Barbados' world-famous rum. The golden spirit has been made at the Mount Gay Distillery for over 100 years. Tours of the operation are conducted twice daily, Monday to Friday.

A Bajan Secret: A perfect place to wind up a tour of the north is **Cove Bay** on St. Lucy's Atlantic coast. On maps it is shown as Gay's Cove, but it is known to all Bajans as Cove Bay. To get there, you'll pass through the village of **Pie Corner**, the site of an archaeological dig where artifacts from Carib and Arawak Indian civilizations have been unearthed. Follow the road out of Pie Corner to a grassy field with a horse farm to the left and cliffs to the right. The road to Cove Bay cuts right through a cow pasture, but stay on it, and you won't be disappointed.

The bay itself is not the visitor's destination, but a beautiful promontory called **Paul's Point**, which some say is the prettiest spot in all of Barbados. The Point overlooks the bay and the length of Barbados' Atlantic coastline. Here under the coconut trees the trade winds are fresh and vigorous. Towering over the south of the bay is the northern side of the jutting Pico Teneriffe, an unusually shaped white cliff which rises from the sea in stark grandeur, guarding the eastern coastline like a sentry and appearing much higher than its 80 meters.

Scott McCranels surfing at Duppies.

CHATTEL HOUSES

They are as delightful a part of the Barbadian landscape as the undulating fields of cane and bright blue sea; they are "chattel houses," the tiny, gay, makeshift homes traditionally built by rural Bajans. "Chattel" is movable property; these wooden houses are built on a foundation typically of loose stones, easy to dismantle and move. This mobility was once very much a virtue, as the original owners of chattel houses were plantation workers who didn't own the land on which their houses stood.

No two of the island's thousands of chattel houses look alike; but they all share a number of architectural features. They built of stone, weathered plank and corrugated metal for roofs and for the fencing that pens backyard pigs, chickens and goats.

Chattel house windows are inventive. Traditionally, each window sports three wooden shutters, two side-hinged and one hinged from above, to allow maximum flexibility in adjusting to sun and wind. Should a storm or hurricane approach, these shutters, called *jalousies*, can be shut tight against potential torrents. Today, glass and louvers are fast replacing the centuries-old wooden jalousies, but many fine examples still exist.

Other characteristics of the chattel house include short eaves, a further protection against hurricane damage, and fantastic color : it's not unusual for siding, molding, windows and doors to be painted in different, exuberant hues.

Modern houses in Barbados are often concrete, and less picturesque than the generations-old chattel house. But its influence isn't forgotten: Bajans incorporate many of its details, adaptive as they are to local weather, into modern island dwellings.

ST. PETER: SUN, SAND AND SURPRISES

St. Peter is blessed with western *and* eastern seafronts; it spans the width of Barbados. The calm Caribbean knocks gently against the western rim of the parish, the hills of rural St. Andrew dominate its eastern fringe, the sophisticated parish of St. James lies to the south, and rugged St. Lucy is to the north.

Highway 1, which runs out of St. Michael along the coast through St. James, is the most popular route into St. Peter. Here you'll see hotels, restaurants, some of Barbados' finest privately-owned seaside houses, and a number of beach bars where thirsty travelers can stop for a fruit punch and gaze out at the sparkling sea.

An even more scenic approach into St. Peter is from St. Andrew, through Cherry Tree Hill or up Farley Hill. The Cherry Tree Hill entrance, with its canopy of mahogany trees, is the most majestic. Immediately after entering the parish by this cool avenue there is,

on the right, one of the most treasured attractions of the north, **St. Nicholas Abbey.**

It is the oldest house on the island, and one of three remaining examples of Jacobean-style architecture in the Americas. A visit to the stone and wood mansion affords a revealing view of aristocratic plantation life.

The house is said to have been built around 1650 by Colonel Benjamin Berringer, a white landowner and member of one of the aristocratic families that dominated the social and political life of the island at that time. Soon after his house was built, Berringer was killed in a duel by Sir John Yeamans who later married Mrs. Berringer. Sir John and his bride were among the pioneers who left Barbados in 1669 to settle in South Carolina in the United States. Sir John became Governor of South Carolina in 1672.

The Abbey was named after one of Colonel Berringer's descendants, according to local historian Maurice Hutt. Berringer's son John left the house to his daughter, Susanna, who married a man named George Nicholas. It was his name that became

Preceding pages: Market women grow the crops they sell. Below, St. Nicholas Abbey.

214

attached to the property. No one seems to know how the 'Saint" and "Abbey" in the mansion's name came about.

To the north of the Abbey are ruins of the sugar factory that once ground the cane produced on the extensive estate. The factory was closed in 1947. However, the present owner, Stephen Cave of England, has some old film footage which shows various aspects of life at Nicholas Abbey early in the 20th Century, including black laborers at work in the factory. This intriguing footage is shown to visitors on request in a room that was once the stable.

Farley Hill National Park and its "great house" ruins are a few miles away from St. Nicholas Abbey. To get there, follow the road from the Abbey, turn left at Diamond Corner, and make another left onto Highway 1.

The peaceful Farley Hill National Park consists of several beautiful acres of tropical trees and plants on a cliff 900 feet (275 meters) above the sea, and overlooks the entire Scotland District.

Farley Hill mansion was built 200 years after St. Nicholas Abbey, on the grand scale of the 19th-Century planta-tion houses. The massive great house was built in sections, beginning in 1818. During the late 1800s, it was owned by Thomas Graham Briggs who lived what can only be described as a high life here. Farley Hill gained a reputation as the most lavish of the old Barbadian merchant palaces, and included a billiard room, library, oversized dining room and several reception rooms.

Hollywood Comes to Barbados: After Briggs' death in 1887, Farley Hill had a number of different occupants but it never regained the elegance that it saw under him. It was nevertheless selected for the filming of a Hollywood movie in the 1950s. For many years after, the unbelievable things that happened when Hollywood came to Barbados were the talk of the island. Journalist George Hunte wrote:

The glory that was Farley Hill had faded by the time that Robert Rossen approved it as Bellfontaine, the Fleury home in the 20th Century Fox film of Alex Waugh's "Island In The Sun" [starring Harry Belafonte].

Then for two months in 1956 the crumbling old 'palace' experienced

Another roadside attraction.

a transformation as 300 persons worked under the supervision of art director John de Cuir from Hollywood and his assistant, Walter Simmons, to convert it into a mansion suitable for a sugar baron. A complete new gallery and stairway was constructed to face the lawn. An open veranda was added in front of the main entrance, where a huge porte cochére with overhanging roof bordered an artifical lake. The waterworks of Barbados had to pump hundreds of thousands of gallons of water into this lake daily for weeks because its bottom was porous. Special paints were flown in from the United States and used to transform ordinary green leaves until they looked through the camera lenses like scarlet flamboyant flowers and magenta bougainvillea blooms. One flamboyant tree was delicately cut into numbered pieces at Crystal Springs on the St. James coast, transported to Farley Hill and there stuck back carefully together as a single tree growing alongside the porte cochére.

The large quantities of wood and other flammable materials that were used in the restoration were a danger, however, and a few years after the majestic occasion fire destroyed everything at the mansion except the walls.

In 1965 the Barbados Government bought the Farley Hill property and declared it a National Park. It was officially opened by Her Majesty Queen Elizabeth II, on Feb. 15, 1966.

Over the years the park has been an understandably popular recreation area for Bajans and visitors. The beautifully landscaped grounds contain dozens of different varieties of trees, especially fruit trees such as mango, soursop, mannee apple and tamarind. There are benches on the edge of the cliff where visitors can sit and savor the view, one of the nicest in Barbados. It is open daily from 7 a.m. to 6 p.m., and the entry fees are BDS $2 for cars and $1 for motorcycles.

Highway 1 west from Farley Hill leads into the most densely populated part of the parish, down sloping hills into settlements such as Mile and a Quarter, Ashton Hall, The Whim and the city of Speightstown on the coast.

Haunted House: A right turn off the

Sea-bath for man and beast.

highway at Mile and a Quarter leads to **Alleynedale Hall**, an old Barbadian great house that is said to be haunted. Before proceeding down to the St. Peter coast, pay it a brief visit to savor its architecture and wonder about its secrets. Alleynedale Hall is set in the still factory yard of the 315–acre Alleynedale sugar estate.

Barbadian historian Edward Stoute has written:

The last male of this family was a clergyman and he committed suicide by cutting his own throat. However, they did not, as was the custom of the day, bury his body where four roads crossed and drive an iron stake through it, but put him in a leaden coffin and buried him in the wall of the cellar. Sir Reynold Alleyne, whose grandmother was a Miss Tyrrill, purchased the place in 1810 and changed the name to Alleynedale Hall. What has become of the leaden coffin and the body of the unfortunate Reverend is not known, but there is, or was, a cavity in the floor of the cellar in the shape of a coffin. It is related that the spirit of the unfortunate Reverend walks around the house at night.

That unfortunate Reverend would have known **All Saints Church**, on Highway 1 to the east of Mile and a Quarter.

The original All Saints survived hurricanes in 1675 and 1780 but could not withstand the great hurricane of 1831. A foundation stone was laid in 1839 and the new church was consecrated in 1843. This new church barely lasted 40 years before the walls were found to be shaky and the church had to be demolished to make way for a new building which was completed in 1884. Despite all the rebuilding All Saints Church remains on the original site and a number of the old tombstones are still present, providing a journey into old Barbados with the names of the prominent planter families of centuries ago.

On a Whim: To the south of Mile and a Quarter (so named because it is that distance from Speightstown [see below]) is an exit to the left off Highway 1 into the **Whim Gully**. This gully is one of the most accessible of the dozens of gullies that dot the Barbadian landscape since the road passes through its

"Warri," a game slaves brought from West Africa.

floor. The foliage rises up on both sides, and in the center of the gully the road crosses a bridge where the temperature is very cool. In times of heavy rain, water flows over the rocks of the gully's floor and under this bridge. The Whim Gully is notorious to the residents of Speightstown as the source of much of the water which floods the town after heavy rains. The road from The Whim goes through the other of St. Peter's major gullies, Sailor's Gully.

Sailor's Gully is bordered on the south side by a cliff about 80 feet (25 meters) high. Hanging from the cliff are festoons of thick vines. And in the limestone is the opening of a cave with mossy stalactites and stalagmites visible from the road. In Sailor's Gully the road branches into two, and both routes lead into miles and miles of St. Peter's sugarcane fields and eventually back to the Farley Hill Park region.

At Orange Hill there is a panoramic view of the land sloping down to the west coast and the scenery of St. Lucy, dominated by the Arawak Cement Plant on the Checker Hall coast.

Before leaving this part of the parish for the west coast or St. Peter's Atlantic coast the visitor should also take the time to see the **Barbados Wildlife Reserve** and **Pleasant Hall Hill.**

Shy Monkeys: The Reserve is a project of the Barbados Primate Research Center in a lush mahogany woodland with footpaths. It offers a unique opportunity to observe at close range, in their natural habitat, the monkeys of Barbados (*Cercopithecus sabaeus*). You'll see young monkeys at play, mothers caring for their babies and older males keeping watch over their territories as they forage for food. An interesting and well written booklet *The Green Monkey of Barbados* provides information on the behavior of this shy and elusive creature. The booklet, refreshments and gifts are available at a reception center. Opening hours are from 10 a.m. to 5 p.m. daily and there is an admission fee of BDS $5 for adults and half price for children under five.

At **Pleasant Hall Hill** there is a cave where it is believed that Carib Indians once worshipped. The entrance is 10 feet (three meters) above the ground and is hidden by bush. Inside is a small carved piece of rock in the shape of a

Creative advertising at a repair shop.

218

human head.

Secret Picnic Spot: The villages of **Boscobel** and **The Risk** are the communities closest to the desolate and rugged Atlantic coast of St. Peter. You can reach them by following the road east from Diamond Corner.

Most people go to Boscobelle to see Barbados' best known landmark on the Atlantic coast, **Pico Teneriffe**. This is a tall pillar of rock that can be seen from as far south as St. John. Nearbly **Cove Bay** (actually in St. Lucy), is one of the island's most beautiful picnic spots (which most visitors don't know about) and it offers the best view of Pico Teneriffe.

Writes George Hunte in his book on Barbados:

"It rises like a large bump on a rugged eroded cliff. Anyone who has seen the towering mountain at Teneriffe in the Canary Islands must wonder at the imagination of the person who first gave Pico Teneriffe its name. Yet, situated where it is on the south side of the deeply indented Gay's Cove, the peak seems higher than its few hundred feet while the figure on its pinnacle may be mistaken on a misty day for a sorrowful Madonna gazing out to sea in anxious care of her beloved fisherfolk.

Full of Charm: People who live in the north go to **Speightstown** to do their shopping. The character of Speightstown as not changed much over the past century, even though its face has been revamped. It is unique among the island's four towns because it is the only one to have retained much of its original street system. It is a charming town of small streets lined with simple, two-story shops, many boasting old-fashioned Georgian-style balconies and overhanging galleries propped up on slender wooden pillars.

The construction of a by-pass highway has routed traffic around the center of the town, making it an ideal place for strolling, especially on a Saturday morning when the "hucksters" sell fresh fruit and vegetables from their trays on the narrow streets, and it seems as if all the north comes to Speightstown. In the center of town are remnants of the Denmark and Orange forts, which once mounted 23 cannons between them. Some old cannons are

Church Street, Speightstown.

still standing on the **Speightstown Esplanade**, a promenade which overlooks the sea.

The man after whom the town is reportedly named was William Speight, a white landowner and member of one of the earliest parliaments in Barbados. Speight came to Barbados from Bristol and owned land in the St. Peter area. The town was once called "Little Bristol" since it was a bustling port for the shipment to Bristol, England, of sugar produced in northern Barbados.

Glory Days: Speightstown had its greatest glory in the days when there were no motor vehicles, and Bridgetown could only be reached by foot, horse-drawn carriage, or boat from the northern end of the island.

At the center of the town today is the modern **Speightstown Mall**, opened in 1980. It is one of the most comprehensive shopping areas on the island, complete with a department store, bank and fast-food restaurant.

Two of Speightstown's most interesting landmarks are Arlington House and St. Peter's Parish Church.

Arlington House was built as a

private home, in a style similar to the great houses of South Carolina in the United States. Over the years it had fallen into disrepair, but in 1986, restoration work was started by Peace Corps volunteer Lauren Cutsinger. The work has been a joint effort of the Peace Corps, the Barbados National Trust, the Duke of Edinburgh Awards Scheme, the Lions, the Boy Scouts, the Barbados Museum and some Speightstown businesses.

St. Peter's Parish Church is in the heart of Speightstown, at the corner of Church and Queen streets. It was one of the island's earliest churches, originally built in the 1630s. The structure was largely rebuilt in 1837, in Georgian style, and then again restored in 1980 after a fire devastated all but its walls and tower. The restoration took three years and cost BDS $750,000.

Nightlife of the North: North of Speightstown, below quaint fishing villages such as Six Men's, is Barbados's largest resort, **Heywoods**.

The 306-room complex offers the most modern tourist accommodations and facilities to be found on the island. It stands on 30 acres of expansive beachfront property and was designed around an old sugar plantation. The facilities, which cost BDS $60 million to build, include seven accommodation buildings, each with a distinct design and ambience, a conference center, plus what seems like whatever a visitor could possibly think to do, from browsing through a beach market under thatched huts to nursing a rum drink at the beach bar.

A nice way to absorb an extensive view of the sloping west coast of St. Peter and to end a tour of the parish is to stop at **Eastry House**. This hotel is located on six acres of landscaped gardens on top of cliff 200 feet (60 meters) above the sea. The view from Eastry House extends as far down the coast as the Deep Water Harbour in Bridgetown and as far north as the Arawak Cement Plant in St. Lucy. Below the cliff is the posh residential district of Mullins Bay.

The owner of Eastry House, Gordon Carlstrom, makes no secret of the fact that the 34-bedroom hotel caters to an upscale market and is proud of Eastry's high ratings over the years in travel guides. The Queen of Denmark vacationed at Eastry on several occasions.

Left, Pico Teneriffe; right, a solitary moment.

AFRICA
UNITE.
JAHLOVE
SEEN.

A LIVING ART

Africa lurks still in the works of Barbadian artists and craftsmen. Walk through the Temple Yard district, at the westerly end of Bridgetown, and watch the Rastafarian craftspeople bend their dreadlocked heads over leather and straw, clay and wood. Listen to their joyous humming, the sounds of their mallets and chisels. Before long you are transported to that faraway continent.

The African cultural memory springs forth in the colors, themes and styles of many of the island's most creative citizens. It expresses itself in the unique blend of art and craft that so dominates the Barbadian art world.

The Barbadian artist will boggle the minds of those who try to distinguish between art and craft. Throughout the centuries, the Barbadian artist-craftsman has ornamented, embossed and embellished the functional, making it a work of art. He has taken simple, everyday items and made them into expressions of his personal and cultural self.

Community of Craftsmen: At Temple Yard, you'll find artists who have been able to combine old and new, East and West. There is Ibo, an artisan, who designed a building made entirely of bamboo: doors, windows, roof . . . all plaited with marvelous skill, rainproofed and heatproofed, too. And there is the artist Akyem, who studied at the Jamaica School of Art. A master of clay, Akyem produces plaques, hangings, sculptures in the round, low-relief scenes, and some unusual paintings which explore and reject all Westernized concepts of art.

Here, at Temple Yard, the creations of a whole community of craftsmen are laid out before you, leather bags, shoes, purses . . . there are countless items in wire, bamboo, coconut husks, shells and fronds; images of local fish, birds, fruit, animals; seashells clustered into fans and jeweled vases. Many of these are functional, yes, but created with the art-spirit of Africa.

To many of the brethren in Temple Yard, "making with the hands" is part of the Rastafarian creed. You will find painted

Preceding pages: Young Rasta by mural; whirling dancers at the show "1627 and All That Sort of Thing" at the Barbados Museum. Left, Bajan art often incorporates themes from everyday life.

images of Marcus Garvey, the Jamaican leader of the Back-to-Africa movement, reggae musician Bob Marley, former Ethiopian Emperor Haile Selassie, lions—the Rastafarian symbol—and maps of Africa resplendent in red, green and gold.

Exquisite Boutiques: The Rastafarians are only one group of craftsmen on the island. Nearby, in the complex of small, exquisite boutiques, galleries and curio shops called Pelican Village, you'll find other craftsmen in their workshops and stores, their goods on display for visitors.

The Barbados Arts Council, an old and respected institution, has its Art Gallery here. And there is Karl Broodhagen's painting and sculpture gallery, where the island's art connoisseurs gather. Broodhagen is "a

whose bronzed features are forever immortalized on a pedestal at the Government Headquarters on Bay Street, just outside Bridgetown. Perhaps the most impressive of Broodhagen's works, some dating to the 1930's, are those he keeps at his house in Strathclyde, St. Michael.

Avant-Garde Sculpture: In Pelican Village, there is a Pelican Restaurant where the fashionable and the knowledgeable gather after seeing the sights and making their purchases. Nearby, there is the Industrial Development Corporation (IDC), a statutory body which oversees handicrafts in the island. On its grounds is a massive piece of sculpture called "Pelican in Flight" consisting of three pylons welded together and rusting under the sea-breeze. Some consid-

living legend" in Barbados. He is a master craftsman, painter, thinker and researcher. He began his working career as a tailor and grew into a virtuoso artist. If you have the opportunity, take a look at his statue, "The Freed Slave," commemorating the 150th anniversary of emancipation. It stands in the center of a traffic circle in St. Barnabas, where the parishes of St. Michael and St. George meet. A larger-than-life figure of a man with his arms upraised, head thrown back, broken chains dangling from his wrists, the statue speaks eloquently of pride and freedom.

Broodhagen has also made exquisite portrait heads of many famous Barbadians, including the famed Sir Grantley Adams,

er · this piece an insult, foisted on the Barbadian public at exorbitant cost, by an 'avant-garde' architect.

The IDC looks after local craftspeople. It has Handicraft Sales Shops at Pelican Village, Grantley Adams International Airport, Sam Lord's Castle in St. Thomas, Heywoods Holiday Village in St. Peter, and at Harrison's Cave in St. Thomas.

The IDC also has training workshops, where beginners and veterans alike can practice their crafts. Products coming out of these workshops include elaborate dress accessories: hats, shoes, handbags; table accessories: place mats, coasters, utensils of coconut and clay, straw and bamboo grass; handy items: baskets, lampshades, beauty-boxes for your dressing tables, and rugs.

Hill of Clay: If you're particularly interested in pottery, you will find Barbados filled with collectable treasures. The tradition of making household vessels from clay started long ago in the parish of St. Andrew, at Chalky Mount, a mighty hill of stratified clays sandwiched between thin strata of shale. Here, the sedimentary core of Barbados is laid bare; red, yellow, brown and white clays can be seen in the massive cross-section of Chalky Mount visible from the East Coast road.

Throughout the centuries, the ground of Chalky Mount supplied the material for numerous household items: the clay pot was the stove for many a home; clay lamps and candlesticks were a necessity; cups,

tacked onto the sides of the houses where the potters live) you'll find shelves displaying the finished work. You'll find the traditional ovens nearby in the yard; strong structures made of thick brown fire-bricks, encasing hundreds of degrees of heat when running full blast.

Creative Spirit: The potter's craft is handed down in the family here from one generation to the next. Courtney Devonish is a son of Chalky Mount, a purveyor of a long tradition, though he operates from a modern workshop at Pelican Village. Some of the best examples of traditional pottery can be found at his place; but he has been trained formally in Italy, and you will also find pieces that come from the classic European styles in his gallery.

plates, bowls and that strangely beautiful utensil called a 'monkey'—used for cooling and dispensing drinks—served everyday functions.

Only fairly recently has the electrically operated potter's wheel appeared on Chalky Mount. You can still find many of the older, traditional hand- or foot-operated wheels in use here. Often the master potter has a boy to do the turning, setting the ponderous flywheel in motion. In these workshops (often no more than sheds

Left, a Bajan artist paints a village scene in vibrant colors with a palette knife. Right, Ras Akyem Ramsey with his prize-winning "House of King David."

The creative spirit is restless in Barbados. People turn from one art form to another. Golde Spieler is like that. She's a marvelous manipulator of material. She has some first-class ink and watercolor studies of local plants, with authentic landscapes in the background. She also paints in oil and acrylic. And her pottery workshop at Shop Hill in St. Thomas is eminently worthy of a visit.

Open-Air Markets: For an island so small, Barbados boasts a surprisingly large number of artists. You'll find the knowns and the unknowns coming out in droves at the festival markets. There is Bridgetown Market, in early August, at the end of the annual Crop Over Festival, a very old and

recently revived activity. Crop Over is a real explosion of calypso, costumed bands, street fairs and dancing. At its culmination, special stalls are set up to show off the wide range of Barbadian arts and crafts.

The costumes of the revelers who participate in the Crop Over Festival are a delight in themselves, and are evidence of the great creative design talents of the islanders. It's a pity that the art of the carnival costume is so ephemeral; beautiful creations are left abandoned in backyards a day or two after having dazzled spectators on the roads.

The Oistins Fish Festival, another island favorite, is growing yearly. It concentrates on things of the sea; and here, on Easter weekend, the fishermen have their day. For the little town of Oistins in Christ Church, fishing has always been a major occupation. The fishing boats can be seen lining the beach like washed-up shells, equally colorful and sparkling. Boatbuilding is one of the oldest activities of the islanders, and the painting of these boats is an art in itself. But the craft of the fisherfolk doesn't stop here; they also make fishing nets and fish-pots. These pots are clever, box–like structures with a tunneled, twisted entrance through which fish can swim, but once inside, they can't find their way back out. The traps are made of wire and bamboo, plaited and tied. They are among the best examples of Barbadian craft.

The Holetown festival, in mid–February, focuses more on the historic traditions of Barbados. It was at Holetown that the first English settlers landed and established their little wooden pioneer huts in 1627. The festival that takes place here is filled with costumes and pageantry, and art and craft displays abound.

Batik and Silk-Screen: You'll also find plenty of art and handicraft pieces in the little shops attached to the hotels on the St. James coast and along the Christ Church roads. They have a wide range of printed fabrics: batik and silk-screen dresses, wall-hangings and scarves. At Walker's World, a shop with branches where hotels are concentrated, there are the famous Jill Walker prints. Her countless scenes and landscapes of Barbados adorn the walls of Bridgetown offices, hotels, guesthouses and public places. They are seen in the most unexpected places. Her representations of island life are a little satirical, but no matter, Jill is one

of the hardest-working and most popular artists around.

The Barbados Museum houses some extremely interesting items of old Barbados, and has a fine art gallery. There are some interesting old prints there, including maps, landscapes and colorful portrayals of the activities of an earlier era.

The most famous old painting in Barbados is the painting of Christ by Benjamin West which hangs in the St. George Parish Church. This painting was once placed in a storehouse on one of the plantations, and neglected for a long time. A thief, entering the storehouse, was frightened by the piercing eyes of the portrait, and began to dig them out. Though the portrait was later sent to Britain for repairs, one eye remains

missing.

Another hangout for local art enthusiasts is the Talma Mill Art Gallery, housed in an old windmill. It is run by Norma Talma, another of the trained artists and teachers and a fine painter who has recently devoted herself to collages made of homemade paper.

The National Cultural Foundation organizes regular art exhibits at the Queens Park Gallery, and around Independence Day (November 30) there is the National Independence Festival of Creative Arts (NIFCA), which features shows and presentations of a great number of local art forms. The NIFCA visual arts and craft exhibition usually presents the works of schoolchildren.

Left, traditional crafts like blacksmithing are alive and well in Barbados. Right, Henry Harding, an old-school potter, holding one of his "monkey jugs."

Ornate Murals: The Cultural Foundation is also in the process of assisting local communities and schoolchildren in creating murals in community centers and schools. These depict the cultural, historical and social aspects of their neighborhoods, as well as the popular personalities of those who reside there. There is a large, ornate and complex mural at Eagle Hall, St. Michael, on the wall of the Post Office; others are at Springer Memorial School in Government Hill; at Ellerton Primary School, St. George; at the Bathsheba Community Center, on the East Coast in St. Joseph; one at Boscobelle, and still others are in progress.

The first murals in Barbados were simple, naive paintings done on the outside

walls of shops and nightclubs on Baxter's Road and Nelson Street in Bridgetown. They advertised the activities to be found inside. The carts and stalls of vendors carry smaller versions of this kind of art. The more recent spate of mural-painting began with the staging of the Caribbean Festival of Creative Arts here in Barbados in 1981. CARIFESTA is the biggest arts festival of the region, hosted on a rotating basis by the various islands. At the St. James Secondary School and the Barbados Community College, there are several murals created during the last CARIFESTA. Several artists worked on each, so that in one mural you will find a variety of styles and techniques.

Preserving Culture: Many of the island's

artists are driven by the urge to portray, in realistic painting, aspects of their culture which are fast disappearing. They make a conscious effort to record the donkey cart, the windmills and the great houses of the old sugar plantations; the ways of life of the farm worker, the fisherfolk, the peasant; the places where such people lived and the materials they used.

The little chattel houses of the villages are a favorite source of inspiration to these culture-preservers. Fielding Babb must have painted hundreds of them, mainly in oils, with the palette knife. You'll also find paintings of chattel houses by Adrian Compton (he does fine graphics, too), Omowale and Sundiata Stewart (twin brothers), Winifred and Harriet Cumberbatch (twin sisters), Oscar Walkes (a self-taught painter with a sharp, bright, detailed style), Briggs Clarke and Kathleen Hawkins. Their scenes of plantation life in old Barbados are collected by connoisseurs, Virgil Broodhagen, son of Karl and a brilliant representor of Barbadian architecture, among others.

Artists also seek out old buildings about to be demolished and capture their image before the wrecker (natural or man-made) arrives. You'll find paintings of the public buildings, the Careenage with its tangle of masts and ropes silhouetted against the sunset, and you'll find sunsets and coconut trees aplenty.

Some artists have painted the history of events and eras as well: of slavery, of struggle, of sailing ships; of insurrection and rebellion; of hurricanes, rain and flood.

Startling Hues: Art in Barbados runs the whole gamut of themes. Some artists, like Ena Power, live in a world of flower-painting. Some, like David and Indra Gall, have moved into the realm of the symbolic, using local images to project their message.

You may notice that the color of the older oil-based, European-style paintings is subdued, even dull. By contrast, the color in Caribbean paintings is sometimes startling. But no more startling than the colors of the landscape. There are seas so turquoise, skies so ultramarine, flowers and foliage so crimson and yellow, butterflies so multicolored, that often a stranger from the North, seeing West Indian paintings and not knowing the islands, disbelieves and thinks that the artist is exaggerating.

Left, sculptor Karl Broodhagen at work in his studio. Right, every summer brings an explosion of creativity for the annual Crop Over celebration.

"BAJANS, COME BACK TO CALYPSO!"

Box-cart and stick for wicket
Dat is my culture
Mauby and marble cricket
Dat is my culture
Slamming domino in competition
With the calypso and sweet steel band
So now you see what I really mean
Dis is my true culture in the
Caribbean . . .
　　—"Culture," Mighty Gabby (1985)

No doubt about it: calypso in Barbados is here to stay. For centuries, church and state tried to banish this African-derived music. But the musical culture of Afro-Barbadians survived—and indeed thrived—underground. Today this tuneful, topical music is, as Mighty Gabby, the island's foremost calypsonian, proclaims, an integral part of Barbados' "true culture."

On one level, the lively calypsoes are pure entertainment—the ultimate party music. But they also function as a kind of auditory newspaper, spreading information about current issues. No topic is too trivial or too touchy to be the subject of a calypso song—themes range from corrupt politicians to potholes in the road, a controversial beauty contest to a nosy neighbor. A visitor who wants to learn about the true social and political situation in Barbados need only listen to the current crop of calypso tunes. And today's visitor will be spared a subterranean search, because you can hear the music everywhere: on the radio, at nightclubs, in the hotels.

Social Commentary: Calypso's ancestors were slave songs brought by West Africans to the West Indies in the early 1600s. Historians suggest that the slaves brought two distinct types of songs: work songs and ribald songs of commentary.

The work songs, sung by laboring slaves to lift their spirits and pass the time, were usually laments on the sorrows and hardships they suffered. The lighter, satirical songs are more like the social commentaries of contemporary calypso. Surprisingly, the slaves rarely attacked their masters in these tunes. The songs were basically channels for the spread of local gossip about plantation people.

Left, the Sunshine Orchestra Band at a south coast hotel. Right, emotion-filled music at the Mount Hillaby Pentecostal Church in St. Thomas.

"Forever England": By the 1640s there were 20,000 Africans and 23,000 British colonists in Barbados; social and cultural life was patterned on that of England in their quest to create "some corner that is forever England." The cultural heritage of African slaves was not welcome in such a society. The British viewed the Africans' music, dance, dress, food, languages and religious rituals as pagan and barbarous.

In 1649, the indentured servants and Africans rebelled against the white landowners. Legend has it the bondservants

roused each other to battle by lively music on horns, drums and conch shells. Another uprising in 1675 led to the enforcement of a slave code that banned the beating of drums. The law provided that:

　　. . . due care be taken to restrain the
　　wanderings and meetings of Negroes and
　　other slaves at all times . . .

In 1688, the plantation society passed another law stipulating that any drums or loud instruments had to be burned if discovered. But the planters could not wipe out the musical heritage out of the slaves; music was a vital part of the Africans' daily life. They sang while they worked. They celebrated with songs on holidays and at funerals (they believed the dead would be transported back to Africa, away from the brutal slave society).

In response to the masters' strict policies, the slaves hid away their African customs. And these were carefully preserved and handed down to younger generations through secret ceremonies and rituals.

Slave music had much in common with present-day calypsoes. The melodies included spontaneous vocal effects such as cries and yells, verses alternated with choruses, and the songs were based on clearly discernible short phrases.

Even after the slaves were freed in 1838, the planter class deemed any vibrant expression of African cultural heritage dangerous and a "relapse into barbarism." Indigenous music therefore stayed under-

rhythms are superimposed on a persistent and recognizable African base. What results is a seductive, semi-martial rhythm that excites even the most staid villagers to dance or "work up," as Bajans would say.

Tuk bands travel from village to village playing popular tunes and inviting villagers to contribute their own compositions—as long as they fit with the lively tempo. People dress up as donkeys or bears and dance suggestively. Men put on dresses and stuff them with rags to suggest pregnancy. The melodies of tuk songs are simple and the subjects are trivial. But these tunes have kept the laboring classes in high spirits on many a Sunday afternoon and have become synonymous with holiday revelry in Barbados today.

ground and survived as folk music. This "little tradition" of communal singing, religion, dance and customs became embedded in the life-style of little villages and tenantries away from unfriendly eyes and ears of the leaders.

Seductive Beat: At the time, the primary form of resistance to cultural pressures was the music of the tuk band. The name comes from the onomatopoeic sound "Boom-a-tuk, boom-a-tuk" that the big log drum gives out. For the last 120 years, tuk music has been played at picnics and excursions and on public holidays.

The music is lively, with an intricate, pulsating, quick beat strongly suggestive of British military bands. The regimental

Calypso Country: In the early 20th Century, the calypso that had developed in Trinidad began to influence such folk music and catalyze a revival of the Barbadian calypso tradition.

The songs from Trinidad influenced not only the melodies of the Barbadian songs, but more importantly—the lyrics. Themes widened beyond gossip and scandal to include more satire and social commentary. But it took many years for calypso to become an influential and forceful medium of satire and a legitimate vehicle of musical expression in Barbados.

Although a few performers like Da Costa Allamby, Frank Taylor and Mighty Charmer were hard-working calypsonians

236

in the late 1930s, not many Barbadians were drawn into the music. Most citizens were preoccupied with British standards of respectability. People were concerned with getting ahead, which to them implied losing touch with all vestiges of plantation life. The more closely an individual approached the British in his manner and speech, the more cultured he was considered. Ironically, the phrase "he ain' got no culture" referred to those whose behavior revealed the vitality of their African ancestry.

Up To No Good: Singing calypsoes was certainly not a way of achieving positive social status and prestige in Bajan society. Early calypsonians were seen more as jokers and comics than as serious singers. They functioned like the strolling minstrels

mercial value.) The only performer to make much of an impact was Mighty Charmer, the first recognized Barbadian calypsonian, who became professional in 1947 with "My Dear Mammy." And even then, Barbadian calypso was held to be far inferior to the "real thing" from Trinidad. This lack of acceptance of indigenous calypsonians as being worthy artists was a serious obstacle to the development of the art form.

Because their chances for gaining exposure and money were greater in Trinidad, those who could afford it—like the Mighty Charmer and the Mighty Sugar—went to Trinidad. Charmer left Barbados in 1950 and stormed Trinidad with his composition "Flying Saucer." The exposure he gained there was important for the develop-

of earlier decades, wandering from rum shop to rum shop and from street corner to street corner. Mothers would pull their children inside and shut the door when they saw these minstrels. They forbade their daughters to talk to the singers. In the mothers' eyes, the calypsonians were up to no good and had "only come wid a guitar to fool their daughters."

Yet calypso pioneers persisted, lured perhaps by the chance of making some money. (By this time, the art form in Trinidad had acquired a measure of com-

ment of calypso in Barbados. He arrived in Trinidad when calypso was functioning as a powerful political weapon. He was also there at the time of the rise of the Mighty Sparrow, the master of satirical calypso.

For this reason, when Charmer first recorded in Trinidad in 1961, his lyrics had become more critical, though he retained his sense of humor. His hit, "The Laughing Stock," satirizes the clearly divided social classes in the West Indies:

You could tell some people's class
By de way dat dem does laugh
Every time you go to a social or party
De Big Shots laugh—Ho! Ho! Ho!
De middle class laugh—He! He! He!
But when de woman began to laugh

Left, a band parades through the street at a "village meet" in Market Hill, St. George. Right, a tuk band makes the rounds on Boxing Day.

*You could tell she was from de ordinary
class
She bawl out, Wullos! muh belly! Oh lawd
Ah going dead! Wuhlaw!*

Charmer was an exception. Popularity—
not to mention stardom—was elusive for
most Barbadian calypsonians for almost two
more decades. Ironically, it was a group of
white, middle-class men called the Merrymen who kept the Barbadian calypso tradition alive in the 1960s and early 1970s.

Hit After Hit: Led by Emile Straker, the
Merrymen's repertoire consisted of old
calypsoes played in a sing-along style that
crossed the boundaries of folk, country-
and-western, pop and calypso. They perfected a beat for their music called the
Caribbeat. This has and remained their

experimented with a Trinidad-style Carnival, a bacchanalian festival occurring immediately before Christian Lent. At first,
this Carnival contained none of the island's
enduring folk forms such as tuk band
music, folk singing, calypsoes or folk
dances. In the third year of Carnival, when
black calypsonians finally played a role in
the festival, they were treated as comics and
burlesque performers.

By 1963, however, the government-
owned station Radio Barbados came on the
air, and together with Rediffusion (the
former Radio Distribution) provided more
of a channel for budding calypsonians.
Also, more calypso shows were being organized at theaters and community centers
on the island. And visits from established

signature for nearly 30 years in the business, during which they produced hit after
hit.

The Merrymen's first big Caribbean tune
was "Archie Brek Dem Up," a catchy song
about carnival revelry. Before this they had
a string of hits with old calypsoes like
"Brudda Neddy," "Millie Gone to Brazil"
and "Sly Mongoose.' By the late '60s they
were the only Barbadian group with a
Caribbean-wide reputation.

Meanwhile, black calypsonians in Barbados found the going rough and either
stopped singing altogether or switched to
ballads and American pop. Perhaps they
were frustrated by the treatment they
received from 1958 to 1964 when Barbados

Trinidadian singers got the public more
interested in stage-presented calypso.

By Independence in 1966 a new crop of
performers had entered the Barbadian
calypso scene, including Mighty Gabby—
who became the high priest of calypso
in the 1980s—Mighty Dragon, Lord Deighton, Lord Summers and Mighty Viper.
These men helped calypso reclaim its
rightful position as the real music of the
people. And in 1968 and 1969 there were
major calypso competitions that attracted
wide public attention. But then a new
sound came on the scene and drove calypso
underground once again.

Sound Called Spouge: The new sound was
spouge. It was originated by the same

Jackie Opel who had started out in the early 1960s as a calypso singer. Opel had migrated to Jamaica, where he was successful as a ska and rock-steady singer. But when Jamaica started turning to the reggae sound in 1968, Opel returned to Barbados to introduce his calypso-reggae hybrid.

Opel and spouge dominated the Barbados music scene from 1969 to 1973, although Opel himself died in a car crash in late 1970. The Draytons Two and Sandpebbles, Troubadours, Blue Rhythms Combo and the Outfit all cut original spouge records, which filled the airwaves until 1974.

However, Barbadian calypso came to life again when the Crop Over Festival was revived in 1974. At first the response from calypsonians was slow, but by the 1980s

nian is always a member of the opposition; he is always keeping politicians on their toes, reminding the powerbrokers that they hold a sacred trust from the people and that it is their duty to be sensitive to the needs of the little people.

Satirical Assaults: In recent times more than 50 percent of Barbadian calypsoes have dealt with politics. Gabby is the foremost exponent of this type of satirical assault on politicians. His tent, Battleground, founded in 1979, is an organization critical of government. Gabby's calypsoes are hard-hitting and direct.

Grynner, Gabby's colleague, often takes the same tack, as in his vicious "Mister T," in which he describes the way he'd like to punish a deceptive politician:

the calypso contest had become the single most important event of Crop Over. And the artists have responded by presenting thought-provoking and rib-tickling songs about politics, politicians, youth, education, tourism, public transport, crime, religion, social prejudice, apartheid and male-female relationships.

Calypso in Barbados has become the voice of the people. A current saying holds that no matter what political party holds power at a given point in time, the calypso-

Left, the Merrymen, a well-known white Bajan calypso and folk group. Right, the Barbados Police Band plays in Queen's Park for special occasions.

Your tricks and lies and pleasant smiles
Can't win my "X" again
You come with big tricks, corned beef and
biscuits to instill hurt and pain . . .
I gine rip yuh pants. I gine mek yuh dance
You gine feel dat I is a nest of ants
I gine milk yuh goat, I gine sink yuh boat
And next I gine beat yuh wid my "X".

Other calypsonians are more subtle in their attacks, though no less serious or critical. Sir Don's "Tom Say," Romeo's "De Microphone Hey," Black Pawn's "Sucking the Country Dry," Stranger's "De Government Loco," and Viper's "Message to the Prime Minister" all criticized government's policies and defended the poor. But all managed to couch their satire in more or less tolerable lyrics, although Romeo and Viper's tunes were banned from the airwaves.

The best exponent of this type of subtle satire is probably Gabby's arch rival, the young and promising Red Plastic Bag, who rocketed to fame in 1982 with "Mr. Harding Can't Burn," a tune which won him the first of his two titles of Calypso monarch. The Bag, as he is known, uses all the possibilities of language: irony, pun, sarcasm, allusion and double entendre. In the hilarious but biting "Holes," he complains about the wretched condition of the island's roadways:

A friend of mine from the U.S.A.
Here on a holiday
Wanted me to show him around

Neighbor, neighbor, neighbor, neighbor
Mind yuh business, not me own.

Creative Vision: Each of the performers plays different roles and has distinct specialities. Grynner, for example, is the "King of the Road," and a comedic entertainer without peer. Viper and Romeo are both young men who have emerged on the scene since Independence. Viper is good with songs of revelry. And Romeo, the "Love Man of Calypso," is a charming and polished performer.

Barbadian calypso is alive and well and in the capable hands of many talented performers. Gone are the days when a calypso singer was ostracized for his lack of respectability. And gone are the days when less indigenous music kept the develop-

I took him all over the town
But goin through the countryside
My face I wanted to hide
The condition of the roads was a sight to see
So many times he had to say to me
Look a hole! A big big hole!
Watch that hole! Shun that hole!

There are plenty of other calypsonians who use the music more as social commentary or just plain entertainment. One of the best examples of this is "Sousie" by Director, in which nosy neighbors are criticized:

Neighbor, neighbor, neighbor, neighbor
Leh me 'lone!
Leh me 'lone!

ment of calypso underground.

Today's Barbadian calypsonians offer a wide range of perspectives on social issues, and this is what keeps the public interested and entertained year after year. The performers use their creative vision to identify, analyze and criticize problems and to suggest solutions. Today, calypso is an indispensable component of contemporary Barbadian society, providing the people with a clear mirror image of the land they live in.

Left, calypsonian Red Plastic Bag sings on "Old Year's Night" at the Crane Beach Hotel. Right, Rasta calypso singer Adonijah, also a scholar and journalist.

THE MIGHTY GABBY: KING OF CALYPSO

Listening to the island's calypsonians is a good way to get a feel for the issues that concern Barbadians today. The Mighty Gabby's award-winning music typifies Bajan calypso: his lively songs are more than entertainment—they are a form of protest and a means for seeking positive change within the culture.

The Mighty Gabby's influence has steadily grown within the world of calypso—he won the Crop Over Festival competition in 1968, 1976, 1977 and 1985. His songs often speak of the challenges Barbadians encounter in their daily lives. A 1976 tune that hit close to home for many Bajan women was "Needles and Pins," a comment on a common feature of working-class life:

Johnny got two women
he wife and he girl frien'
Johnny got two women
You know dat is problem
But what really, really cause de strife
He love de girl friend' better dan de wife
An every time de two o' dem meet
It is bacchanal in de street!

The more political song "Jack," named for a public official who attempted to limit the use of beaches by vendors and beachcombers, asserts the joint ownership which Barbadians feel for their country's landscape:

Jack doan want me to bade on my beach
Jack tell dem to kick me outa reach
Jack tell dem I will never make de grade
Strengthen security, build barricade
Dah can't happen here in this country
I want Jack to know
Dat de beach belong to me.

His criticism of those who minimize Barbadian culture is evident in his 1985 song "Miss Barbados," written in response to a Canadian woman being chosen to represent Barbados in an international beauty contest:

Miss Barbados never hear 'bout flying-fish
Miss Barbados never hear 'bout cou cou dish
Miss Barbados 'ent know 'bout bread-

fruit and that's no lie
Miss Barbados is as Bajan as apple pie!

Gabby's songs can also be saucy and spicy, as in the delightfully tongue-in-cheek "Hit It" (1983), in which he relates the events of a cricket game between himself and a young woman. On the surface, the song is about cricket—but it is filled with sexual innuendos:

Hit it-why yuh missing so?
Hit it-you used to brag before
Hit it-if you could handle me
Hit it and let me see
Hit it, Hit it, Hit it!

Gabby, whose real name is Tony Carter, began singing at the age of six. As a teenager he competed in his first calypso contest, placing third behind Sir Don (Marshall) and The Mighty Romeo. In 1971 he moved from Barbados to New York, where he worked to refine his writing and performing skills, returning to the island in 1975. Gabby has become to Barbadian calypso what Bob Marley was to Jamaican reggae and what Sparrow means to Trinidad's calypso. He is the spokesman of a musical form as well as of a culture. His recognition as Folksinger of the Year in 1977, 1978 and 1979 further illustrates the place Gabby has carved out for himself as a Bajan musician.

His music speaks for the thousands of Barbadians who see their culture awash in foreign influences. In "Culture" (1985), he sings:

All o'dem shows pon TV you must agree
are not for we
Show me some Castle in My Skin by George Lamming
Instead of that trash like Sanford and M.A.S.H.
Then we could stare in the face
And show dem we cultural base.

This is music that provides the visitor with a glimpse of a world often known only to Bajans. Gabby's songs, however critical, are infused with a love for his homeland; hearing them inspires a true appreciation of Bajan culture.

DANCE AND DRAMA: STREET BEATS, STAGE TREATS

If all the world's a stage, everyday life in Barbados is high theater, from the musical pulses and pitches of community gossip to the rhythmic swaying of hips as the beat of calypso fills the street.

The performing arts of Barbados are much more than flaming limbo and a poolside calypso band playing "Yellow Bird." Though the many local dance performances, plays, concerts and annual festivals are not always marked as stops for visitors, the adventurous traveler who seeks out these delightful extravaganzas will be treated to an inside look at Bajan culture.

A walk down a busy street is a drama in itself. Listen to the rhythm of the language. The sounds of words, it becomes apparent, are as important as the words themselves; double meanings, expressive folk sayings, stories told with much gesturing and emotion are entertainments without an admission charge. The repartee and haggling at an open-air market makes co-stars of vendor and customer.

Dancing? Music is everywhere: at parties, at church, on the mini-buses, at home. Portable radios take music to the streets and to work. It is said that Bajans dance before they can walk: watch any toddler, barely able to walk, to hoist himself up, grasp his mother's knee, and stand and sway to calypso.

Out of this verve comes performing arts infused with spontaneity and energy. Little wonder that a strong ballet tradition doesn't exist on Barbados, and that most island dance companies are interpretive, modern, ethnic.

Love of Dance: From earliest times, there were two dance traditions on Barbados: the more formalized, European dances of the planters, and the energetic, spontaneous dances of the slaves, rooted in West African tradition. Both groups loved to dance, and though the plantation owners originally tried to prohibit slaves from gathering to play music and dance out of fear that they would organize rebellion, they quickly came to realize that the slaves worked more productively if they were allowed to enjoy their own form of dance and music one or two nights a week.

The dancers "hollered and bellowed in an Antique manner, as if they were all madd," wrote an early observer. Some dancers would tie rattles to their legs and wrists; others looked on, clapping their hands and chanting "Alla, Alla!" A description from 1750 commented on the use of the entire body, which is typical of West African dance, observing that "their bodies are strongly agitated by skipping, leaping and turning around."

Many of these early reports by white

witnesses of the African-inspired dances and rituals revealed both fascination and astonishment: after all, white visitors and plantation owners had never seen anything quite like this. They were ballroom dancers, at best.

"Supreme Excellence": An account from 1880 said that "the twistings of the body seem to constitute the supreme excellence of the dance," and went on to describe the dancers' "indecent, wanton, and lascivious" movements in great detail. Today, the West African tradition of pelvic gyrations is still seen in West Indian dance—Bajans call it "working up," and you're most likely to see it on holidays as tuk bands joyously parade through the streets.

Left, drummers provide African rhythms for performance given by children's dance group (right), headed by dancer actor Robert Ifill (smiling drummer).

Today, the rift between "formal" dancing and folk dancing is still evident in Barbados. Ballet, for example, for many years suffered under negative connotations and a class bias. It had been taught exclusively to wealthy white children, and became a symbol of class separation. Now, however, many aspiring jazz and modern dancers study classical ballet technique weekly at the Penny Ramsey or Sheila Hatch Schools of Ballet.

Modern dance on Barbados—abstract and expressionistic—began as a rejection of formalism and sterility. It was introduced to the island in 1968 by Mary Stevens, founder of the Barbados Dance Theatre Company. One of the island's leading dance groups, the company conducts training classes, promotes community spirit through dance, and develops greater interest among young people in cultural affairs—a worthy mandate.

Some of BDTC's performances remain indelibly etched in the memories of its audiences. "How Greed Traps Anansi on an Island" tells the story of Anansi (also known as "Anancy"), a clever and daring spider–hero of many popular West Indies folktales.

Another Bajan folk "celebrity" is the Hag, an old woman who turns into a vampire. Choreographer Rosemary Wilkinson used the story to symbolize, "the schizophrenic complexities of women." Combining native folktales and modern dance technique in this manner makes the dance especially West Indian.

Current Issues: Some performing artists feel that the themes of island dance are too diffused. Says Anthony Payne, one of the directors of the Rontana Dance Movement, a company formed when the Rontana Dance Company merged with the Awade Drummers in 1975, "Dance is a communicative art, and it ought to mirror its community. There must be current issues worth dancing about, but dance in Barbados has no focus."

One of Rontana Dance Movement's most exciting pieces is entitled "Follow the Drum." Choreographed by Beverley Griffith, its dancers interpret the sound of four sets of percussion instruments: the continuous flow of tambourines, the more guttural bass drums, the faster, lighter bongos, and the loud, staccato timbales. The piece is gloriously African-inspired.

One of the pioneers in interpretive dance was Yoruba Yard, a small theater in the Bridgetown suburbs that, during the late 1960s, housed a broadly based cultural

organization founded by Elton "Elombe" Mottley, now the director of The National Cultural Foundation. Yoruba Yard explored Barbadian folk material and researched the island's Caribbean and African past. It contracted Shola Olaoye from Nigeria to provide technical assistance in dance, and staged the still memorable "Landship" dance, which translated the movements of sailors on a ship into dance steps that seem to float to tuk band rhythms. Though financial problems forced their theater to close, the Yoruba Dancers still flourish as a semi-professional group.

Dance Experience, a young group of talented dancers, was formed in 1981 by internationally acclaimed Barbadian dancer Richild Springer, now a professional

dancer in Europe. Despite its youth and many obstacles, the company has grown from strength to strength, entertaining Barbadians and conducting workshops in folk, modern and jazz technique. Many of their folk performances are accompanied by the Wesahh Singers. The dance "Croptime," which portrays the last days of the sugar crop season and the rejoicing of its workers, is accompanied by the refrain:

To we economy it's essential
We all know as every Bajan should...

Grassroots Effort: Country Theatre Workshop, founded by Patrick Cobham, was introduced to promote and develop the performing arts in the rural parishes where "the audience prefers folk dances." They now perform at a weekly dinner show at the Plantation Garden restaurant as well.

Both Cobham and Tyrone Trotman, the director of Tyrona Contemporary Theatre (a group of dancers and musicians who perform on the hotel circuit), believe the performing arts should reflect an awareness of society. "Study your people—the way they walk, act, gesticulate—see people the way they are, go into villages, talk to the old folk," Trotman tells his dancers.

Danny Hinds, a young dancer trained in the Yoruba Dance Company, also believes in this approach to dance and drama. As President of the company called Youth Creative Expressions, he staged. in 1982, a multimedia production entitled "Black Heritage," a portrayal of the West Indian

bring African and jazz dance to 50 energetic children in an afterschool workshop called Creative Arts for Youth, which stages occasional public performances. The same year Danny Hinds also formed a new group—Bim International—which entertains visitors with polished folk dance performances at a west coast hotel.

The First Plays: Theater in Barbados began in the late 1600s, with plantation improvisations called "tea meetings" in which individuals recited passages, presented slapstick skits and gave spontaneous speeches. Just as spontaneous were the alfresco performances given by sailing troupes of actors who pulled into port and presented plays in the shadow of their ships.

black man through the generations. The music was drawn from the haunting melodies and rhythms of Jamaican reggae superstar Bob Marley, from the lively beat of calypso, and from the soundtrack of the movie "Roots."

Devoted to the development of Afro-Caribbean dance, two groups emerged from Youth Creative Expressions: New Generation and Seitu (the Nigerian word for "artist"). In 1981, Robert Ifill, the former president of New Generation, began to

Left, a song in the musical "Barbados, Barbados" at Balls Plantation. It is the story of the infamous Rachel Pringle. Right, "Laff It Off" at Queen's Park.

The first mention of theater in Barbados occurred in, of all things, the diary of George Washington. He noted that, on Dec. 15, 1751, on a trip to the island, he attended a presentation of "The Tragedy of George Barnwell."

By 1783, a theater called the Patagonian, complete with boxes, was presenting English plays, including performances of Shakespeare. An advertised billing of a performance of "Richard III" notes that the Duchess of York was played by "Miss McIntosh (being her first appearance)" and also included "on the programme, Lady Pentwenzle from Blow-Bladder-Street." The Patagonian Theatre soon received swift competition from another theater, referred to in newspaper accounts as the "New Theatre." Comedies and pantomimes drew crowds, exclusively from the plantation-class whites. A newspaper review of one performance noted that no "profligate or abandoned women were admitted."

Until the early 20th Century, in fact, the small theater groups in Barbados were exclusively white. Then, after World War II, the Green Room Players emerged, and began to stage productions of local and international plays. From light farce to serious drama, the Green Room Players' extensive and efficiently produced offerings have pleased several generations of Barbadians and visitors. Among their popular comedies, playing to packed audiences, are "Let's Go Bajan," "Move Over Mrs. Markham," "Absurd Person Singular," and "See How They Run." Their 1978 production of "Colly!" was a celebration of the work of the late Frank Collymore, a distinguished Barbadian writer of mime, dance, song and poetry.

In the 1960s, the now-defunct Barbados Writer's Workshop produced several West Indian plays under the directorship of Earl Warner. Today, the non-profit Stage One Theatre Productions, established in 1979, carries on the tradition of producing works relevant to the Caribbean experience. The Company's goal is to encourage greater interest and participation in the theater; it sponsors training workshops and public auditions.

Raw Energy: One of Stage One's most successful productions has been Errol John's "Moon on a Rainbow Shawl," set in a Caribbean backyard in the late 1940s and suffused with raw energy. The play, first-prize winner in a 1957 play competition sponsored by a London newspaper, is both warm and powerful. Its lingering question: How far have the Caribbean territories evolved from colonialism towards an independent future?

The beginnings of an answer to the questions lie with Esther, a child gifted at needlework and embroidery. The patterns she creates, however, are not those that her society encourages. Still, she finds her own patterns "prettier, though much harder to

do." The embroidered shawl created by Esther becomes a symbol of the diversity and identity of the Caribbean territories. As the stage lights dim and then extinguish, the vision of this multicolored shawl of hope remains with the viewers.

Folk and popular theater are the winning efforts of a newer island group, Community Theatre Productions, which grew out of a demand for entertaining theater that makes use of Barbadian material. The company's first event, an improvised folk comedy called "Laff it Off," played to packed audiences at the Queen's Park Theatre. "Laff it Off" delighted Bajans and visitors alike with its amusing exploration of the wit and talent found within the everyday goings-on at a village rum shop. The rum shop, called "Nook and Cranny Bar," is transformed from bar to court to church to parliament to cultural center.

Community Theatre Productions also sponsors a series of training workshops to help community groups hone their dramatic skills.

Weekend entertainment abounds in Barbados. In the villages, you'll find Friday and Saturday are often filled with the sounds of music and laughter as residents are entertained by a "village meet," a beauty contest, a "dub" contest, a tuk band, or a local dance, called a "fete," "bram" or "jump-up."

Dinner Extravaganzas: Most likely to snare the visitor, however, are the many dinner

shows, entertaining demonstrations of Bajan history and mores. Produced by entrepreneur Andrew Nehaul, the show "1627 And All That...," for instance, portrays the folk culture of Barbados in music and dance in the historic courtyard of the Barbados Museum.

"Barbados Barbados," another Nehaul wing-dinger, is performed on Tuesday nights at Balls Estate. During hors d'oeuvres, drinks (especially notable is the delicious and potent "Pringle punch,") and

Left, the dance company BIM International, headed by Danny Hinds (in front), performs at the Divi St. James on the west coast. Right, "1627 and All That."

a sumptuous buffet, the audience participates in the true story of Rachel Pringle Polgreen, born a slave but saved from her unhappy life by Captain Pringle of the Royal Navy. (See feature article on page 115.) The climax of the play is the infamous night of boisterous reveling in Rachel's hotel during Prince William Henry's visit.

Living Theater: Festivals are living theater, and Barbados offers many special celebrations and events.

The Oistins, Holetown, St. Thomas and St. Andrew festivals are annual affairs which showcase the island's talented performing, visual and culinary artists.

The National Independence Festival of the Creative Arts, in late November, is a forum for professional and amateur performing artists. More recently, the Esso Arts Festival was added to give dancers, dramatists and musicians more of a chance to display their talents. During February and March the island's three best plays—chosen from those submitted in a competition for both aspiring and established playwrights—are performed. During these two months, dance groups also offer a variety of performances ranging from classical to modern to jazz to folk.

The Crop Over Festival in July is the island's largest fête, a month-long celebration inspired by what was once the island's main economic event, the harvesting of the sugarcane crop. Crop Over opens with the ceremonial delivery of the Last Canes, during which the Champion Cutter and the Piler of the last crop are named and honored. This is followed by a decorated cart parade.

The celebration continues with the Farley Hill Concert, held amidst the 19th-Century ruins in Farley Hill National Park. This event is an artistic explosion of dance, drama and music.

Bridgetown Market, also part of Crop Over, is an open-air emporium of hundreds of decorated crafts and food stalls on the Princess Alice Highway in Bridgetown. Local tuk bands, steel bands, hot Jamaican reggae, the latest calypso hits and American disco rhythms compete for attention.

The Cohobblopot, held at the National Stadium, is another potpourri of drama, music and dance, although more formal and organized than the Bridgetown Market.

Kadooment Day climaxes and closes the Crop Over Festival. Costumed bands portray themes of Bajan life, uninhibited revelers dance in the streets, fireworks explode in the sky . . . and the month's festivities end in a dazzling display of color and light.

BAJAN DIALECT: A GOOD COOK-UP

"When yuh poor, yuh very speech poor." So say the Bajans about the pervasive effects of poverty. But they speak an untruth about their unique language, for Bajan, rising out of the clash between African and European speech, has crystallized into a rich form of expression.

Bajan was born about two centuries ago, the child of a mixed marriage. The mating began on the west coast of Africa, continued on the Atlantic Crossing, and was finally consumated in the West Indies, giving birth to a "hybrid" language.

In its infancy, Bajan combined features from both languages: English words were pronounced with African intonations; African expressions were translated literally into English. But the African elements of Bajan's formative years have slowly eroded; now the English influence is much stronger.

It is said that when a hybrid language remains exposed to the influences of one parent, it grows more like that parent and less like the other. When a hybrid and parent language exist side by side, the hybrid is often seen as inferior, the tongue of the illiterate, a medium for jokes and light matter. The parent is considered the language of the church, the school and the judiciary—the language of the learned, the one more suitable for any and all serious subject matter.

Cinderella Language: Bajan, like other dialects in the Caribbean, is known as a "Cinderella language." For a long time, most Bajans accepted this judgment, and thought that their language, like Cinderella, should be restricted to the kitchen and the backyard. But as in the Cinderella story, fairy helpers appeared—this time as writers, poets and linguists. They began to wipe out the image of Bajan as a "broken" version of English. They showed that like Cinderella, Bajan had its own beauty, seen in the variations of its stress patterns and pitch levels, which combine to shape a language that is neither English nor African, and yet is both.

Local poet Bruce St. John defends the language against those who say that it is limited:

We language limit?
Who language en limit?
Evah language
Like a big pot o' Bajan soup:
Piece o' yam, piece o' potato,
T'ree dumplin', two eddoe,
One beet, two carrot,
Piece o' pig-tail, piece o' beef
Pinch o' salt, dus' o' pepper,
An' don' fuget okra
To add to de flavour.
Boil up, cook up, eat up
An' yuh still wan' rice...

Crash Course: Let's use this poem as a crash course in Bajan. Line 1 translated is, "Is our language limited?" In Bajan, unlike in English, one form of a pronoun may be used as subject, object and possessive: "we know"; "tell we"; "it is we book."

Bajan does not invert the subject and verb when forming this type of question; the sentence looks like a statement, but by raising your voice at the end, a listener will know that you have asked a question.

Verbs, even if used as adjectives, have no participle endings such as -ed, so you hear; "it finish," "it cook."

In line 2, "en" means "is not," and "who" is used instead of "whose."

The numbers "two" and "t'ree" make plurality obvious in lines 6 and 7, so no final "s" is needed. This feature is not as widespread in Barbados as it is in the other islands, so you will still hear "four steps" as well as "four step."

Note that from any powdered substance, you can get "a dust" (line 9), meaning a small portion.

Line 12 gives a brief insight into the subtle differences between Bajan and English: "boil up" means "bring to the boil," but you can also hear "boil down" used when referring to the practice of allowing most of the liquid to boil out of your sauces or soups, giving them a thick consistency. "Cook up" means "cook all of the items together."

The Bajan speaker does not pronounce the ending of most words which end in two consonants. This is shown in line 6—"dumplin'," line 10—"an'" and line 13—"wan'."

There is no "th" sound in Bajan so wherever an English word has this sound, the Bajan speaker has either "f," "v," "t," "d," "z" or "k":

English	Bajan
breathe	breav
with	wit/wid/wif
clothe	cloze/clove
think	t'ink
the	de
strengthen	strengken/strengfen

The verb system of Bajan is somewhat different from that of English. For instance, Bajans use the present tense of a verb even when speaking about past action—"he run home last night," instead of "he ran home last night."

Expression of present time also differs in both languages. Whereas speakers of English would say: "the dancer casts strange shadows as he moves to the pulse of the drum," the Bajan speaker would say: "De

dancer t'rowing strange shadows all de time he moving to de pulse o' de drum." This is because the Bajan speaker usually speaks of present action as ongoing activity, while the English use what is called the "simple present tense."

"I does sing": To express habitual action, the English speaker would say: "I sing on Tuesdays, he dances on weekends and we relax when we get the chance." A Bajan speaker says: "I does sing 'pon Tuesday, he does dance 'pon a weekend and we does relax when we get de chance." Bajans don't worry about subject and verb agreement in sentences like this.

When speaking about the intensity of anything, Bajans seldom use "very." In-

stead of saying, "It's a very pretty morning," a Bajan would say, "De mornin' pretty, pretty, pretty!" A speeding car might inspire a description such as "de car went 'long fast, fast, fast," or "de car went long real f-a-s-t," spoken with great emphasis on the word "fast."

Even though most Bajan words are English words, sometimes their meanings are quite different from what we might expect. For instance, in Bajan, to be "ignorant," is to be mean or very aggressive, not stupid. A woman has "gone cross," or is "pushing bread cart," when she is pregnant. If a Bajan promises to "pass by" your place, he would not be intending to go past, but would be planning to visit.

Outside of the law courts, being "malicious" does not mean that one is harboring malice, it simply means that one is inquisitive or nosy. It is therefore possible to hear a mother telling her two-year old infant: "Come out of my bag, you too malicious." In this context, "come out of" means "do not look into" or "take your hand out of."

During your stay, you may be asked whether you've had a "sea-bath" (swim) yet. If you're both going into town, "all two" are going. When you need a pencil, ask for a "black lead." And if you've gained weight since your last trip, your Bajan friends won't hesitate to tell you that you've "put on some size."

Note the Bajan use of the word "mind": it means "move" in the statement "mind you' foot out o' my way"; it means "take care" in the request "mind this child 'till I come back"; it means "ignore" in the expression "don' mind she" and in the idiomatic expression "mind you' mout," it means "be careful about what you say."

All visitors should therefore be advised to "mind" how they interpret words they seem to share with Bajan speakers. But do take the opportunity to savor the symmetry of the Bajan language, its various contours of thought and its unique turns of phrase. As language is the fabric of thought, be sure to take time to listen and to enjoy the lively patterns, to see the cloth this hybrid language has fashioned. You may come to see how well Bajan suits the life of the island. With an open mind and an attentive ear, any stranger to these shores can leave quoting the final line of Bruce St. John's poem: "de cook-up is a beautiful soun'."

Left, "News don' lack a carrier." Right, it's time to eat a "home-cook" meal at the Swizzle Inn. Next pages: "Go so, up de hill, an' swing *so*," say the Bajans when giving directions.

252

WORDS OF WISDOM: 40 BAJAN PROVERBS

In Bajan homes, words of wisdom flow freely. Proverbs embodying folk values are uttered in almost every conversation, especially in the countryside. The proverbs listed below give one a palpable sense of the rhythms of rural Barbadian life.

Expressed with a sing-song jingle, proverbs capture the cadence and melody of Bajan speech. They provide information about the world view and morals of the Bajan. Yet their common-sense wisdom applies to people everywhere. Shrewd, biting and witty, their purpose is to instruct, admonish and judge people in the matters of everyday life.

• "One bellyful don' fatten a hog."
It requires sustained effort to achieve anything worthwhile.

• "Hansome don' put in pot."
Having physical beauty does not offer any practical benefits.

• "De sea en' got no back door."
The sea is not a safe place. ("en" = ain't)

• "Yuh can' want it in de glass and de bottle too."
You can't have it both ways.

• "Goat head every day better dan cow head every Sunday."
It is better to be given reasonably good treatment all the time than first class treatment occasionally.

• "If greedy wait, hot will cool."
If one waits patiently, one will get what one wants.

• "Every bush is a man."
Be careful how you talk; someone may well be listening.

• "A eyeful en' a bellyful."
Just because you can see it doesn't mean you can have it. (Said by women to men.)

• "Ole stick o' fire don' tek long to ketch back up."
It doesn't take long for two people who have been lovers to become lovers again.

• "Dirty water does cool hot iron."
Once a man is aroused, practically any woman, good or bad, can satisfy his lust.

• "Cut pumpkin can' keep."
Once virginity has been lost, it is almost impossible to abstain thereafter.

• "Head en' mek fuh hat alone."
One should always use common sense.

• "Egg have no right at rockstone dance."
People should not get into situations with which they cannot cope.

• "One-smart dead at two-smart door."
No matter how smart you think you are, there is someone who can outsmart you.

• "De more yuh peep, de less yuh sih."
People will devise ways to fool those who try to spy on them.

• "Every skin teet' en' a laugh."
Outward signs of friendliness aren't always genuine.

• "Good name fuh blasted fool."
It is foolish to make big sacrifices when there is nothing to be gained but the reputation of being a good Samaritan.

• "Mek-sure better than cock-sure."
It is better to make absolutely sure rather than assuming all is well.

• "News don' lack a carrier."
There is always someone to pass on a gossip.

• "Pretty-pretty things does fool li'l children."
Superficial things impress superficial and naive people.

• "Tek time en' laziness."
Much can be achieved by taking one's time.

• "Talk does mek talk."
It is best to stay silent when someone tries to pick a quarrel.

- "Yuh does rust out before yuh wuk out."
Laziness harms the body more than work.
- "Coconut don' grow 'pon pumpkin vine."
Children inherit the traits of their parents.
- "Fisherman never say dat 'e fish stink."
People never give bad reports about themselves.
- "Duppy know who to frighten."
People will take advantage of those known to be weak. (Duppies are spirits of the dead.)
- "Manure can' mek ole plant grow."
It is pointless to try and improve a hopeless

faults are brought into the open.
- "De las' calf kill de cow."
Taking the same risk too often can have disastrous consequences.
- "Evah (every) pig got a Saturday."
Animals are slaughtered on Saturdays: everyone has his day of retribution.
- "Gold teet' don't suit hog mou'."
Elegant trappings look out of place on those who aren't used to them.
- "Hungry mek cat eat salt."
Necessity causes people to do things they wouldn't normally do.

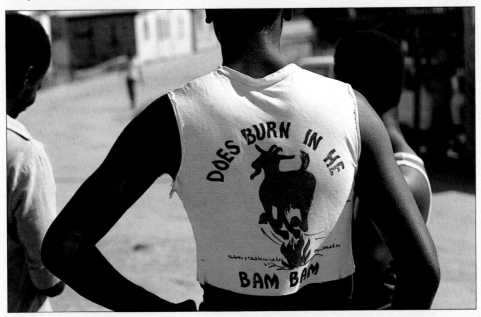

situation.
- "Trouble don't set up like rain."
Misfortune can arrive unexpectedly.
- "Yuh can hide and buy ground but yuh can' hide and wuk [work] it."
It's impossible to hide all of one's actions.
- "Better fish in de sea dan wha ketch."
There is always someone who will make a better lover than the present one.
- "Cat luck en' dog luck."
What one man can get away with might cause a problem for another.
- "De higher de monkey climb, de more 'e show 'e tail."
The more one shows off, the more one's

- "Two smart rat can' live in de same hole."
Two tricksters can't get along.
- "When hog dance, look fuh rain."
Unusual signs are omens of unusual events.
- "De new broom sweep cleaner, but de olebroom know de corners."
Both the new and the familiar have their advantages. (Used in a sexual context.)
- "Coo-coo never done til de pot turn down."
An issue is never settled until there is a definite sign of finality.

George Lamming

IN THE CASTLE OF MY SKIN

FROM LEGENDS TO LITERATURE:
A STORYTELLING TRADITION

On a moon-swept night in Pie Corner, St. Lucy, two women entertain one another with stories of ghosts and spirits. And over a family supper in Bridgetown, a grandmother admonishes children not to "throw stones at a dog or cat when yuh meet them at night—it might not be a cat or dog at all." Shared myths, legends and musings like these are part of Barbados' social currency, as traditional a part of life as flying fish and *cou-cou*.

Barbados also has a rich literary tradition, a number of respected novelists and one of the world's highest literacy rates: over 95 percent of the people can read and write. Here, folk beliefs and literature exist side by side, each preserving the culture and expressing its hopes and fears. Both sensibilities are an integral part of the many-sided Barbadian character.

As for the folklore side, it's replete with looming imaginings and supernatural beliefs. The *duppy* of Bajan folklore is a spirit, a "shade" of a departed person. The *Conrad* is an avenging ghost that possesses the body, racks it, and shouts nasty things at people. Many are the tales of a Conrad in someone's belly, talking in strange voices, and interrupting its host when he tries to speak. There are also many accounts of *heartmen* who seem to appear and vanish with the sugarcane crop season. Heartmen supposedly kill children, offering their hearts to the devil for sacrifice, or using them to make concoctions of magical power.

No less puzzling is the *baccoo* of Barbados, a small man who reportedly often lives in bottles. In the baccoo one finds good or evil, prosperity or failure, heroism or villainy, depending on the amount of attention showered on him by his human owner. Local legends also fear entities that throw stones on the houses of the obsessed, and slap the victims of magic with invisible hands. Stories of witchcraft, spells and miracles abound.

African Heritage: The many Bajan tales and folk beliefs are survivors of an oral tradition that harks back to the African heritage of the majority of the Barbados

population. From the villages of West Africa to the village communities of the Caribbean, from Blue Fields of Nicaragua and Limón of Costa Rica, to Afro-Brazilians and South American bush people, the oral tradition is used to transmit cultural mores and values. In Barbados, these folk tales and songs describe legends, fragments of history and social events. Many contain a moral or a lesson: they are teaching tools. Others are sheer entertainment, vehicles for grassroots creativity. Of all popular Bajan folk tales and practices, however, those that have the most powerful hold are religious. These are the stories and beliefs directly descended from old-time African lore.

The African deity Shango, for instance, once enjoyed a cult following in Barbados. Several other African gods are heroes of ancient, and now obscure, Barbadian tales. The West African "Anancy" folk tales, for example, inspired the Bajan phrase "'nancy story," meaning a tall tale or a fib. "Don't give me no 'nancy story!" a Barbadian mother might scold her half-lying child.

The demons of West Africa's folklore have had an equally strong hold on the Barbadian imagination. Myriad are the

Left, the young George Lamming on the cover of his novel about growing up in Barbados. Right, the author today, near the Atlantis Hotel in Bathsheba.

tales of voodoo and *obeah* (witchcraft), of magicians that transform themselves into balls of fire and animals, of duppies and spirits of the dead.

Barbadians, for example, will tell you that a dead person will "dream" you a few nights after he dies, and that an important message will be conveyed to you in this way. They will hold vigils or wakes, called "nine-nights," to ensure the soul's safe passage to the other world. As in Haiti, there are ceremonies in which the living talk to the dead, inviting the dead to rectify unhappy situations they might have caused while still alive.

Local Lore: Legends that originated locally, in Barbados and the West Indies, are especially vivid and entertaining. Even cunning is widely accepted in Caribbean circles. The tale "The Metaphysical Prank" (see box on page 263) is a case in point.

Stories describing local mysteries circulate freely as well. The Merrymen, a popular singing group, tell of a now-famous steel donkey who would appear at night and wreak havoc:

The steel donkey coming down...
An' he jumping and prancing 'bout
A long thing like a muffler sticking out
behind him
And 'e tongue sticking out he mout'

In the 1960s and '70s, there were Barbadians who swore they saw this steel donkey, surrounded with blue light, bawling and galloping along the country roads of Barbados. One woman said: "I believe it. I *see* it.

today in Barbados there is a persistent folk rumor that certain people can transform themselves into animals and move inconspicuously among people, for instance. There is currently a Bajan who, his neighbors insist, has been seen in his backyard changing into a duck.

Folk tales about theft and cunning abound in the Caribbean, and in Barbados they are especially evident because of popular stereotypes concerning the character of the Barbadian male. He has acquired a reputation for craftiness not unlike that of the folk heroes of the African Anancy tales. Though this behavior has more to do with Bajan thriftiness than stealth, this identification of the male as a "smart man" of

We was living in Orange Hill, St. James, that time. One night late I hear a strange noise. I peep out through the flaps o' my jalousies. If I lie I die: I see this light, blue, and inside it, a thing like a donkey, hollering, kicking up, galloping. It stop outside a shop. Days after, noises was coming from out that shop. I was in there one evening. All of a sudden, I see things falling off the shelves o' the shop. Not all together, one by one, like something picking them up and dropping them. Tins o' sardine, tins o' milk. I get out o' there fast. Few weeks later, the shop close down. Ask anyone in Orange Hill, then, if you doubt me."

History and social events are preserved in folk songs as well. One Bajan folk song documents the activity of a petty thief:

Sly Mongoose, the dog know yuh name.
Sly Mongoose, you ain't got no shame.
You go straight in the lady kitchen
Take up half of she big fat chicken
Hide it down in yuh w'estcoat pocket
Sly Mongoose.

And then there is the song that preserves the story of a West African king, captured by the British because of his intrigues against them, and brought to Barbados under a kind of house arrest in the late 1800s. There he became something of a folk hero; crowds thronged around him everywhere he went. He fell in love with a local woman, Rebecca:

King Ja-Ja won' leave Becka 'lone
King Ja-Ja won' leave Becka 'lone
King Ja-Ja won' leave Becka 'lone

reveals the power of obeah: with one drink, a man is overwhelmed by a powerful desire to marry the woman who gave him the drink. These and other folk songs can be found in the fascinating and readable *Folk Songs of Barbados*, a collection edited by Trevor Marshall, Peggy McGeary and Grace Thompson.

True and Exact History: For generations, Barbados' folk traditions have been passed on orally, but rarely written or recorded. The earliest writings about Barbados were not done by Barbadians, but by visitors who reported the island's history and conditions. The first study of the island is Englishman Richard Ligon's *A True and Exact History of the Island of Barbados*, published in 1673. A more definitive work is Robert

Wha' Becka got is all she own...

The song "Lick and Lock-up done wid" commemorates the ending of slavery on the island. "Murder in the Market" is about a woman who killed her common law mate in the 1870s. "Ah ain't kill nobody but muh husband," the song goes. "Panama Man" reminds us of the hundreds of Bajans who went to help in the construction of the Panama Canal, and whose riches, on their returning to Barbados, were legendary: they tossed coins in the street. "Da Cocoa Tea"

Left, Englishman Richard Ligon wrote the first book about Barbados; it was published in 1673. Right, enthusiastic readers at the Hilltop School, St. Michael.

H. Schomburgk's *The History of Barbados*, published in 1848. Past editions of two island newspapers, the *Barbados Mercury* and the *Bridgetown Gazette*, also contain a wealth of historic information and insights. The Barbados Public Library, with its headquarters on Coleridge Street, just outside the main bustle of Bridgetown, preserves copies of these books and newspapers. It is well worth a visit for those interested in the history of Barbados.

Indigenous literature, meanwhile, first came to public notice in the 1940s and '50s through the efforts of a BBC program called *Caribbean Voices*, aired in England and hosted by Henry Swanzy, and through a Barbadian "little" magazine called *Bim*.

First published in 1942, *Bim* encouraged local creative writing. Highly acclaimed novels were to flow from the pens of *Bim* contributors in later years—novels which may not have been written without a forum like *Bim* and the encouragement of its original editor, the late Frank Collymore. Back volumes of *Bim* are a Who's Who of Caribbean writers, including George Lamming, Oliver Jackman, Geoffrey Drayton, Derek Walcott, John Wickham, Monica Skeete, Austin Clarke, Andrew Salkey, Edward Braithwaite, Bruce St. John and Timothy Callender.

It was to *Bim* that many foreign publishers of Caribbean prose turned in their search for authors. The English, for instance, were becoming increasingly interested in West Indian culture, as West Indian immigrants poured into the mother country. Many books about West India, by West Indians, appeared in England. Back home, meanwhile, the spirit of independence was rising among now-educated, upwardly mobile blacks. Trade unions, political parties and calls for self-government were the order of the day.

Coming of Age: Much of Barbados' best writing grew up in this ferment. Quite literally grew up: it is surprising how many early indigenous novels deal with childhood, with coming of age, with the search for self, with questions about color and race, bondage and freedom. George Lamming's *In the Castle of My Skin*, *The Emigrants* and *Season of Adventure* are perhaps the classic cases in point. In *Season of Adventure*, for instance, the beat of drums in a voodoo ceremony sends a mulatto woman into a frenzied search for meaning and value in her life. Geoffrey Drayton's *Christopher* is a novel about a white Bajan growing up and coming to terms with black society. Austin Clarke's *Amongst Thistle and Thorns* tells the tale of a black Bajan boy doing the same with white society. John Wickham's autobiographical stories touch on this theme too.

The search for self also pervades Oliver Jackman's *Saw the House in Half*. Its title comes from an old Bajan folk rhyme:

Saw the house in half
An' gimme the bedroom part.
I ain't want no mash' up potato
Gimme me dumpling whole...

Although born of some domestic quarrel, the image of the divided house was, for Jackman, an image of Barbados itself; that is, a clash of British and African cultures.

Today the island's writers do not treat the themes of independence and identity with such urgency, an interesting comment on the ongoing and successful synthesis of these two Bajan ways of life. Contemporary novels and writings often bubble with humor, and capture the lives of ordinary people, in a positive way. In fact, many Barbadians now take special delight in local radio broadcasts of West Indian stories which often focus on popular culture and village life. Such readings brought to life the stories of Jeanette Layne-Clarke, Monica Skeete and Timothy Callender. Barbadians love these broadcast stories; they take pride in hearing about themselves. The dialect of Barbados lends itself to public readings too, and Barbadians enjoy the sounds of their own voices, proverbs and situations.

Today, there is a vigorous, vibrant springing up of writing in Barbados. There is a movement to record the oral tradition of the island, and capture its dialect in writing. And Bajan authors are writing more honestly and confidently, describing fuller, rounder characters than ever before; writing less for the overseas reader and more for their own people. It's a spirit kindled in the following poem by H.A. Vaughn, called "Revelation," written about 40 years ago and certainly ahead of its time. The most quoted and anthologized poem to come out of Barbados, it is the first Barbadian poem written to the black woman:

Turn sideways now and let them see
What loveliness escapes the schools;
Then turn again, and smile, and be
The perfect answer to those fools
Who always prate of Greece and Rome
'The face that launched a thousand ships'
And such like things, but keep tight lips
For burnished beauty nearer home.
Turn in the sun, my love, my love!
What palm-like grace! What poise! I swear
I prize these dusky limbs above
My life. What laughing eyes! What gleaming hair!

Recently, the literary magazine *Bim* published *Sandy Lane and other Poems*, H.A. Vaughn's collection. Another essential book for the lover or student of Barbadian verse is Frank Collymore's *Collected Poems*. And anyone wishing an overview of the spirit of Bajan folk culture, and its influence on Barbadian literature, will want to read *The Barbados Book* by Louis Lynch.

Right, the fisherman heads out to sea to dispose of the *baccoo*, the story goes, but is soon overcome by curiosity and opens the bag to take a peep.

TWO BAJAN FOLKTALES

The Metaphysical Prank

A very sick man went to a practicing metaphysician who operated in the city of Bridgetown. The practitioner explained to the man what "pain" was all about. He told him that pain really only existed in the mind. He claimed that all that had to be done was to affirm and believe that the pain was gone and that gradually it would be relieved. With neophyte's zeal, the sick man successfully made the affirmations.

However, when the practitioner asked for the fees for his service, the man, who by now was fully recovered, said: "Wha' fees? All you have to do is affirm and believe dat you receive de fees and you have dem."

The Baccoo from St. Peter

Mrs. Barbara lived in Speightstown, St. Peter. After her death, her daughter was cleaning the house. In the bedroom of the deceased, she saw a blanket under the bed and attempted to remove it. To her surprise, the blanket showed resistance and seemed to have pulled itself back under the bed. When Mrs. Barbara's daughter examined the blanket, she discovered that it contained a baccoo. The miniature man defied all her attempts to root him out. Eventually a Roman Catholic priest was called in to rid the house of this demon. The priest put the baccoo in a bag and paid a fisherman fifty dollars to carry it out to sea.

The mysterious small man in the bag proved too much for the curious fisherman, however. He opened the bag to take a peek, and the baccoo escaped. Legend has it that soon after, the house of the fisherman was destroyed by a fire. People have linked the fire to the fisherman's failure to dispose of the baccoo.

THE BOYFRIENDS

Elmina Griffith had two boyfriends. One was short and one was tall. One was ugly and the other was good-looking. One had a lot o' money and the other didn't have none. And Elmina did like all two of them.

But from the start she grandmother was giving trouble when it comes to this boy-talk. She start from the time she first see Elmina with James. James was the short one, the one who was ugly and didn't have no money neither. One night he come home there and sit down and talk to the grandmother and grandfather good good, and they was talking to he nice too, trying to find out things 'bout he and where he come from and who he family is, and when James get up and went 'long, seeing that he ain't going get no chance to talk lovey-dovey with Elmina that night, the grandmother ups and says:

down in all o' we morris chairs like if they own the place. What you want with boy-friend already, Elmina? And he ain't even nice-looking. I wonder where he come from? I aint know he nor none of he family, though he say he born up in St. Peter where I used to live meself. And I know everybody that is anybody in them parts. But I ain't know *he*. And you hear what sorta job he doing?" she say, turning to Grandpa. "Says he does work with Patterson's Garage. What he does do? Motor-mechanic or does drive taxi?"

"But Elmina, what you getting on with though? This is what I bring you up to do? You mother gone and dead and lef' me with you, and looka how you wanta mek she memory shame after I try so hard with you. What a young little girl like you want with boyfriend already? When I was your age I couldn't even *look* at a man, and now you got them coming in the house sitting

"Grandma, nothing ain't wrong with them jobs! You got a lot o' old-fashion ideas that collar and tie work is the only work decent men could do. What wrong with honest work? The man only trying to make a living. He got to mek money and he doing the job that he like doing best too. He tell me that."

"What you talking 'bout? You wanta tell me you really like he? Why you tekking up for he so strong? You think he like you? How you know he don't go 'round the place chatting down every girl he come across? You know how these men does behave when they reach a certain age. Listen, I want you to get married and thing, but what

264

is you hurry? You still too young to tek on the responsibilities of a wife. You is only twenty-six."

"But grandma, that is old enough."

"Old enough? Girl, when I was *thirty* my mother beat me because I was walking the road and I speak back to a man that speak to me."

But Elmina only chupse and say, "But Grandma, I *like* James, though. I can't help it I like he bad, and he say he like me too."

"Hey, but you ain't got no respect for me and you grandfather? How you can talk that

in coat and collar and tie like if he feel that this give the atmosphere the sort of seriousness that it demand; like if it is a business conference or something. And he looks at James and say;

"Ahem...ahem. Young man, this is the second time I see you and I would like to find out some things 'bout you. You have family?"

"Well, my father dead, but my mother still living. And I got two sisters that went to school at St. Leonard's and St. Michael's."

sorta thing in front of we? Look, Zedekiah, you better watch that girl, hear! She feel that she too old to get lashes. You better watch that girl, Zedekiah."

"Listen, however she mek up she bed she got to lie down 'pon it, yuh know," the grandfather say. "But if I see the young man again, I going ask he a few questions."

So when James pass by another time to see Elmina, the grandfather comes out and sits down in the rocking chair, all dress up

"Elmina would sneak outa the house and go and meet he, and they use to walk to the beach and hold one another hand and mek plans 'bout getting married and thing . . . "

"Them is good schools to go to," the old man say. "So what you sisters doing now?"

"Well I ain't know. They wasn't home when I left."

He had the old man there. He like he is a fool, yuh, Zedekiah start to think. What sorta idiot this girl encouraging in my house though? Listen, I talking too decent to this idiot. I better talk in language he understand.

"Ahem. Listen, young man, you have money?"

The young man put he hand in he pocket and scratch 'bout.

"Lemme see... 'bout three dollars. How much yuh want?"

The grandfather bend down and hold he head in he hands.

And Elmina, sitting down 'pon the couch beside James, was very embarrass because she did know what the grandfather was getting at; in fact, she did want to find out sheself. So she turn to James and she says:

"All grandfather want to know is what your intentions is."

"Well, right now I intends to ketch the ten o'clock bus," the young man say.

"Listen young man. I ain't want you to ever come back inside this house o' mine!" Zedekiah shout out. "Don't ever come here again or I will do as I say as sure as my name is Amos Zedekiah Joshua Zechariah Hedoniah Griffith."

"I believe you, man. You ain't got to tell me you name too," the young man say. "And Elmina, I want you to know that whatever happen I still love you with a eternal love, and I building a house and anytime you ain't feel like standing here no longer, you know what you kin do. I gone for now."

And James went 'long.

"You hear what he say?" says the grandmother, coming out from the bedroom where she was listening behind the partition. "But looka this wussless nigger-man though

nuh, trying to encourage a nice decent young girl like you to come and live with he. You see what he been intending for you all the time now? You see that we did right?"

So James never went back inside Zedekiah's house again, but every now and then when Elmina coulda think up a excuse she would sneak outa the house and go and meet he, and if it was night, they use to walk to the beach and sit down 'pon the sand and hold one another hand and look out to sea and look at the lights and tell one another how much they like one another and mek

plans 'bout getting married and thing, and so on.

Then one day Elmina get a job in a store in town and that is where she meet Bannister. Bannister was the Assistant to the Assistant Manager, so that mean that he had to do all the work. But he still had time to come and chat down Elmina though. And while Elmina ain't like he as much as she like James, she did still like he enough to take on, and she realize too the old people woulda like he better too.

And man, you should see the first evening when Elmina drive up in the car with this good looking young man at the wheel all dress to death in white—white suit, white shirt and collar and tie; and all the neighbors come peeping out through the jalousies and admiring the way he look and the other girls in the village jealous and saying that this time she must be work something 'pon he to get he to like she so. And Bannister gets outa the car and slam the door hard and gone 'round to the other side and open the door for Elmina and Elmina gets out with she head straight in the air and goes inside the house with Bannister. And Zedekiah comes out and starts shaking hands and laughing and talking good good good.

Then out runs the grandmother talking with the best words she could find and says to Bannister that he must excuse the condition that the house in.

So they sit down and talk a lot of small talk and then Bannister ask the grandparents if he could take out Elmina from time to time, and the grandfather say yes, of course, sure, that he know a decent man when he sees one, and that he certainly does admire the way Elmina does pick her friends.

After that Bannister make a date to go to the drive-in theater with Elmina, and then he left. So that is how the two of them start going 'round together. Elmina living it up now, every Saturday night she feting and coming home early in the morning, and she always going this place and that place with this Bannister fellow. And the grandparents watching with interest, wondering when the time going come that Bannister going mek the move to get married to Elmina.

Now Elmina was getting through all right: she dressing up in a lot of nice clothes and looking real sweet, and though she ain't got time to see James as often as she use to do in the past, sometimes 'pon a night when the old people think that she out with Bannister, she really gone off somewhere to meet James. And is true that she like James more, but she like Bannister too, and it looking like if Bannister is the man most likely to succeed in the long run. James feeling bad 'bout it, and asking she why she don't just stick to he and wait till he get enough money to married she, but she was so excited with the new life she living for the first time that she can't stick to James alone and leave out all o' that fun.

But some trouble start up that make a big scandal in the village, and all the people say, I tell yuh so, I know it would happen. And the grand-parents feeling shame and crying and thing. "Where that man Bannister? What he doing 'bout it?" Zedekiah ups and says. "Elmina, you know where he live? Looka, come lewwe go up there right now."

So the two of them ketch the bus and gone up by where Bannister live and knock 'pon the door and wait. And then a woman open the door and says she is Mrs. Bannister,

and that Mr. Bannister ain't home. And the old man ask, "Well, when he coming back? I got something important to tell him."

"I ain't certain," the woman say.

"Where he gone?"

"Well, this morning he ketch the plane for South America, where he gone to see after opening a business, and after that he got to go up to Canada to see he uncle, and after that he got to go to Norway and Czechoslovakia and I think he might got to pass through Jerusalem too. So I really can't say when he coming back."

"Well when you see him again, tell him I want to see him," the old man say. That was all he coulda say, too.

So then they gone back home and the old people quarreling and saying that they did know all the time that Bannister wasn't no good but that they was hoping that he woulda behave heself like a gentleman. And they turning on 'pon Elmina and asking she why she couldn't keep sheself to sheself and things like that, and saying that they got five minds to put she outa the house.

So one morning Elmina get up and went straight to where James living and say that she staying there, that she ain't going back home, that she fed up with everything there. And James straightway gone and start taking out marriage license and thing and next thing you know they married and living in the house that James build.

And a lot of people was saying that James is a idot to act that way after she stop seeing him for such a long time, but they didn't know what was going on for after the baby born and they look at it, it did so ugly, that everybody realize that Elmina had marry the right boyfriend after all.

—*Bim* Magazine 52 (1971)

"You should see the first evening when Elmina drive up in the car with this good looking young man at the wheel all dress to death in white . . . "

THE LAND OF FLYING FISH AND COU-COU

Barbadians contend that the way to a man's heart is through his stomach. The Bajan woman's ability to cook is therefore highly praised, and a woman who cannot cook is hesitant to admit it. In fact, not long ago, this was reason enough for a man to "leave out" a prospective girl friend, or to eat at his mother's, to the girl friend's embarrassment. A popular folk song recounts just such a pickle:

> Such a pretty little girl
> Like Jessie Mahon,
> She lazy since she born,
> De girl can' cook,
> She won' read a book
> So pack she back to she ma...
> Pack she back to she ma ma...

Bajan cooking is especially creative, and hence praiseworthy, for two reasons. One is that there are limited native foods available. The main protein sources for Barbadians have traditionally been milk, cheese, fish, imported salt beef and pork, corned pork, local fresh mutton and pork, and some imported frozen beef. In recent years, fast-food chicken and chips, hamburgers and hot dogs have become staples, too, although a Bajan cook would never consider these quick meals competition for "a sweet Bajan stew" or "cou-cou and salt fish."

Another reason a good Barbadian cook has a talent to treasure: for most islanders, the food budget doesn't stretch that far. Many households raise and slaughter their own chickens and pigs, for example, as an economy measure. The Bajan housewife tries hard to "make a six a nine," that is, to stretch the family dollar. And in doing so, she calls on a vast number of cooking techniques, drawn from diverse cuisines, from African to Spanish.

Culinary Hybrid: The many influences which have shaped Barbadian life are perhaps nowhere as apparent as on the dinner table. Bajan cooking is a culinary hybrid, drawn from African and English traditions, as well as Amerindian, Spanish, French, Chinese, Indian, American and Caribbean cooking techniques.

The Bajan national dish, *cou-cou* and salt

fish, is African-inspired. Cou-cou is a cornmeal and okra pudding, a relative of a basic foodstuff of Africa called "foo-foo." It is ladled with gravy and served with salt fish.

Cou-cou in the making is a wonderful sight, and a challenge: much energy is put into the stirring, for if any lumps are allowed to form, the cou-cou is considered a failure. The finished mixture is packed into a bowl and then turned out onto a plate. The center of the mound is sunk with a spoon and a light gravy ladled into the center and around the golden mound.

The love of this dish inspired the following poetic flight of fancy:

> Salt fish like slabs of wood,
> Onions like bangles and
> Tomatoes like cartwheels
> Cover the cou-cou, which floats
> like an island in a sea of sauce.

Salt fish—much tastier than "slabs of wood"—is a food originally imported to feed slaves; it was an inexpensive source of protein. Today, salted cod is as expensive as some meat and poultry. Cod fish balls and cod cakes are now considered a delicacy, and served at cocktail parties and other festive occasions.

Tasty Fish Dish: Another Bajan specialty is flying fish. These silvery blue specimens, seven to nine inches long, abound in clear warm waters in many parts of the world. Yachtsmen and those traveling by ship have often reported seeing schools of fifty to one thousand flying fish suddenly leap from the water, and glide through the air for up to seventy-five feet (23 meters). In Barbados, these fish are most plentiful from December through June. They are bought in large quantities during these months and stored in freezers or dried.

A spicy Barbadian seasoning makes flying fish an especially tasty national dish. The seasoning is made of finely chopped onion, parsley, thyme, black pepper, paprika, garlic, finely chopped red pepper and any other herbs or spices available plus a little salt and a few drops of lime juice. This is all mixed together to allow the flavors to blend and then packed into the seams of the fish and left a while to penetrate before the fish is fried or steamed.

Other fish on Bajan menus include king fish, dolphin, red snapper, chub and

Preceding pages: A family gathers for Sunday dinner at midday. Left, every night at Baxter's Road women cook fish Bajan-style over open fires in "buckpots."

bonito. Small fish such as sprats, jacks and fray are also tasty favorites.

Barbadians are pork lovers, too. It is often said that the only part of the pig which the Bajan cannot covert into a tantalizing dish is the hair. One traditional pork dish starts with several pounds of pork, which is "corned" or pickled in a stone jar with coarse sea salt, saltpeter, spices and water. After two weeks in the jar, the pork is removed and desalted by soaking several times in cold water. It is then boiled with white beans, onions, tomatoes, parsley, thyme, pepper, butter and gravy.

Even finely chopped pig's tails, snouts, heads and feet are served in a dish known as "stew food," with what are called "ground

brought to Barbados in 1793 by a British sea captain. Breadfruit can be cooked in stews, fried, boiled, or pickled.

Sunday Buffets: If late-week meals are inexpensive and imaginative, weekends in Barbados bring their own customs. Pudding and souse is a pork dish that is a traditional Saturday night meal. Leftovers are usually fried and served for breakfast on Sunday. And the custom of entertaining friends on Sundays is still popular; these occasions often assume a festive atmosphere, complete with popular music and buffets of local dishes.

To encourage Bajans to appreciate and cultivate more home-grown foods, the island's Hotels' Association now sponsors an annual culinary exhibition known as

provisions"—that is, root vegetables, such as yams, sweet potatoes, white eddos, cassava (a native root vegetable) and breadfruit. This particular dish is often cooked with green vegetables, such as okra, cristophenes (a green pear-shaped squash), cabbage and spinach. "Stew food" traditionally was cooked mid-week, those days furthest away from payday, when fresh or expensive food supplies could be counted on to be somewhat depleted.

For nearly two centuries, breadfruit has been a staple in the Bajan diet. It is a starchy fruit, white in the middle with a bright green skin, that grows on trees throughout the island. The breadfruit tree originally came from Tahiti, and was

Bajan Table. Hotels, restaurants and individuals are invited to display foods in different categories, and prizes are awarded. The exhibition takes place in early October.

The National Independence Festival of Creative Arts (NIFCA) also celebrates Bajan culinary arts. This festival culminates on Barbados' Independence Day, November 30. Gold, silver and bronze medals are awarded for preparation and presentation of native dishes.

Left, roadside fruit stands abound in Barbados, especially in urban areas. Right, Bridgetown's Cheapside Market is especially busy on Saturday mornings.

ISLAND DELICACIES

—Bajan folk song

Peas and Rice: This is a very popular main dish. Rice is combined with one or several kinds of peas, including green or dried pigeon (gunga) peas, blackeye and split peas, whole and cow peas, or beans or lentils. Salted pig tails or other salted meats are cooked in the rice to season it.

Pudding and Souse: This is an old island dish made at home or readily available from hawkers in the markets and along city streets. The pudding is made from grated and well-seasoned sweet potato which is stuffed into the cleaned intestines of a pig. This is steamed in a large saucepan of water until it is cooked; the finished product looks like a long dark sausage. This is cut into slices and served with the "souse," which is pig's head, feet and flesh cooked until tender, cut into slices and "soused" or pickled with lime juice, onion, hot pepper, salt, chopped cucumber and parsley.

Sea Egg: This the roe of a white sea urchin caught on reefs around the island. The yellow roe is picked from the shells and piled into other cleaned shells. Each shell is topped with a sea grape leaf, steamed and sold from trays in the markets.

Roti: This favorite food is of Indian origin, but so popular as to at least seem Bajan. It consists of a flat bread with a spicy meat and curry mixture inside. It is often made at home but is also available at many food shops.

Conkies: The name of this Bajan dish comes from "Kenke," a similar African food. Conkies are made of cornmeal, coconut, pumpkin and spices, mixed to a thick consistency, placed on steamed young banana leaf squares, then folded

From left to right: Rastaman serves up some "itals," an all-natural vegetarian stew; bikeload of sorrel, for making a traditional Christmas drink; old-time mauby seller; grated coconut or coconut "milk" is used in many Bajan dishes.

like a parcel and steamed over water in a deep pot.

Fruit Drinks: Popular drinks are coconut water, lemonade made from fresh limes, and a variety of punches made from such local fruits as cherries, guavas, mangoes, soursops, or golden apples, gooseberries, pawpaws, passion fruit or tamarinds.

Mauby: A drink made from boiling pieces of a bitter bark with spices. It is then strained and sweetened, and can be brewed to make it frothy like beer. It is very refreshing on a hot day.

Sorrel: Prepared from the fresh or dried red sepals of the plant and boiled or infused in hot water with spices and rum added. This is the local Christmas drink.

Ginger Beer: Made from green or dried root ginger in a similar way.

Falernum: A local liqueur made with lime juice, granulated sugar, rum and water, flavored with almond essence.

Corn and Oil: A drink consisting of equal parts of refreshing rum and falernum.

Recipe for a Bajan Favorite:

Coconut bread

1 ¼ lb. flour
3 teaspoons baking powder
3 cups grated coconut
6 oz. brown sugar
6 oz. shortening
½ teaspoon salt
1 teaspoon powdered cinnamon
1 teaspoon powdered nutmeg
2 teaspoons almond essence
¼ lb. raisins *or* mixed fruit
1 cup milk
1 large egg

Cream together the sugar and shortening. Beat the egg well, then mix it in. Add the grated coconut, spices, almond essence, either the raisins or the fruit, and milk. Sift the flour with the salt and baking powder, and mix it in last. Put the mixture into one greased two-pound size loaf pan and one one-pound size pan. Bake it in a moderate oven, at 375° F (140° C) for about one hour, or until it is golden brown. Then take the sweet-smelling loaves out of the pans and cool them on a rack before serving.

HERBAL CURES AND "ITALS"

Nature was Barbados' first pharmacy, or "doctor shop." While "modern" medicine has superseded traditional folk cures throughout most of the island, ancient medical remedies are once again attracting a following among Bajans.

Folk cures seem to have sprung from three diverse sources on the island. The original Arawak inhabitants probably used indigenous plants and herbs in teas and "cures." It is also likely that African folk cures and bush medicines made their way to Barbados with the island's African finger grow; it has very sharp thorns and reportedly is an aphrodisiac for men. (You may therefore guess which "finger" it helps to "grow.") Of course, there are some bushes which thrive all over the island, such as Christmas bush, cure-for-all and circee.

Groundnuts and Coconuts: The Rastafarians have brought the use of groundnuts (primarily peanuts) and coconuts back again. They call these foodstuffs "itals," a derivation, in their dialect, of "victuals." On almost every street corner, members of the

inhabitants. More recently, the development and growth of the Rastafarian movement has spurred a resurgence of interest in natural cures: Rastafarians look mainly to nature for their needs; they have initiated research and experimentation with non-traditional teas and cures, and in doing so have extended the range of Barbadian folk medicines.

Unfortunately, much of the open pasture where many wild plants and herbs once thrived has in recent years been cleared for housing or cultivation. Some bushes seem to have been overused and are very difficult to find. A good example is a bush called Rastafari brethren do a busy trade in coconuts.

Coconut water is praised by most Bajans as a preventive and cure for illnesses of the bladder and kidneys. Coconut oil is also a long-standing cold remedy: it may be rubbed into the head to break up a cold. It is also used on the scalp a day or two before washing the hair to help loosen dandruff flakes. And of course coconut water is lauded as a refreshing beverage. The ever-useful coconut inspired this ditty:

Coconut woman is calling out
An' everywhere you can hear her shout
'Get your coconut water

Man it good for yuh daughter
Coco got a lot of iron
Make you strong like a lion...

The song goes on to advocate "if you tired and feeling down/Get coconut water an' little rum."

Peanuts are another Bajan "health" food. Barbadians have always eaten them raw for general health; and in large quantities peanuts are supposed to stimulate sexual desire or increase sexual prowess. For this purpose, the nuts are soaked in milk, gin or beer for one night or one week, depending

upon the potency desired.

"Brings the Blood Down": A melon-like fruit called pawpaw is put to many uses in a Bajan home. The fruit itself is delicious, and it often is pureed into a beverage as well. Either way, it prevents constipation or, as the Bajans phrase it, it helps to "keep the bowels moving."

Green pawpaw is reportedly useful for reducing the effects of hypertension, or high blood pressure; it "brings the blood down," goes a local expression. The pawpaw for this purpose is taken one or two ways, either as two small cooked slices of green pawpaw, or in an elaborate concoc-tion that involves grated nutmeg, candle grease and an optional few drops of coconut oil.

This versatile fruit is also used to prevent infection from cuts and bruises. Two or three thin slices are placed over a cut and bandaged for two or three days to promote rapid healing without infection. Pawpaw is used in this same way in parts of Africa, with excellent results.

The cactus-like aloe plant is another Bajan all-rounder. For colds, itching throats and constipation, the outer skin is removed and a small piece of the inner pith is swallowed with a pinch of salt to reduce the bitterness. Many Bajans recall the experience of being forced to swallow bitter aloe as one of their worst childhood memories! A thin "inside" slice of aloe can also be bandaged on cuts to aid the healing process.

The green brew made from yet another native plant, the circee bush, is also a bitter medicine; it is used to help reduce fever and relieve the symptoms of influenza. Some people refer to the circee bush as "miraculous bush," a tribute to its healing powers. A cousin, in name at least, to the miraculous bush is the "wonder-of-the world" plant (pronounced "wonda-worl'") which, when chewed with a pinch of salt, is supposed to bring relief from mild asthmatic attacks. Others believe firmly in a bowl of green-lizard soup to get rid of asthma.

Creative Cures: Some Bajan herbal teas and home cures have merit, while others are definitely doubtful to the modern mind. For example, a child with asthma would be taken to a young pawpaw tree and made to stand upright against the tree. A nail would be driven into the tree just above the child's head. People believed that as the tree grew, the illness would gradually disappear.

For a child afflicted with worms, a piece of bitter worm-wood would be steeped in rum and the liquid fed to the child for nine consecutive mornings. If that failed to work, raw aloe in milk was administered instead. Hiccups mandated a different "cure": a match stick was pushed into the child's hair, or a small piece of brown paper was moistened with saliva and placed on the child's forehead.

Workable cures or wishful thinking, the folk medicine tradition of Barbados is extensive and vibrant.

"A Very Sweet Thing": The Story of Rum

Ring-a-ding-ding, Ring-a-ding-ding,
Rum from Barbados is very sweet thing.
—Bajan toast

On this tiny island of just 166 square miles, there are estimated to be nearly 1000 "rum shops." Barbados is the country in which the name "rum" was coined, and the first to export the golden liquor. It is the home of some of the best rums in the Western hemisphere.

Rum is made by distilling the juice extracted from molasses, the thick liquid residue left after most of the sugar has been taken out of the sugarcane juice.

Most of Barbados' dark rums are made in the traditional pot stills. The longer they are aged, the better: a five-year-old rum is good, but a rum aged for 10 years in barrels made of American white oak is even smoother and mellower. The rum acquires its dark color from the wood and from a small amount of caramel added later. Lighter rums are made in modern stills and aged for less time.

Kill-Devil: Delicious and sweet today, Barbadian rum wasn't always carefully refined. In the 1640s, the first batches of native distilled spirits were referred to as "kill-devil" by Englishman Richard Ligon, a Royalist refugee who wrote the first book about Barbados. The rum in those days was not very tasty, but it was very strong. Those who imbibed it quickly felt its effects; as Ligon put it, "It lays them to sleep on the ground."

It is likely that the name "rum" itself was first coined in Bridgetown's taverns or on its waterfront, where it was loaded onto foreign ships for export. Around 1650, an anonymous island visitor left behind a description that "the chiefe fudling they make on the Island is Rumbullion, alias Kill Divill, and this is made of sugarcanes distilled, a hot, hellish and terrible liquor." Rumbullion may simply have been a descriptive word, or an English version of the Dutch and German *roemer*, meaning a large drinking glass.

Rum helped to make Barbadian planters prosperous. It was bought by planters who did not have their own sugar works, and sold to the taverns and to ships both for consumption by the crew, and for resale overseas. With all this indulgence, con-

sumption on the island reached 70,000 gallons a year by the late 1700s—much more than today.

"Leh We Fire One": Rum is unquestionably still the social drink of Barbados today. It is drunk at births, christenings, weddings, wakes, funerals and at all other rites of passage. The invitation "Man, leh we fire one on dat!" could be prompted by a promotion, a lucky bet on the horses or on the pools, or anything which causes happiness, and the "one" to be "fired" (that is, drunk) is usually rum. Rum is

drunk straight from the bottle; with each person taking turns in a spirit of community, or from small "snap" glasses on the rocks, or with a chaser to dilute its strength and taste.

Rum is even a political instrument in Barbados. Politicians regularly provide rum and corned beef before and after elections, and woe be to the greenhorn political aspirant who doesn't fulfill this tradition. Voters have been known to "eat out, drink out, and vote out" many a candidate who was miserly with the supplies of rum.

It is considered bad form to drink a

politician's rum and then not vote for him. A folk song from the 1940s tells of one such candidate's revenge:

Speightstown people drink Marshall rum
And then vote fuh "Labour"
Speightstown people drink Marshall rum
And then vote for "Labour"
Doan pass here, doan pass here
For de dog will bite yuh ...

Apparently "Marshall" unleashed his dog on those who had "drunk him out and voted him out."

Where Tongues are Loosened: The "rum ering when instead you could be tipping a glass to:

Rum is sweet, rum is sweet
Doan let this drink
Sweep you off your feet

Some of the best rum-drinking rhymes come from the Christmas season and the best known is:

Hark the Herald Angels sing
A gallon o' rum is just de t'ing
Peace on earth and mercy mild
A pint for a man and a gill for a child.

Sociologists tell, in stark statistics, the

shop" is the place where liquors are dispersed. It is more than a store selling liquor, however. It is also a village store, often selling groceries and fuel, and an informal community center, where tongues are loosened, politics discussed and rumors spread. It is not a bar, a café, or a restaurant, though it may be all of these.

There are fewer rum toasts than rum shops, but it's a point hardly worth consid-

Left, passing the time at a rum shop in St. Philip. Right, oak barrels for aging rum at the West Indian Rum Refinery in St. Michael.

story of rum consumption in Barbados. It is true that the typical rum shop patron is male, middle-aged, and sometimes too likely to spend at the rum shop what he could be putting towards child support or other obligations. Women rarely frequent rum shops, generally attending only occasionally, and with a male escort. The rum shop, in other words, is primarily a male bastion, and its liquid pleasures—like most pleasures—sometimes abused.

Still, it seems impossible to separate "Barbados" and "rum." In the words of one devotee, "No matter how long the world lasts, rum shops will go on."

BARBADOS TEAM v. REST OF WORLD — March 8th — 13th,1967

| Cortez Jordan (Umpire) | D. Holford | P. Lashley | R. Brancker | A. Taylor | A. Howard : Greenidge (Emergency Fieldsmen) | G. Bethel | A. Bynoe | R. S. Buller (Umpire) |

| S. Nurse | C. Hunte | E. Weekes (Manager) | G. Sobers (Captain) | W. Hall | C. Griffith |

280

CRICKET: "THE NATIONAL RELIGION"

When Barbados became independent in 1966 after more than 300 years of British colonialism, it chose to proclaim its political manhood by challenging the rest of the world to a cricket match.

Barbados lost: an appropriate reward, perhaps, for such arrogance. Yet, no one doubted the ability of this country to hold its own against the might of an international all-star team. Barbados may be no more than a pinprick on the world map, but the game of cricket brought it instant and universal recognition. Often called its "national religion," cricket in Barbados is nearly a way of life.

Most of Barbados' national heroes are cricket heroes. The pages of *Wisden Cricketers' Almanac*, the Bible-size tome that has chronicled the game for the past 122 years, are filled with the records of brilliant Barbadians who have fashioned this most intricate sport into an institution.

Exuberant Pride: In Barbados today, cricket is a source of exuberant pride. After all, even if Barbados did lose that 1966 match against a world team, it has trounced several international touring teams. It has taken the Shell Shield, the annual regional tournament, for 11 out of its 19 seasons.

The game of cricket was introduced almost two centuries ago by the British military. The local white planter and merchant classes soon set up their own clubs, and organized regular competitions. It seems there would be other pastimes more suited to the tropical heat, yet cricket flourished in the Caribbean. Cricket, more than any other sport exported to the far corners of the empire, was seen as a character-builder, a reflection of the noble values of British culture. "It's not cricket" is still widely used to mean it's not the proper thing.

In the early years, cricket clubs mirrored the clear class and racial structures of Barbadian society. Wanderers, formed in 1877, drew membership mainly from the white mercantile community. Pickwick was the club of the plantocracy, and like Wanderers, strictly white. Spartan's members were mainly from among the growing black and mixed-race professionals—doctors, law-

On the national team at the time of independence were some of the world's best cricket players. Sobers was captain.

yers and the like. When Spartan members blackballed Herman Griffith, a public health inspector, because they felt he was beneath their station, objectors broke away and formed the Empire Club. Griffith became one of the great players of the game, a fast bowler (pitcher) who could sprint 20 powerful strides before hurling the 5½ ounce leather ball at over 90 miles an hour (145 k.p.h.). He was the first black captain of a Barbados team. These four clubs are still active, although the class and racial structure of their memberships have

What Is Cricket, Anyway?

The best way to understand cricket—no small undertaking—is to experience a match firsthand. Like an abstract painting or love, cricket's intriguing charms are in the eye of the beholder.

It is an intricate game with idiosyncratic rules and traditions. Matches run long hours, and can span as many as five days, at the end of which no clear winner is guaranteed. Indeed, cricket is steeped, like a four o'clock tea break, in a private vocabulary.

Perhaps the enigma that is cricket is best summed up in this description, attributed to an English cricket club:

You have two sides, one out in the field and one in. Each man that's in the side that's in, goes out and when he's out he comes in and the next man goes in until he's out. When they are all out the side that's out comes in and the side that's been in goes out and tries to get those coming in out. Sometimes you get men still in and not out. When both sides have been in and out including the not outs, that's the end of the game—Howzat!

changed dramatically.

All of this formal activity was once centered around Bridgetown and confined to a small segment of the population. Yet, artisans, laborers and others would not be excluded, and soon formed their own clubs. In the sugar-speckled countryside particularly, plantation bosses recognized the game's potential for fostering community spirit. They encouraged workers to play, providing them with land for a field, and passing on second-hand gear from their own clubs.

Largely ignored by the Barbados Cricket Association, the established organization, these lesser teams arranged their own competitions. The rivalry was usually intense, particularly on the sugar plantations where outsiders could qualify for membership only by living on or near the plantation or by marrying or courting a girl from the village.

This spirit gave momentum to the formation of the Barbados Cricket League at a time of significant social and political upheaval; the League is now recognized as a step towards Independence. Ironically, this game that once segregated the classes and colors so neatly, eventually brought disparate groups together in a way not possible otherwise. White plantation managers and business executives found themselves playing against black lawyers and civil servants: camaraderie and respect emerged. It would be some time, however, before the steve-

an international Test Match for the West Indies against Pakistan at Kingston's Sabina Park in Jamaica, the lithe left-hander scored an incredible 365 runs. He was stopped only when the jubilant crowd invaded the pitch to hoist him shoulder-high in triumph.

He was an explosive batsman, a bowler of three distinctive styles, and an incomparable fielder. He played 93 international matches, from 1954 until 1974, when the cartilage in his knees finally gave out. Trinidadian calypso king the Mighty Sparrow described him as "the greatest cricketer on Earth or on Mars" in a 1965 song. And in 1975, Queen Elizabeth overturned a tradition and knighted Sobers, not at Buckingham Palace, but in an open-air cer-

dore or the cane-cutter found a place "at the stump."

The New Heroes: Today's well-known players are black, and many are from humble backgrounds. In the 1950s, the West Indies scorelines were dominated by three batsmen of grace, style and endurance known as the Terrible Three Ws: Frank Worrell, Clyde Walcott and Everton Weekes. Worrell was knighted by Queen Elizabeth in 1964; his image still graces the Barbadian five-dollar bill.

Garfield Sobers, born into a family of six in the Bridgetown suburb of Rayland, grew up to be the undisputed finest player of all time. In 1958, at the age of 21, he recorded the highest individual score ever made. In

emony on the Garrison Savannah, the site of the earliest recorded matches on the island. The versatile Sobers now captains the Barbados golfing team and plays to a two-handicap himself.

Making It Big: Barbadian cricket inspires personal hopes and dreams as well as national pride. It is a vehicle for young boys who want to escape from poverty and "make it big." They know that mastering cricket may mean more to their future than any other skill. So they play cricket everywhere, year-round.

They sharpen their reflexes and techniques playing in the street and on the beaches, using anything that approximates a real ball and a real bat. Top players earn at least US$50,000, a very good living in Barbados. The West Indies team has been by far the strongest on the limited international circuit for at least a decade and is in demand. This means that its star players are in demand as well: Malcolm Marshall and Joel "Big Bird" Garner, for example, have steady contracts with English county teams and have played for wealthy clubs in Australia.

Even those not quite on their level can find jobs coaching and playing abroad. About two dozen Bajan cricketers head overseas every year to make money they could never earn from cricket at home.

The two controlling organizations of cricket in Barbados, the Association and the League, cram 100 matches into the

States and Canada.

Teas and Trees: One of the peculiarities of cricket is that there is no legal definition of the playing area. A batsman on some fields may need to hit the ball 70 yards over the boundary, while other fields are smaller, requiring hits as short as 50 yards. Some clubs are equipped with dressing rooms and showers and elaborate teas. In country areas, things are a bit rougher: the shadiest tree serves as a pavilion, the grass on the field is kept trim by a flock of sheep, and the "tea" is considerably more potent.

No matter what the conditions of the field or its surroundings, the fans come. A day at cricket is a social ritual. An international match runs from 10:30 a.m. to 5:30 p.m. each day for five straight days, with

limited space at their disposal every Saturday afternoon throughout the official season, from early June until mid-September. A "softball" association controls a modified form of the game which uses tennis rather than leather balls, and slim bats of local mahogany in place of the regulation willow bats imported from England. Sunday morning is the time more than 100 softball league teams compete with one another for places on the Barbados teams that regularly tour the United

Left, a print by local artist K. Hawkins depicts the first intercolonial cricket match in the Caribbean, at the Garrison. Right, beach cricket at Bathsheba.

breaks for lunch and tea. When the action on the field is sluggish, and the sun is hot, diversions become mandatory. So fans make a picnic of it, toting their baskets of peas and rice, salted pig-trotters, pickled breadfruit and other delights, as well as the island's famous rum.

Kensington Oval is always crammed to its 15,000 capacity on days of a Test Match against England or Australia, and the atmosphere is noisily electric. It can seem even more crowded at key club matches where as many as 4,000 enthusiastic fans encircle much smaller grounds.

Until the 1960s, businesses closed and Parliament was adjourned when international teams came to town. Still, absenteeism is high—and often excused—during a big match. Productivity drops when the West Indies are on tour in England, as the play-by-play commentary is heard on thousands of radios concealed in desk drawers and behind service counters. A series in Australia, when play continues through the Bajan night, is a fine excuse for cricket parties that gather around the radio.

All the activity surrounding the game has produced some characters who like nothing better than to entertain the fans when the players are failing to do so. The late "Flannagan" (no one seemed to know or really care much about his real name) traveled with Barbados teams throughout the 1930s and 40s, serving as a sort of mascot, heckling and teasing opponents on

both reflected those changes and helped bring them about.

There are those who fear that standards are declining of late. When Barbados finished fifth out of six in the regional senior and junior championships in 1985, everyone threw their hands up in horror, predicting the end. Yet, Barbados had won the senior pennant five times in the previous eight seasons, and the junior title for two consecutive years before that. It is true, however, that the protracted absences of star players fulfilling overseas contracts are clearly affecting club standards.

The Nation newspaper, discussing the issue in an editorial, pointed out that the cricket club of 50 or 60 years ago was "first and foremost a social statement." It stated:

and off the field with his loud, sharp-witted comments.

"King Dyal," Redvers Dundonald Dyal, has been a regular for more than a quarter-century, unfailingly supporting the other team, particularly if it is the English. He always makes a grand entrance to the most conspicuous seat in the most conspicuous stand—and each interval reappears in a different, resplendent, three-piece suit: flamboyant scarlet, canary yellow, emerald green.

More than a Game: In the nearly 200 years since the first match was recorded in Barbados, cricket has remained much more than a game. The island has changed enormously in that time, and cricket has

When cricket became a mere game, then an occupation, it was the beginning of the end of what it once was. It may have become better organized, the players more technically competent, but they have become less committed to club, country, and ideals.

Perhaps, but then, Barbados has changed as well, and most of these changes make up something gained, not something lost. Always a barometer, cricket and its social climate will certainly continue to evolve along with Barbados.

Left, the Barbados team today. Right, Sir Gary Sobers, a Bajan cricket hero who was even knighted by the Queen.

GUIDE IN BRIEF

TRAVELING TO BARBADOS

Barbados, according to one of the island's television commercials, is "the land where the sun rises first." Easternmost island of the Caribbean, this small paradise (22 miles long by 14 miles wide) lies off the coast of Venezuela, 2,100 miles from New York.

To get there, paradise-seekers can travel by scheduled commercial flight, private aircraft, yacht, mailboat (from neighboring islands) or cruise ship. More than 20,000 flights land annually at **Sir Grantley Adams International Airport**, considered to be the Caribbean's largest and most efficient facility.

By Air

There are 12 carriers offering flights to and from Barbados, with daily service from New York and Miami available from American Airlines and Pan American. Eastern also offers daily flights from New York, connecting through Miami, and British West Indian Airways (BWIA) has daily flights from Miami and New York, as well as scheduled service from Boston, Baltimore, Toronto and London. West coast flights to Barbados (via Miami) can be booked on Eastern, which also features Miami-routed service from Houston and Dallas/Fort Worth.

Caribbean Airways, the island's national carrier, flies to and from London, Brussels and Frankfurt. Leeward Island Air Transport (L.I.A.T.) connects Barbados with the rest of the Caribbean, while BWIA makes connections from Trinidad/Tobago, Jamaica, and Puerto Rico. Cubana Airways links Barbados with Havana, Guyana and Trinidad. Air Canada flies in from Toronto on Saturdays and Sundays (and also has service from Montreal and Winnipeg); Wardair also flies from the same Canadian cities; and British Airways provides three direct flights per week from London. To contact the airlines in Barbados, call:

Air Canada, (Grantley Adams Intl. Airport), 428-5077.
Air Martinique, (Grantley Adams Intl. Airport), 428-4660.
American, (Grantley Adams Intl. Airport), 428-4170.
British Airways, (Bridgetown), 436-6413; (Grantley Adams Intl. Airport), 428-7632.
BWIA International, (Bridgetown), 426-2111; (Grantley Adams Intl. Airport), 428-6765.
Caribbean Airways, (Bridgetown), 426-0110; (Grantley Adams Intl. Airport), 428-5660.
Cubana Airlines, (Grantley Adams Intl. Airport), 428-0060; (BWIA for reservations).
Eastern Airlines, (Grantley Adams Intl. Airport), 428-7434.
Guyana Airways, (Bridgetown), 436-6224.
L.I.A.T., (Bridgetown), 436-6224; (Grantley Adams Intl. Airport), 428-9893.
Pan American World Airways, (Bridgetown), 436-1854; (Grantley Adams Intl. Airport), 428-7632.
Wardair, (Grantley Adams Intl. Airport), 428-3131.

By Sea

Edward Teach (more commonly known as Blackbeard the pirate), Stede Bonnet, and Sam Lord were all Barbadians with one thing in common: piracy. Which makes it more than appropriate to travel to the island by ship. Unfortunately, most cruise lines only stop over at the recently expanded and renovated Port of Bridgetown for a day or two, with the exception of Cunard Line's two-week "Sail n' Stay" package that combines a week aboard the *Cunard Countess* with a week on land at the Cunard Paradise Beach Hotel. Ocean Cruise Lines offer fly/cruise packages which include a week at a selected island hotel and a week's luxury cruise of the Caribbean. Cruise lines (and their ships) that include the island on their schedule are:

Chandris Cruises, (*SS Amerikanis*), 212-586-8370.
Cunard Lines, (*Cunard Countess*), 212-880-7500.
Costa Cruises, (*The Daphne*), 1-800-462-6782.
Epirotiki Lines, (*SS Oceanos*), 212-599-1750.
Holland American Lines, (*SS Rotterdam*), 1-800-442-8171.
Ocean Cruises, (*Ocean Princess*), 305-764-3500; 1-800-556-8850.
Princess Cruises, (*Sun Princess*), 213-555-1770.
Royal Caribbean Lines, (*Nordic Prince*), 305-379-2601; 1-800-327-6700.
Sitmar Cruises, (*Fairwind*), 1-800-527-6000.

Windjammer Cruises, (*Mandalay*), 305-373-2090.
Sun Line, (*Stella Oceanis*), 212-397-6400; 1-800-872-6400.
Sea Goddess Cruises, (*Sea Goddess I*) 305-266-8988.

TRAVEL ADVISORIES

Immigration

No immunization certificates are required, except for travelers coming from certain African and South American countries who must possess yellow fever vaccination certificates. All visitors must present proof of citizenship—preferably a passport. Although residents of the United States and of Commonwealth countries need only show a birth certificate and photo i.d. (like a photo drivers license), a passport remains the ideal document, if for no other reason than it permits easy re-entry once home).

Commonwealth citizens may stay in Barbados for a period of six months without a visa, while U.S. citizens may stay for three months. To stay longer, application for extension must be made to the Chief Immigration Officer at Customs House, The Wharf, Bridgetown, telephone 426-9912, along with proof of ability to maintain financial support.

Visas are required for citizens of the following countries: South Africa, Albania, Bulgaria, the People's Republic of China, the Republic of China, Czechoslovakia, Hungary, North Korea, Poland, Romania, the U.S.S.R., East Germany, Yugoslavia, India and Pakistan. Immigration cards will be handed out on the plane and stamped on arrival. Be sure to retain it: you will be asked to present it on departure, along with a **$16 BDS departure tax** (cruise ship passengers are not required to pay this).

Customs

Barbadian customs officials are the first people you meet and their friendly, courteous behavior is your first indication of the overall island temperament. A new airport customs system which speeds passengers with nothing to declare through the arrivals hall was established in 1986. Meat and frozen foods are prohibited (without a permit from the Ministry of Agriculture), as are plants, flowers and fruits. And as in most countries, the import of firearms and ammunition as well as any form of narcotic drug is forbidden.

United States residents are allowed up to $400 worth of duty-free goods when returning home (if, they have been out of the country more than 48 hours), while Canadian residents can bring back up to $300 worth of goods (if out of the country for more than one week). Citizens of Great Britain and Germany are allowed certain amounts of cigarettes, perfumes, wines and liquors, which is similar to the restrictions imposed on citizens of Trinidad/Tobago and other Caribbean countries.

Pets are not allowed into the island, with the exception of those raised in the United Kingdom (or those which have spent six months quarantine there).

Currency

Visitors can bring in as much foreign currency as they can carry and both Canadian and U.S. dollars are honored in most major hotels and larger stores. In fact, the U.S. dollar, which is worth approximately twice the Barbadian dollar, is accepted throughout the island. Daily rates for other currency are printed in the local newspapers, as well as listed in banks. Unlike many countries, there's not much difference in the exchange rate offered by hotels and restaurants as compared to banks. Major credit cards and traveler's checks are accepted at many hotels (if not most), restaurants and shops.

GETTING ACQUAINTED

Climate

Boasting one of the world's best climates, Barbados was once a refuge for the wealthy and for years reigned as queen of Caribbean resorts. All secrets are eventually found out and Barbados—and its climate—is no exception. There has to be a good reason why thousands of people flock to its Caribbean and Atlantic beaches every winter—and one of the reason's is an average year-round temperature of 80 degrees (27c).

More than 3,000 hours of sunshine, tempered by gentle northeast trade winds, are recorded annually.

Temperatures range from 77.5 Fahrenheit (24c) in January to a high average of 81.1 (29c) in August and September. The lowest recorded temperature was 59 (15c) and the highest 95 (35c), giving Barbados one of the most pleasant climates in the world. The wettest months are September, October and November. However, showers are usually brief. Rainfall averages between 40 and 85 inches per year, with an average relative humidity between 57 and 74 percent.

Nights are cooler along the East coast, where the ocean winds keep up a constant blowing off the Atlantic. Evenings are generally cool all over the island, making excellent sleeping conditions a reward for all the activity (or non-activity) of another perfect Barbadian day.

Clothing

Light, casual, tropical wear is recommended year-round. And while casual is the general rule, Barbadians are a conservative people: bathing suits and bikinis are frowned on outside of the beach or swimming pool. Evenings can be slightly more formal (in the classy, resort-style sense), depending on the kind of hotel or restaurant visited. Men will find a jacket handy (and often requested), while women will find a long, flowery dress or stylish evening ensemble appropriate for those romantic nights out on the town. During the off-season summer months, everybody relaxes into an even more casual mode.

Tanning

No one wants to waste a vacation smothered in layers of Noxema cream or recuperating in an air-conditioned room. But the intensity of the island sun often takes alot of people by surprise. Instead of being tanned and glamorous, they look like they belong in an intensive care unit.

To avoid sunburn, it's best to lie out in the sun only during the early morning hours between 8 A.M. and 10 A.M., or in the late afternoon, between 4 A.M. and 6 A.M. An hour the first day, with ample use of sunblock cream (not oil, as this tends to cause blisters) is recommended for those who burn easily or prefer to build up a slower, longer-lasting tan.

Pests

Barbados is free of poisonous snakes (due to the large mongoose population), but does have minor nuisances like mosquitos and sand-flies. Mosquito coils and other devices are often provided by hotels, if not, try turning on the air-conditioner for a few moments before sleeping.

Sea-urchins are a common underwater hazard—look carefully before you step. And although it looks like the common crabapple, the manchineel apple tree which frequently hangs temptingly over West Coast beaches, is poisonous. If it's raining, even water dripping off the leaves onto your skin can cause painful blisters.

Common Sense

Barbados is no different from the rest of the world. If you leave stuff lying around, there's always a chance someone might take it (including another tourist). To stay on the safe side, lock your hotel room before going out and use the hotel's safety deposit box for extra cash or jewelry. It's also a good idea not to leave anything valuable on the beach when you swim—without asking someone to keep an eye on it.

Etiquette

Due to the islanders' innate sense of politeness (and perhaps because of the conservative British heritage), they expect visitors to behave as if they're guests. Do say "please" and "thank you." Don't order people—from waiters to banktellers to the boys who arrange your beach chairs—around. Also, do ask permission before taking anyone's picture. See "Photography."

Tipping

Tipping is both accepted and welcome—in Bajan slang, "tip" is said to be an acronym for "to insure promptness." Most restaurants and all hotels add a 10 percent service charge to the bill, but it's normal to leave 10 percent to 15 percent more. Hotel maids should be left the equivalent of $1 US per day and bellboys should be tipped at least 50 cents per bag. Airport porters expect the same (the equivalent of $1 BDS), while taxi drivers usually receive 10 percent of the fare.

Time Zones

North American time is between one and five hours behind Barbadian time. For example, Barbados is one hour ahead of New York (Eastern Standard Time). From April to October, Europe is five hours ahead; four hours ahead from November to March.

Business and Banking Hours

Most department stores and boutiques are open from 8 A.M. to 4 P.M. on weekdays, from 8 A.M. to 1 P.M. on Saturdays and closed on Sundays. Supermarkets are open for business from 8 A.M. to 6 P.M. from Monday through Wednesday, until 7 P.M. on Thursdays and Fridays and from 8 A.M. to 1 P.M. on Saturdays (with a few exceptions that remain open later). The main post office (in Cheapside, Bridgetown) is open Monday through Friday from 8 A.M. until 4:30 P.M. (closed Saturday and Sunday). Local branch hours are Monday from 8 A.M. until noon, Tuesday through Friday 8 A.M. to noon, 1 P.M. until 3:15 P.M.

All banks on the island (with the exception of Barclays International are open from 9 A.M. to 3 P.M. every weekday except for Friday, when the hours are 8 A.M. to 1 P.M. and 3 P.M. to 5:30 P.M. Barclays hours are from 8 A.M. to 3 P.M. Monday through Thursday, and 8 A.M. to 1 P.M. and 3 P.M. to 5:30 P.M. on Fridays. Main branches of the major banks are located on Broad Street, Bridgetown—with the exception of the Barbados National Bank on Fairchild Street. The following banking institutions have offices in Barbados: Barclays Bank International, Bank of Credit and Commerce International, Bank of Nova Scotia, Barbados Development Bank, Barbados National Bank, Canadian Imperial Bank of Commerce, Caribbean Commerical Bank, Chase Manhattan Bank and the Royal Bank of Canada.

Barclays, Broad Street (Bridgetown); Roebuck Street (Bridgetown).
Barbados National Bank, James Street (Bridgetown); Broad Street (Bridgetown).
Caribbean Commercial Bank, Broad Street (Bridgetown).
Chase Manhattan Bank, Broad Street (Bridgetown).

Holidays

Despite its off-season timing—or perhaps because of it—the annual summer **Crop Over Festival** is considered the island's most festive occasion, culminating with the carnival-like **Kadooment Day** parade on the first Monday in August. Even before Crop Over begins (at the end of the sugar cane crop harvest in July), calypso "tents" spring up in local schools and meeting halls, in preparation for the festival's big musical competition which ends with the crowning of a calypso King and Queen. Other official national holidays include New Year's Day (Jan. 1), Good Friday, Easter Monday and Whit Monday, May Day (May 1st), United Nations Day (first Monday in October), Independence Day (November 30), Christmas Day (December 25) and Boxing Day (December 26).

Electricity

The Barbados Light and Power Company supplies reliable electricity service throughout the island, at 110 volts A.C. and 50 cycles of electrical current. Some hotels also provide transformers for 220 A.C. equipment. Plugs on the island come in the form of two flat prongs (same as in the United States and Canada).

Photography

Be sure to ask permission before shooting portraits of local people—they'll appreciate the courtesy (not many folks like being considered a sort of visual souvenir) and it may lead to an interesting dialogue. Color film is the best way to capture the island's brilliant color contrasts and spectacular sunsets. Flash bulbs or units are a must if you're planning to capture impressions of popular night time entertainment spots. If you're serious about photography remember to bring your camera everywhere—particularly along some of the less-traveled roads. You may run into a gaggle of schoolgirls, prim and neat as a pin in ribbons and uniforms or a serious game of dominoes at a local rumshop.

Hurricanes

All over the Caribbean, children are taught the rhyme: "June too soon, July standby, August come it must, September ‾

remember, October all over," but in fact the hurricane season really starts in June and continues through October. Barbados, however, is lucky, in that most serious hurricanes have tended to pass just north of the island—sometimes by a very narrow margin indeed. Disastrous hurricanes struck the island in 1675, 1780 and 1831. Hurricane Janet, in 1955, was the most recent to hit the island with full force.

A hurricane is a concentrated area of low atmospheric pressure, starting its existance as a depression off the coast of Africa and then moving across the Atlantic, where it gathers strength and develops into a tropical storm before working up into a hurricane frenzy. To be officially considered a hurricane, winds must reach more than 74 miles per hour.

The government Meteorological Department (428-7101) tracks storms (with the assistance of the U.S. Hurricane Center in Miami) from the moment they begin off the African coast. At the beginning of each hurricane season, local newspapers publish information on precautions and emergency plans. Local radio and television issue warnings according to the hurricane's development and location. If there is a hurricane, stay away from low-lying coastal areas, remain indoors (or go to one of the island's official shelters), and stay tuned to your radio or television. Stocking a supply of batteries, canned food and bottled water is highly recommended.

Bajan Colloqualism

English may be the official language, but the island's African and old English heritage have left a language legacy that is distinctly Barbadian. The following is a short list of phrases:

Directions

Swing — turn
below — on the left
above — on the right

Telephones

can I borrow the phone? — may I use your phone?
who de body is? — who is it?
de body is I — it's me

General

bad — good (eg: "she likes him real bad")
break fives — shake hands
chupse — a noise that expresses irritation
cheese — a VIP, an important individual
cool out — relax
caffuffle — confusion
don't hag me — don't bother me
duppy umbrella — mushroom
fire rage — quarrel
hail — support
jump up — dance
mistress — anyone in charge of a household, a superior
onliest — only
shake hands — wave
sand side — beach
swizzle — cocktail
weather — bad weather
wunna — all of you

Sunsets

The best sunset view is from the island's western beaches. Wait until the reds, purples, oranges and pinks have faded—you may be lucky enough to spot the fabled "green flash" that's supposed to appear on the horizon—just as sun finally disappears. (If you notice the sunset is more spectacular than usual and that the sky has been reddish-colored all day, it's because of another local phenomena—fine red dust carried by the wind from the Sahara desert.)

Other Island Mysteries

Lovers of the occult will find there are some fine examples of the unexplainable in Barbados—from the legends about "Duppies," or spirits of the dead who are supposed to walk at night, to the mysterious "face in the window," which can be seen on a window of a Bay Street house. Legend says one of the house's earliest inhabitants crashed his face through the window as he died, and although the glass has been replaced many times, the shape and imprint of his face can still be seen. Even more mysterious is the Chase Vault in Christ Church Cemetary, where the Chase family coffins, encased in a sealed vault, were rearranged by an unseen hand. The church eventually had to bury each family member separately—but strange noises continue to be heard deep inside the now-empty vault.

A Marriage Made in Heaven

What could be more memorable than a barefoot wedding on a soft-sand beach, perhaps as the sun sets on the west coast and a tuk band plays rhythmically in the background? Barbados is an idyllic honeymoon spot, but also welcomes couples who really want a wedding to remember. All it takes is a six-day residency and an application for a marriage license ($50 U.S. at the Marine House in Hastings, Christ Church, 427-5420), plus a special stamp ($13 BDS) which can be purchased at any post office. It takes three days to apply for the license, after which the bride and groom have a choice of venues, from a tall-masted yacht to one of the island's many churches of varying denominations.

TOURIST INFORMATION

Tourist Board and Embassies

More than 400,000 people enjoy the island's hospitality each year, due in no small part to international marketing efforts by the Barbados Board of Tourism. Their professional staff can help plan your vacation by providing brochures describing activities, festivities and accommodation on the island, as well as available flights, cruises and tour packages. They also sponsor (in cooperation with the Barbados National Trust) an "Open House" program which takes visitors to some of the island's loveliest residences. For more information, contact The Barbados National Trust (426-2421) or the Board of Tourism's local and overseas offices listed in the Appendix.

In addition, the embassies, commissions and consulates of 20 countries are located in and around Bridgetown. See the Appendix for a list of addresses.

TRANSPORTATION

Island Flying

Due to the island's small size, there is no internal flight system. You can, however, tour Barbados by air through a number of local operators, including Aero Services (428-8628/9) from Grantley Adams Intl. Airport. Jaunts to the nearby Grenadine Islands can be arranged through L.I.A.T.

Buses

Commuting by bus is one of the best ways to really get to know the people. The buses are blue with a yellow strip and cost 75 BDS cents to get anywhere on the island. All buses lead to or from Bridgetown, except for the Bathsheba to Speightstown and the Oistins to Speightstown routes. Major bus routes and numbers to keep in mind include number 12 to Sam Lord's Castle and the Crane Beach Hotel; number 13a to St. Christopher via the South Coast; number 1 to Speightstown via the West Coast; number 6 to Bathsheba, via a scenic country route; number 4 to Harrison's Cave; and numbers 7 and 7a to Bowmanston and Sargeant Street, respectively, via Gun Hill Station.

Main bus terminals in Bridgetown are located at Fairchild Street, The Lower Green Bus Stand, Pelican Stand and River Stand.

Rental Cars

Besides the way Barbadians use their car horns (frequently), the biggest complaint visitors have about island driving is getting lost. Even residents have trouble finding such scenic landmarks as Turner's Hall Woods, because of the winding network of unmarked roads. Still, driving is one of the best ways to see the island (losing your way just adds to the adventure). Just remember to stay on the left side of the road (and take care when driving at night). The speed limit is 60 kph, except on the smooth Spring Garden Highway between Bridgetown and St. James, where it's 80 kph.

Any temporary resident or visitor can drive using an international driver's license. If you have a valid license from your country of origin, all you need is a $30 BDS permit (a newly-instigated system allows permit pick-up at the time of car rental;

otherwise it's available at the airport, the Central Police Station or police stations on the south and west coasts, as well as the Ministry of Transport and Works (429-2191). Major rental agencies have desks at the airport and at many larger hotels, with some of the larger firms (such as Hertz, 428-7878; and Avis, 425-1388) also located in or near Bridgetown. There are excellent local firms such as Sunny Isle, in Worthing (428-8009), Courtesy, in St. Michael (426-5871), Jones Garage Ltd. (426-5030), and Sunset Crest Rental, in St. James (432-1482). Daily rates run from $65 to $75 BDS per day or $300 to $315 BDS per week for the Australian-style Mini-Moke; $85 BDS per day for a four or five-passenger car ($350 to $400 BDS per week). Motorcycles can also be rented, for rates starting at $35 BDS per day for three days or $200 BDS per week. Bicycles cost $10 BDS per day or $60 per week.

Taxis

They're not metered (although plans are optimistically underway to install meters), but the normal rate for a trip from the airport to the west coast is between $27 BDS and $42 BDS; to the south coast from between $13 and $20 BDS.

Sightseeing trips can also be arranged by taxi, but it involves bargaining with drivers. The average fare for an all-day, around-the-island tour is $150 BDS for five hours, carrying between four to six passengers. The general rule of thumb for rental rates is $2.25 BDS per hour, with waiting time priced between $7 and $8 BDS per hour. From Bridgetown to Bathsheba on the east coast, for example, is $38 BDS; to Sam Lord's Castle in St. Philip on the southeast coast is $33 BDS; to the west coast beaches off St. Lawrence is $13 BDS.

To find a taxi, look for the letter "Z" (usually on the license plate). They line up outside hotels (as well as central points in Bridgetown) or ask your hotel to call one for you.

Mailboat and Ferry

Adventurous travelers may wish to explore neighboring islands by booking passage on the inter-island cargo-passenger ship (Eric Hassell & Son, Ltd., 426-5068) that sails from Bridgetown's Careenage every other week. Alternatively, call Carribbean Safari Tours (427-5100) or Tropic Air (428-8062) to find out about flights to

nearby Union Island, where a C.S.Y. (Caribbean Sailing Yachts) charter departs for further exploration. Even more challenging is to fly to St. Vincent and catch the passenger ferry—carrying a melange of people, chickens and mail—through the Grenadines.

L.I.A.T. also offers one day flights (returning to Barbados the same evening) to St. Vincent, Grenada, Trinidad & Tobago and Martinique.

ACCOMMODATION

Within 166 square miles, there are more than 174 hotels, apartment-hotels and guesthouses—of which about 86 are currently registered with the Barbados Hotel Association. A new program for classifying properties from one to five stars is expected to take effect late in 1986. A selection of hotels, listed by parish and chosen at random (with prices and amenities subject to change), is listed in the Appendix. An alternative to dwelling in a hotel, however, is to rent a house or villa.

Villas

Rock stars, movie stars, politicians and other celebrities flock to Barbados. But you don't usually see them. Why? Because they've discovered the secret of a "get away from it all" vacation—a private house or villa, complete with beachfront palm trees or tropical garden, where (with the help of a live-in or occasional staff) the pressures and troubles of high-powered city living literally melt away under caressing trade winds. All over the island—from the hillside ambience of Sandy Lanes Estates in St. James to the secluded hideaways of St. Philip—there are villas, ranging in size from one to six-bedroom, designed to soothe both the body and soul.

Besides allowing visitors the freedom to choose their own menus (by shopping in local markets for such delicacies as mango, passion fruit and breadfruit), living in a house is the best way to truly experience the island lifestyle. Prices range from $350 to $10,000 per week, depending on size and location. Daily rates during the low season (from mid-April to early December) range from approximately $90 to $450 per day, and from $100 to $1,000 per day during the peak season (from mid-December through early April) depending on the size of the house. Reservations can be made through local firms such as Alleyne, Aguilar & Altman, Ltd. in St. James (432-0840); Ronald Stoute & Sons Ltd. in St. Philip (432-6800); Bajan Services in St. Peter (422-2758/2618); the Board of Tourism or your local travel agent.

COMMUNICATIONS

Postal Services

There are post offices in all 11 parishes, as well as the ultra-modern **General Post Office** in Cheapside, Bridgetown (436-4800), which houses the island's main post office, parcel post and registration/money order departments. The local letter rate is 25 cents BDS, cards are 15 cents. Rates to the rest of the Caribbean are 50 cents for airmail, 45 cents for postcards.

Overseas airmail rates are:

To the United States and Canada, 65 cents for airmail; 45 cents for postcards;

To Great Britain and Europe, 75 cents for letters; cards and airgrams 50 cents;

To Asia, Africa, Australia and the Middle East, $1 BDS for letters, 55 cents for cards and airgrams.

Telecommunications

The Barbados Telephone Company Ltd. operates island-wide service that is unusually reliable, with the occasional exception. Overseas calls can be dialed directly to North America and Europe, for a minimum three-minute charge of $17.82 BDS (local calls are free). The area code for Barbados is 809.

Telegrams may be sent through your hotel operator or from the post office and cost 60 cents BDS per word (minimum of seven words) to North America and 80 cents to the United Kingdom and Europe. The Barbados External Telecommunication Ltd. (429-4852) is open between 7 A.M. and 9 P.M. daily and can provide additional information on telegram rates, well as telexes and other communication systems.

NEWS MEDIA

Press

The Advocate and the tabloid-ish *Nation* are the two daily papers. The *Nation* also appears on weekends as the *Sunday Sun*, which includes the *Pelican* magazine.

The Visitor is a bi-monthly newspaper filled with useful information on what to see and where to go, available free of charge at hotels, restaurants and shops. Also for tourists, the newsletter *What's On* appears monthly and the Barbados Advocate-published *Sun Seeker* comes out every other Thursday.

Radio and Television

Barbados is served by one television station, **Caribbean Broadcasting Corporation**, or CBC, which is government-owned and telecasts (in color) on Channel 3. Because CBC-TV has an agreement with the USA-based Cable News Network (CNN), world news broadcasts can be viewed Monday to Friday from 6 A.M. to 10 A.M., Saturday and Sunday from 9 A.M. to 1 P.M. Regular program hours are from 5 P.M. to 11:45 P.M. Monday to Friday and 1 P.M. to 12:30 A.M. Saturday and Sunday.

There are four radio stations on the island, including the **Barbados Rediffusion Service**, a wired cable service available at some hotels (and which operates the daily "Voice of Barbados" program on 790-KHZ—an excellent source of local information and events); the **Barbados Broadcasting Service**, which airs continuous music and news on 90.7 FM; and the **Caribbean Broadcasting Corporation** (CBC) on 900 AM MW and 98 FM.

Books and Magazines

The Cloister Bookstore and the Wayfarer Bookstore in Bridgetown are two of the largest on the island; the latter has branches along the west coast. This is where you can find selections of books on Barbadian history, culture, music, cooking and a wealth of other subjects—including enough fiction and non-fiction to satisfy an appetite for a good beach reading.

The Bajan, a monthly magazine with news and features about the island, is also sold here, as well as at supermarkets and some hotels. *Bim* is an excellent local literary magazine which appears infrequently and features articles and stories by Barbadian and other Caribbean writers.

There's an excellent library at the Barbados Museum open Monday to Friday, (427-0201), as well as a good, second-hand bookstore on Bay Street.

Bridgetown also has a spacious, well-run library (founded by Andrew Carnegie in 1904), located on Coleridge Street. There are seven other local libraries where visitors can take out books for a returnable fee of $20 BDS.

Video and TV Rentals

Radio Shack (429-8702), the Video Connection (427-4170), and Video King (429-5328), among other shops, offer color TV video machines and seven tapes of your choice for an average price of $125 U.S. per week, including delivery.

HEALTH AND EMERGENCIES

Today's travelers are luckier than George Washington, whose 18th-Century visit literally scarred him for life (due to the smallpox he contracted). As previously mentioned, the island enjoys one of the world's healthiest climates—and some of the purest water (pumped up from underground coral recesses). But vacations have a way of bringing out the dormant illness in all of us. Everything from minor afflictions like insect bites or sea urchin spines to motorbike accidents are treated free of charge at island health facilities, which include eight health centers and 10 government clinics. General and emergency care is provided at **Queen Elizabeth Hospital** in St. Michael (436-6450).

It's always best to check with your own physician before traveling, however, and stock up on any necessary prescription drugs, such as sleeping pills or antibiotics.

It's also a good idea to bring along an extra pair of prescription glasses.

Emergency Phone Numbers

Coast Guard	427-8819
Ambulance	426-1113
Fire	113
Police	112
Light and Power Company	436-9000

Telephone Services

Directory Assistance	119
Telephone Repair Service	114
Operator and over-seas call assistance	0
Telephone Company	429-5050

Useful Telephone Numbers

American Express Travel Service Representative	436-6543
Customs at Airport	428-8061
Airport Immigration	428-7101
General Post Office	436-4800
Immigration Department	426-1011
Barbados Chamber of Commerce	426-0747
Barbados Hotel Association	426-5041
Barbados Board of Tourism	427-2623
Caribbean Broadcasting Corporation	429-2041
National Library Service	426-3981

DINING OUT

Sampling local cuisine, for the adventurous, or enjoying a gourmet meal, for the sophisticated, is all part of going to another country. Barbados has restaurants featuring everything from Chinese to Italian to typically Bajan cuisine. National dishes to try include the ubiquitous (and delicious) flying fish—either fried, grilled or stuffed; hot salt fish cakes; pickled breadfruit (a unique vegetable dish you won't find at home); cake-like conkies, made of pumpkin, coconut, cornmeal and raisins steamed in banana leaves; and pepperpot, a stew so well-seasoned that it literally used to be passed like an heirloom from generation to generation.

The grander hotels offer international cuisine prepared under the skilled direction of French chefs, or for contrast, try a

Saturday night stroll down **Baxter's Road** in Bridgetown for a sensory assault by numerous roadside food stands emitting culinary rays of savory and exotic spices. Wisely, so far, Barbados has refused entry to the Golden Arches, but it does have its share of fast food outlets, including Kentucky Fried Chicken, the Barbados Pizza Hut, and Chefette, a local favorite for inexpensive pizza, chicken and even steak. A partial list of island restaurants is included in the Appendix.

SHOPPING

The price-conscious will find the island to be a treasure trove of duty-free bargains as well as local handicrafts. Shops like Cave Shepherd's, C.F. Harrison, Da Costa's and Correia's (the latter for fine jewelry) on Broad Street in downtown Bridgetown, feature everything from Liberty print fabrics to Scandinavian silver and French perfume. **Mall 34** and the **Norman Centre** (also on Broad Street) are two of the best enclosed malls—air-conditioned for additional browsing comfort. Other established Bridgetown stores (many of which have west coast branches) include The Royal Shop, for jewelry and watches; and Louis Bayley, for jewelry, watches and crystal.

The best of Barbados Ltd. shops (at Skyway Plaza, Sam Lord's Castle in St. Philips and the Sandpiper Hotel among other locations) feature collections of Barbadian handicrafts and clothing. Other hotels (such as Sandy Lane and Glitter Bay) boast small, exclusive boutiques featuring the styles of local and overseas designers. Worth a look is the Petticoat Lane Boutique, located next to the Waterfront Cafe on The Wharf in Bridgetown's Careenage area. It's small but well-stocked with a colorful array of fanciful lace and daring evening dresses by local designer Carol Cadogan. Try Simon's Shop next to Giggles Beach Bar and Restaurant in St. Peter for another selection locally designed, sophisticated styles.

Handicrafts range from handwoven straw mats, hats and baskets to batik fabrics, smocked or embroidered children's dresses, and coral and shell jewelry. Be sure to take a look at Barbadian pottery as well—it retains a lingering Arawak Indian heritage combined with both African and European influences. Interesting leather work by local Rastafarians is on display at the Temple Yard off Princess Alice Highway, as well as at different markets and beachfront stalls around the island. The best places to find a comprehensive collection of handicrafts are the **Pelican Village** stalls, off Princess Alice Highway near the Deep Water Harbour (on Bridgetown's northern outskirts) or the **Handicraft Emporium** on Harbour Drive.

Sugar may no longer be king on Barbados (by the 1970s, tourism had usurped its throne), but the island rum is definitely royal—and worth bringing home. Mount Gay and Cockspur are two of the most popular brands and can be purchased (along with other liquors) at duty-free shops around the island. Falernum, a rum-based syrup used in mixed drinks and cooking, is a Barbadian specialty that makes a tasty and unusual souvenir. And although it may be hard to lug home, the local Banks Beer is considered by those who know to be among the Caribbean's best!

Any goods purchased at duty-free shops in town (duty-free shops are also located in the airport) can be packaged and sent to the airport or harbour to await your departure. Make sure you allow ample time (usually two days) for delivery—then simply collect your purchases from the Chamber of Commerce in the airport's departure hall.

CULTURAL ACTIVITIES

Museums and Galleries

The best place to learn about the country's rich and complex history is at the **Barbados Museum and Historical Society**, housed in the former British Military Detention Barracks, a mile from Bridgetown. The museum building dates back to 1820, but the history depicted inside goes back to the early 17th Century and before, a time when the island was inhabited by Arawak Indians (before its "discovery" by Portuguese and English sailors). The old jail cells now house exhibits on local archaeology, geology, zoology and other subjects, including whole rooms that recreate plantation life of the last century. There is an art gallery (with changing exhibits), a children's gallery and a museum shop that sells prints and crafts by local artists. The museum is open from Monday to Saturday, 9 A.M. to 6 P.M. Admission is $4 BDS for adults and $1 BDS for children.

Bajan culture can also be appreciated at several art galleries, most of which are located in the Bridgetown and Deep Harbour area. A number of fine Barbadian artists are represented at the **Barbados Arts Council Gallery** (Pelican Village), as well as the **National Cultural Foundation Gallery** at Queens Park House. **The Talma Mill Art Gallery** (in Christ Church) is under the direction of artist Norma Talma, specializes in lyrical, pastel hand-made paper collages with Barbadian themes.

Other galleries worth visiting include the **Devonish Gallery** in Pelican Village, featuring the pottery work and sculpture of Courtney Devonish; the **Studio Art Gallery**, on Fairchild Street; the **Bay Gallery**, on Bay Street (by appointment only); and **Dayrell's Gallery** in St. George (437-5235).

Theaters, Dance and Music

Barbados has a serious tradition of music and performing art (which is described earlier in this book) dating back to the days of the first African slaves. Popular musical expressions such as calypso and folk songs, steel bands and tuk bands, find an excellent outlet during the four major island festivals—**Crop Over** (in July and August); the **Holetown Festival** (at the end of February); the **Oistens Fish Festival** (Easter weekend) and the **National Festival of the Creative Arts** (NIFCA), which takes place in October and November. All these occasions allow the visitor an opportunity to experience the drama, dance and music that truly express Barbadian culture.

During the rest of the year, there's always a chance you might be lucky enough to hear Mighty Gabby, a legendary folk and calypso singer; the Barbados All Star Steel Orchestra; and the Merrymen, arguably the most popular band on the island. Eddy Grant, the London-educated Guyanese musician who settled on the island several years ago, has his own recording studio called "Blue Wave" that attracts such internationally-known recording stars as Sting for album sessions. Other well-known musicians—Elton John, Rod Stewart and Mick Jagger among them—have long found Barbados a source of inspiration as well as relaxation. And while it's hardly rock and roll, the Barbados Police Band (founded in 1880) is one of the island's most popular musical attractions. When they give a concert, it's news and is listed in the local newspapers.

Dance is an increasingly vibrant part of life in Barbados, and visitors can enjoy the graceful expertise of the Barbados Dance Theatre during their twice-weekly performances of "1627 and all that sort of thing," held at the Barbados Museum. The Country Theatre Workshop (who often perform at Marriott's Sam Lord's Castle), the Rontanta Dancers and Bim International are other whose shows are worth watching out for.

There's an abundance of theater production groups, including the Green Room Players and Stage One, both of which perform works by contemporary West Indian playwrights. "Barbados, Barbados," a humorous, somewhat bawdy song and dance rendition of Barbadian history, is performed every Tuesday night at Balls, an old sugar boiling house outside of Bridgetown.

NIGHTLIFE

Nightime is a time for celebration, whether you're embarking on an evening "round-the-island with rum and calypso" cruise aboard the *Jolly Roger*, marveling at the fire-eaters performing at the Plantation Restaurant, Island Inn or just cruising Baxter's Road on a Saturday night.

Dancing to the beat of local bands like the Merrymen, Spice, Jade or Private Eye can be enjoyed at a wide variety of nightclubs, some of the best of which include the **Warehouse** (above the Waterfront Cafe); **Mr. Bojangles** on Lower Bay street in Bridgetown; **Club Miliki** at Heywood's Resort in St. Peter; the **Rendezvous Room** at Rockley's Resort in Christ Church; **After Dark**, in St. Lawrence Gap, Christ Church; the **Village Nightclub** at Barbados Beach Village in St. James; and **The Carlisle**, an open-air beachfront club on Upper Bay Street that features live music, cookouts and low prices. A warning about their door policy: not everyone gets in.

There are rumored to be more than a thousand neighborhood rumshops on the island, not including the very English-style **Ship Inn**, at St. Lawrence Gap in Christ Church, considered one of the liveliest pubs in Barbados; **The Windsurfer**, at the Barbados Windsurfing Club in Christ Church;

and the **Waterfront Cafe**, a popular Bridgetown hang out.

Almost all the larger hotels offer regular live entertainment combined with dinner and dancing, including **Marriott's Sam Lord's Castle** in St. Philip; **Glitter Bay** in St. Peter, the Hilton's **Flambeau Bar** in St. Michael, **The Colony Club** in St. James and **Heywood's. Club Xanadu**, at the Ocean View Hotel in Christ Church, presents occasional professional dinner theatre revues, as well as simple cheek-to-cheek dancing. The **Bel Air Jazz Club** on Bay Street in Bridgetown, attracts a late-night crowd to its all-night jazz sessions—although lately it's been open infrequently.

SPORTS

Bajans are sports-mad—to the point where cricket has become a sort of national religion (it's even played on the beach). Followers reach a fever-pitch of excitement during the annual **Shell Shield Competition**, which usually takes place in January. The Barbados Turf Club attracts flocks of eager spectators (and bettors) to its exciting Saturday horse races at The Garrison Savannah in St. Michael, during the two seasons that stretch from January to May and July through November. A lazy game of dominoes under the trees, road tennis—played with cricket bats, and goat racing—on the beach—are uniquely Barbadian pastimes that can be enjoyed as spectator or participant. A list of more mainstream sports (and some places to find them) follows:

Golf

Heywoods, St. Peter.
Rockley Resort Hotel, Christ Church.
Sandy Lane Hotel Golf Club, St. James.

Tennis

Casuarina Beach Club, Christ Church.
Crane Beach Hotel, St. Philip.
Cunard Paradise Beach, St. Michael.
Ginger Bay Hotel and Beach Club, St. Philip.
Heywoods, St. Peter.
Paragon Tennis Club, Brittons Hill, St. Michael.
Rockley Resort Hotel, Christ Church.
Sandy Lane Hotel, St. James.

Southwinds Hotel and Beach Club, Christ Church.
Sunset Crest Club, St. James.

Hiking

The Barbados National Trust, St. Michael.
The Outdoors Club of Barbados, St. Michael.

Horseback Riding

Country Corral Riding Stables, St. James.
Sunbury Stables, St. Philip.
Ye Olde Congo Road Stables, St. Philip.
Brighton Stables, St. Michael.

Squash

Barbados Squash Club, Hastings, Christ Church.
Casuarina Beach Club, Christ Church.
Heywoods, St. Peter.
Rockley Resort Hotel, Christ Church.
Sea Breeze Hotel, Christ Church.

Polo

Barbados Polo Club, St. James.
Brighton Stables, St. Michael.

Water Skiing

Blue Reef Water Sports, St. James.
Jolly Roger Water Sports, St. James.
Willie's Water Sports, Paradise Beach Hotel, St. Michael.

Windsurfing

Club Mistral, Christ Church.
Jolly Roger Water Sports, St. James.

Scuba Diving and Snorkeling

Dive Boat Safari, St. James.
The Dive Shop, Hilton Hotel, St. James.
Divi St. James Hotel, St. James.
Les Wotton's Watersports, St. James.
Willie's Water Sports, Paradise Beach Hotel, St. Michael.

Sailing

Jolly Roger Water Sports, St. James.
Willie's Water Sports, Paradise Beach Hotel, St. Michael.

Deep Sea Fishing

Blue Jay Charters, St. James.
Jolly Roger Water Sports, St. James.
Pakis Water Sports, St. Michael.

FOREIGN INVESTMENT

In recent years, Barbados has begun a structured campaign to attract foreign investors. Traditionally conservative, the government is now actively seeking to capitalize on its reputation for political stability, in an effort to capture a greater share of the overseas investment market.

Advantages for would-be manufacturers include full exemption from corporate taxes for ten years, exemption on all import duties for parts, materials and production machinery, and unrestricted repatriation of capital profits.

Industrial and Export Incentives

The government-sponsored **Barbados Industrial Development Corporation** (IDC) is committed to continuous planning schemes for industrial growth—in particular to attracting a larger segment of the overseas investment market—with an emphasis on Data processing Firms. Under the last decade's **International Business Companies** Act, overseas firms that do not engage in local trade or investment enjoy between one and two and a half percent annual taxation rate. In addition, local regulations regarding offshore banking, foreign ship representation, exempt insurance and foreign sales corporations have been eased in order to encourage the island's growing reputation as a stable, international financial center. Low office and industrial space rental rates contribute to the government's overseas industry incentives.

By 1985, exports of Barbados-manufactured goods had increased by more than 40 percent in a five-year period, with North America and Puerto Rico accounting for the largest market sector, followed by CARICOM (Caribbean Community and Common Market) and the EEC (European Economic Community), led by Great Britain.

The Barbados Export Promotion Corporation was established in 1979 in order to assist the nation's manufacturing section in penetrating new foreign markets and improve overall export performance. This is done through various schemes planned by the corporation's Board of Directors, which includes such services as market research, export incentive grants and contacts originating from their overseas offices in New York, Trinidad/Tobago, Nassau and Puerto Rico.

Meetings and Conventions: A New Market

In 1984, Barbados became the second Caribbean nation to sign a mutual tax agreement with the United States, under the Caribbean Basin Initiative. Among other advantages, the agreement allows U.S. taxpayers to deduct expenses incurred while attending on-island business seminars, conventions or meetings. In the 1970s tourism accounted for almost half the GDP—and the current government (under Prime Minister Errol Barrow) sees the agreement as a way to increase hotel bookings as well as attract future investors.

Industrial Development Corporation

Potential foreign investors are advised to obtain information and assistance from the **Barbados Industrial Development Corporation**, 800 Second Avenue, New York, N.Y. 10017, (212) 867-6420.

FURTHER READING

History and Politics

Alleyne, Warren, *Historic Houses of Barbados*; Bridgetown: Barbados National Trust.

Campbell, P.F., *The Church in Barbados in the 17th Century*; St. Michael: Barbados Museum and Historical Society, 1982.

Duncan, Neville C., *Women and Politics in Barbados, 1948-1981*; Cave Hill: Institute of Social and Economic Research, University of the West Indies (Barbados), 1983.

Handler, Jerome S., *Plantation Slavery in Barbados*; Cambridge: Harvard University Press, 1976.

Harlow, Vincent T., *History of Barbados, 1625-1685*; Negro University Press, 1926.

Hoyos, F.A., *Barbados: A History from Amerindians to Independence*; London: Macmillan Caribbean, 1978.

Hoyos, F.A., *Builders of Barbados*; London: Macmillan Caribbean.

Hoyos, F.A., *Grantley Adams and the*

Social Revolution; London: Macmillan Caribbean.

Kortright, Davis, *Cross and Crown in Barbados: Caribbean Political Religion in the Late 19th Century*; P. Lang Publishers, 1983.

Levy, Claude, *Emancipation, Sugar and Federalism*; Gainesville: University Press, 1980.

Ligon, Richard, *A True and Exact History of the Island of Barbados (1647)*; London: Frank Cass & Co. Ltd., 1970.

Poyen, John, *History of Barbados: From the First Discovery of the Island in the Year 1605, Till the Accession of Lord Seaforth (1801)*; London: Bibio Dist., 1971.

Sanders, Joanne, *Barbados Records: Wills and Administrations*; Sanders Historical Publications, 1979.

Schomburgh, Sir Robert, *The History of Barbados*; 1971.

Tree, Ronald, *A History of Barbados*; New York: Beekman; London: Fletcher and Son, 1972.

Watson, K., *The Civilised Island of Barbados, A Social History 1750-1860*; Bridgetown: Caribbean Graphics.

Natural History

Barker, Leslie H., *The Geology and Mineral Resource Assessment of the Island of Barbados*; St. Michael: Barbados Government Print Office, 1981.

Hughes, Griffith, *Natural History of Barbados (1756)*; Ayer Co. Publishers, 1971.

Photographic

LaBrucherie, Roger, *A Barbados Journey*; Imágenes Press, 1979.

La Brucherie, Roger, *Images of Barbados*; California: Imágenes Press, 1979.

Sports

Bell, G., *Sir Garfield Sobers*; Nelson Caribbean.

Cozier, Tony (ed.), *West Indies Cricket Annual*; Barbados: Caribbean Communications, (published yearly).

Fiction

Braithwaite, Edward, *Mother Poem*; Oxford: New York: Oxford University Press, 1977.

Braithwaite, Edward, *Sun Poem*; Oxford: New York: Oxford University Press, 1982.

Callender, Timothy, *How Music Came to the Ainchan People*; St. Michael, Barbados: 1979.

Drayton, Geoffrey, *Christopher*; London: Secker & Warburg, Collins, 1961.

Fowler, Robert, *Spoils of Eden*; New York: Dodd Mead, 1985.

Hutchinson, Lionel, *Man from the People*; London: Collins, 1969.

Kellman, Tony, *Black Madonna Poems*; Bridgetown: 1975.

Jackman, Oliver, *Saw The House in Half*; Washington, D.C.: Howard University Press, 1974.

Jackson, Carl, *East Wind in Paradise*; London: New Beacon Books Ltd., 1981.

Lamming, George, *The Emigrants*; London: Allison & Busby, 1980.

Lamming, George, *Of Age and Innocence*; London: Allison & Busby: 1981.

Lamming, George, *In the Castle of My Skin*; London: Schocken, 1983.

Lamming, George, *The Pleasure of Exile*; London: Allison & Busby: Schocken, 1984.

Small, Jonathan, *The Pig-Sticking Season: Jamaica Poems, 1985*; Bridgetown: 1966.

General

Callender, Jean H., *Barbadian Society, Past and Present*; Cave Hill: Main Library, University of the West Indies (Barbados), 1981.

Callender, Jean H. *Barbadian Society, Past and Present*; Cave Hill: Main Library, University of the West Indies (Barbados), 1981.

Collymore, Frank A., *Notes for a Glossary of Words and Phrases of Barbadian Dialect*; Bridgetown 1955.

Dann, Graham, *Quality of Life in Barbados*; Macmillan Caribbean, 1984.

Fisher, Lawrence E., *Colonial Madness: Mental Health in the Barbadian Social Order*; New Jersey: Rutgers University Press, 1985.

Goodridge, Sehon, *Facing the Challenge of Emancipation: A Study of the Ministry of William Hart Coleridge, First Bishop of Barbados, 1824-1842*; Bridgetown: Cedar Press, 1981.

Hoyos, F.A., *Barbados, Our Island Home*; London: Macmillan Caribbean.

Hill, Barbara (ed. Henry Fraser), *Historic Churches of Barbados*; Bridgetown: Art Heritage Publishers, 1984.

Hoyos, F.A., *Barbados: The Visitors Guide*; London: Macmillan Caribbean, 1982.

Jackson, Carl, *East Wind in Paradise*; London: New Beacon Books, 1981.

Joefield-Napier, Wallace, *The Demand for*

Imports: The Case Of Barbados 1954-1970; Jamaica: Institute of Social and Economic Research, University of the West Indies, 1982.

Kent, David, *Barbados and America*; Arlington, Va.: CM Kent, 1980.

Lynch, Bruce G., *Barbados: A Smiling Island*; Brown Books, 1975.

Marshall, Trevor, *Folk Songs of Barbados*; Barbados: Cedar Press, 1981.

Worrell, DeLisle, *The Economy of Barbados, 1946-1980*; Bridgetown: Central Bank of Barbados, 1982.

APPENDIX

Accommodations

All hotels in Barbados add an 8 percent government accommodations tax, as well as the service charges (usually 10 percent) indicated below:

Abbreviations for Hotel Facilities and Charges

AC — air conditioned
BE — beach
(N)B — near beach
BP — beauty parlor
B/S (P) — bath/shower (private)
CS — coffee shop
FI — fishing
GO — golf
GR — games room
GM — gym
KI — kitchenette
NC — nightclub/disco
RE — restaurant
RM — room service
RS — resort shops
SA — sailing
SC — scuba
SH — shuffleboard
SK — skiing
SN — snorkeling
SM — supermarket
SP — swimming pool
SQ — squash
TE — tennis
TEL — telephone in every room

Bridgetown

Moderate

Grand Beach Bay Resort, P.O. Box 639 (426-0888); 138 rms; AC, BE, B (P), CS, FI, RE, RM, SA, SC, SN, SP, TE, TEL. 10% service.

Christ Church

Moderate to Expensive

Casuarina Beach Club, St. Lawrence Gap (428-3600); 64 rms; AC, BE, B(P), CS, FI, KI, RE, SA, SP, SQ, TE, TEL. 10% service.

Best Western Sandy Beach, Worthing (428-9033); AC, BE, B(P), CS, FI, KI, RE, RS, SA, SC, SN, SP, TEL. 10% service.

Rockley Resort and Beach Club, Golf Club Rd., Worthing (427-5890); 220 rms; AC, (N)B, B(P), CS, FI, GR, GO, KI, NC, RE, RS, SM, SP, TE, TEL. 10% service.

Southern Palms Beach Club, St. Lawrence (428-7171); 156 rms; AC, BE, B/S (P), CS, FI, KI, NC, RE, RM, RS, SA, SC, SN, SP, TE, TEL. 10% service.

South Winds Beach Hotel, St. Lawrence Gap (428-7181); 156 rms; AC, BE, B/S (P), CS, FI, KI, NC, RE, RM, RS, SA, SC, SN, TE, TEL. 10% service.

Ocean View Hotel, Hastings, Christ Church (427-7821); 36 rms; AC, BE, B/S (P), CS, NC, RE, RM, TEL. 10% service.

St. James

Expensive

Coral Reef Club, (432-2372); 75 rms; AC, BE, B(P), B/S (P), FI, KI, RE, RM, SA, SC, SH, SN, SP. 10% service.

Colony Club, Porters (432-2335); 76 rms; AC, BE, B(P), B/S (P), FI, RE, RM, RS, SA, SH, SN, SP, TEL. 10% service.

Glitter Bay, Porters (432-4111); rms; AC, BE, B(P), B/S (P), FI, RE, SA, SC, SK, SN, SM, SP, TEL. 10% service.

Sandy Lane Hotel, (432-1311); 118 rms; AC, BE, BP, B/S (P), CS, FI, GO, RE, RM, RS, SA, SC, SH, SK, SP, TE, TEL. 10% service.

Moderate to Expensive

Divi St. James, (432-7842); 131 rms; AC, BE, B/S (P), GM, KI, RE, RS, SA, SC, SN, SP, TEL. 10% service.

Sandpiper Inn, (422-2251); 20 rms; BE, AC, B/S (P), CS, KI, TE, FI, RE, RM, RS, SA, SC, SN, SP, SK, TEL. 10% sevice.

Coconut Creek Club Hotel, (432-0803); 49 rms; BE, AC, B/S(P), CS, KI, TE, FI, RE, RM, RS, SA, SC, SN, SP, SK, TEL. 10% service.

Tamarind Cove Hotel, Paynes Bay (432-

1332); 86 rms; AC, BE, B(P), RE, RS, SA, SP, TE, TEL. 10% service.

Teasure Beach Hotel, Paynes Bay (432-1346); 27 rms; AC, BE, B/S (P), RE, RS, SA, SP, TE, TEL. 10% service.

St. Michael

Expensive

Hilton International, Needhams Point (426-0200); 184 rms; AC, BE, B/S (P), CS, FI, GR, GM, RE, RM, RS, SA, SC, SK, SN, SP, TE, TEL. 10% service.

Inexpensive

Island Inn Hotel, Garrison (436-6393); 22 rms; AC, (N)B, CS, RE, RM.

St. Peter

Expensive

Cobblers Cove Hotel, (442-2291); 38 rms; AC, BE, B(P), FI, KI, RE, RM, RS, SA, SC, SK, SN, TEL. 10% service.

Moderate to Expensive

Heywoods, (442-4900); 300 rms; AC, BE, B/S (P), B(P), CS, FI, GO, KI, NC, RE, RM, RS, SA, SC, SK, SN, SP, SQ, TE, TEL. 10% service.

Inexpensive

Tides Inn, Gibbes (442-2403); AC, (N) B, B (P), KI, RE, RM. 10% service.

St. Philip

Expensive

Ginger Bay Beach Hotel, Crane (423-5810); 16 rms; AC, BE, B/S (P), FI, KI, RE, RM, SA, SN, SP, TE, TEL.

Marriott's Sam Lord's Hotel, (423-7350); 259 rms; AC, BE, B/S (P), GR, GM, RE, RM, RS, SP, TE, TEL. 10% service.

Moderate

Crane Beach Hotel and Beach Club, Crane (423-6220); 25 rms; BE, B(P), FI, KI, RE, RM, RS, SA, SC, SP, TE.

APARTMENT HOTELS

Christ Church

Moderate to Inexpensive

Asta Apartment Hotel, Palm Beach, Hastings (427-2541); 60 rms; AC, BE, B(P), CS, GR, KI, RE, RS, SM, SP, TEL.

Carib Blue Apartments, 60 Dover Terrace (428-2290); AC, BE, B(P), KI, RE. 5% service.

St. Lawrence Apartments, St. Lawrence Gap (428-5070); 42 rms; AC, BE, B(P), CS, KI, RE, SA, SN, SP, SQ, TE, 10% service.

Seabreeze Apartment, Maxwell Coast Rd. (428-2825); 29 rms; AC, BE, B(P), CS, FI, KI, SA, SC, SN, SM, SP, TEL.

Sichris Apartment Hotel, Worthing (427-5930); 24 rms; AC, (N)B, B(P), KI, RE, RM, SP. 10% service.

Woodville Beach Apartments, Hastings (427-1498); 28 rms; AC, BE, S(P), KI, RM, SP, TEL.

Worthing Court Apartment Hotel, Worthing (428-4910); 24 rms; AC, (N)B, B(P), KI, RE, TEL. 10% service.

St. James

Moderate to Inexpensive

Golden View, Sunset Crest (432-7930); 70 rms; AC, (N)B, B(P), CS, FI, KI, NC, RS, SA, SC, SN, SP, TE, TEL. 10% service.

Palm Beach Hotel, Holetown (432-1384); 30 rms; AC, BE, B(P), KI, RE, SC, SK, SN, TEL. 10% service.

NOTE: *Off-season (April 16 to December 15) rates are often half the high season (December 16 to April 15) prices. Check with the Barbados Board of Tourism for details.*

Restaurants

Bridgetown

Queens Park Restaurant, Lunches only; local food.

The Waterfront Cafe, The Careenage, (427-0093); English and Bajan food.

Christ Church

Ascanios, Rockley, (436-3549); Italian specialities.

Josef's, St. Lawrence (428-3379); European cuisine.

Luigi's, Dover Woods (428-9128); Steak, fish and Italian entrees.

Ocean View Hotel, Hastings (427-7871); Bajan and Continental fare; outstanding Sunday lucheons.

The Melting Pot, St. Lawrence Gap (428-3555); English-Bajan.

Pisces, St. Lawrence Gap (428-658); Elegant Caribbean seafood.

Ship's Inn/Captain's Carvery, St. Lawrence Gap (428-9605); English pub speicals and Bajan buffets.

The Silver Beach Hotel, Rockley (427-1121); Home-cooked Bajan meals.

T.G.I. Boomers, St. Lawrence Gap (428-8439); American food.

St. Andrew
(East Coast)

Atlantis, Bathsheba; Local and seafood.
Kingsley Club Hotel

St. James

Bagatelle, (425-0666); French and Continental prix-fixe dining.

Bamboo Beach Bar, Paynes Bay (432-0910); Varied, informal menu.

Chateau Creole, (422-4116); Caribbean cuisine and seafood.

Koko's, Prospect (424-4557) Nouvelle Barbadian cuisine.

La Cage Aux Folles, Paynes Bay (432-1203); Chinese and International cuisine, prix-fixe dinners.

Reid's, Derricks (432-7623) Elegant seafood.

Rose & Crown, Prospect (425-1074); Seafood specialties.

The Coach House, Paynes Bay (432-1163); Prix-fixe dinners, local cuisine.

St. Joseph
(East Coast)

Atlantis Hotel, Bathsheba (433-9445); Well-prepared local seafood.

Kingsley Club Hotel, (433-9422); Local cuisine, colonial atmosphere.

St. Michael

Brown Sugar, Aquatic Gap (426-7684); Bajan-style buffet lunches and Continental style dinners.

St. Peter

The Captain's Table, Heywoods Resort (442-4900); Seafood and gourmet continental menu.

Cobblers Cove Hotel, (422-2291); Bajan and continental cuisine.

Mullin's Beach Bar (Mama Leone's), Mullins Bay (422-2484); Italian-continental-Bajan specialities.

St. Philip

Pavillion Restaurant, Crane Beach Hotel, (423-6220); Bajan and seafood dishes, by candle light.

Ginger's, Ginger Bay Beach Hotel (423-5810); Local and international food.

NOTE: *A 10 percent service charge and 8 percent government tax is added to most restaurant check totals.*

Tourist Offices

Barbados

Bridgetown, Harbour Rd., P.O. Box 242 (427-2623/4); Deep Water Harbour (426-1716).

Christ Church, Grantley Adams Int'l. Airport, (428-5012/5570).

United States

New York, 800 Second Ave. 10017 (212-986-6516).

Los Angeles, 3440 Wilshire Blvd., Suite 1215 90010 (213-380-2198/9; 800-221-9831).

Canada

Toronto, Suite 1508, Box 11, 20 Queen St. West M5H 3R3, (416-979-2137).

Montreal, 615 Dorchester Blvd. West, Suite 960, Quebec H3B 1P5, (514-861-0085).

England

London, 6 Upper Belgrave St., SW1X 8AZ (01-235-4607).

West Germany

Frankfurt, Steinweg 5, 6000 Frankfurt Au Main 1 (0611/284451).

Embassies/High Commissions

United States, Trident House, Broad Street, Bridgetown(426-3574).

Austria, "Kay's" House, 13-14 Roebuck Street, Bridgetown; (436-6838).

Belgium, Black Bess Plantation, St. Peter (422-2852).

Brazil, Sunjet House, Fairchild Street, Bridgetown (427-1735).

Canada, Commonwealth Dev. Crop., Culloden Rd, St. Michael (429-3550).

People's Republic of China, 17 Golf View Terrace, Rockley, Christ Church; (426-1793).

Cyprus, "Kay's House", Roebuck Street, Bridgetown; (427-7478).

Colombia, 39 South Ridge, Christ Church (427-8804).

Dominican Republic, c/o Hilton International Hotel, St. Michael (426-0200).

Finland, c/o DaCosta Ltd., Hinck Street, Bridgetown(426-0850).

France, Newlands, Cottage Rd., Rockley, Christ Church; (426-1837).

Germany, 37 Bayan Court, Bay Street, St. Michael (427-1876).

Korea, Mutual Building, Collymore Rock, St. Michael (429-9650).

Japan, 8 Locust Hall Heights, St. George (437-9329).

Netherlands, Ennia House, Cheapside, St. Michael (426-2940).

Norway, Cockspur House, Nile Street, Bridgetown (427-5131).

Sweden, c/o Gardiner Austin Ltd., Cavan House, Broad Street, Bridgetown; (426-2830).

Trinidad & Tobago, Cockspur House, Bridgetown (429-9600).

United Kingdom, Barclays Bank Building, Roebuck Street, Bridgetown (436-6694) or 426-35257.

Venezuela, Civic Building, High & Swan Street; Bridgetown (426-5466).

ART/PHOTO CREDITS

128	Tony Arruza	182/183	Tony Arruza	240R	Willie Alleyne
129	Tony Arruza	186	Tony Arruza		Associates
130	Tony Arruza	187	Tony Arruza	241	Tony Arruza
131L	Tony Arruza	188	Tony Arruza	242	Tony Arruza
131R	Tony Arruza	189	Tony Arruza	243	Tony Arruza
132	David Hunt; Courtesy	190/191	Ronnie Carrington	244	Tony Arruza
	of Barbados Board of	192/193	Courtesy of the	245	Tony Arruza
	Tourism		Barbados Museum and	246	Tony Arruza
133	Tony Arruza		Historical Society	247	Courtesy of A. Nehaul
134/135	Tony Arruza	194/195	Tony Arruza	248/249	Tony Arruza
136/137	Tony Arruza	196	Tony Arruza	250	Tony Arruza
138L	Tony Arruza	197	Tony Arruza	252	Tony Arruza
138R	Tony Arruza	198	Tony Arruza	253	Tony Arruza
139	Tony Arruza	199	Tony Arruza	254/255	Tony Arruza
140	Tony Arruza	200	Tony Arruza	256	Tony Arruza
141	Tony Arruza	201	Tony Arruza	257	Tony Arruza
142/143	Tony Arruza	202	Tony Arruza	258	Courtesy of Stephanie
144	Tony Arruza	203	Tony Arruza		Calmenson
147L	Tony Arruza	204/205	Tony Arruza	259	Tony Arruza
147R	Tony Arruza	206	Tony Arruza	260	Stephen Smith;
148	Tony Arruza	207	Tony Arruza		Courtesy of Barbados
149	Tony Arruza	208	Stephen Smith		Archives
150	Tony Arruza; Courtesy	209	Tony Arruza	261	Tony Arruza
	of Mr. George Gibbs	210	Tony Arruza	263	Tony Arruza
151	Tony Arruza	211	Stephen Smith	264	Tony Arruza
152	Tony Arruza	212/213	Tony Arruza	265	Tony Arruza
153	Tony Arruza	214	Tony Arruza	266	Tony Arruza
154/155	Tony Arruza	215	Tony Arruza	267	Tony Arruza
156	Tony Arruza	216	Tony Arruza	268/269	Tony Arruza
157	Tony Arruza	217	Tony Arruza	270	Tony Arruza
158	Tony Arruza	218	Tony Arruza	272	Tony Arruza
159	Tony Arruza	219	Tony Arruza	273	Tony Arruza
160	Tony Arruza	220	Tony Arruza	274L	Tony Arruza
161	Tony Arruza	221	Tony Arruza	274R	Tony Arruza
162	Tony Arruza	222/223	Tony Arruza	275L	Tony Arruza
163	Tony Arruza	224/225	Tony Arruza	275R	Tony Arruza; Courtesy
164/165	Tony Arruza	226/227	Tony Arruza		of Mr. George Gibbs
166/167	Tony Arruza	228	Tony Arruza	276	Tony Arruza
168	Tony Arruza	229	Tony Arruza	277	Tony Arruza
169	Tony Arruza	230	Tony Arruza	278	Tony Arruza
170L	Tony Arruza	231	Tony Arruza	279	Tony Arruza
170R	Tony Arruza	232	Courtesy of Barbados	280	Stephen Smith;
171	Tony Arruza		Board of Tourism		Courtesy of Barbados
172/173	Tony Arruza	233	Willie Alleyne		Archives
174	Tony Arruza		Associates	282	Stephen Smith;
175	Tony Arruza	234	Tony Arruza		Courtesy of Kathleen
176	Tony Arruza	235	Tony Arruza		Hawkins
177	Tony Arruza	236	Tony Arruza	283	Tony Arruza
178	Tony Arruza	237	Tony Arruza	284	Gordon Brooks
179	Tony Arruza	238	Willie Alleyne	285	Willie Alleyne
180L	Tony Arruza		Associates		Associates
180R	Tony Arruza	239	Tony Arruza	286/287	Tony Arruza
181	Tony Arruza	240L	Tony Arruza	288	Tony Arruza

Spine (from top to bottom): Tony Arruza; Tony Arruza; Tony Arruza; Stephen Smith; Tony Arruza.
Backcover pictures: Tony Arruza (top right corner); Tony Arruza (Surf); Barbados Historical
Society (Tradition); Tony Arruza (Charm); Tony Arruza (Spirit); Tony
Arruza (Elegance); Tony Arruza (Sports); Barbados Board of Tourism
(Festivals); Tony Arruza (Dazzle); Tony Arruza (Treats); Tony Arruza
(Calypso); Tony Arruza (Creativity); Tony Arruza (Kicks).

INDEX